Counsellors in Health Settings

Edited by
Kim Etherington

Foreword by Tim Bond

Jessica Kingsley Publishers
London and Philadelphia

First published in the United Kingdom in 2001 by
Jessica Kingsley Publishers Ltd,
116 Pentonville Road, London
N1 9JB, England
and
325 Chestnut Street,
Philadelphia, PA 19106, USA.

www.jkp.com

© Copyright 2001 Jessica Kingsley Publishers
Foreword © Copyright 2001 Tim Bond

Library of Congress Cataloging in Publication Data
Counsellors in health settings / edited by Kim Etherington ; foreword by Tim Bond.
p. cm.
Includess bibliographical references and index.
ISBN 1-85302-938-6 (alk paper)
1. Health counseling. 2. Sick-Psychology. I. Etherington, Kim
R727.4.C66 2001
616'.001'9--dc21
2001029719

British Library Cataloguing in Publication Data
A CIP catalogue record for this book is available from the British Library

ISBN 1 85302 938 6

Printed and Bound in Great Britain by
Athenaeum Press, Gateshead, Tyne and Wear

Contents

Foreword

This is a groundbreaking book that ought to be read by anyone involved in delivering or developing counselling services in health settings. There are many features of this book that I admire. I will start with my overall impression before considering the distinctive approach and contribution that this book makes to the growing range of texts on counselling around health issues.

My admiration for what has been achieved by the contributors to this book rose steadily as I progressed through the chapters. It is not only that well respected practitioners, many of whom have pioneered the development of counselling services, have communicated their experience so effectively and shared their thoughts so generously, but also that the accumulated impact of this book demonstrates convincingly the contribution that counselling can offer in a wide variety of health care settings. This is a book that ought to be read by trainees, practitioners and their managers in order to increase awareness of the range of opportunities and challenges faced by providers of counselling in this setting.

One of the reasons why this book is so effective in communicating the lived experience of counsellors in health settings is the way contributors have been encouraged to break the mould for these kinds of books. Many books on counselling in health care follow the medical tradition of excluding any attention to the personal experience of the practitioner. The gaze is firmly fixed on the patient and the style of writing is impersonal and from within a scientific tradition that emphasises objectivity and detached observation. I do not want to dispute that this approach has its place. I have written in this tradition and will do so again. The many advances in medical care are testimony to the effectiveness of such single-minded discipline.

However, there is a cost in excluding the subjective and relational elements of medical care. This is particularly evident in writing about counselling and health where one of the contributions of counselling is to incorporate the personal dimension. In my view it is only when the practitioner shares her experience of her work that the quality and importance of the relationship with the patient becomes apparent. It is possible to test the significance of the relationship in interventions from an objective stance, particularly in effectiveness studies. However, the resulting bald assertions and generalisations stripped of personal information inevitably fail to communicate the lived experience in the way that a more subjective and personal way of writing achieves. We need many different types of narrative concerning health care and it is a distinctive strength of this book that the editor, Kim Etherington, has encouraged the writers to include their personal experiences and reflections. Indeed the opening chapter by the editor opens a path for others to follow, each with their own personal voices in which to report their work.

This book follows the methods of writing and systematically reflecting on the experience of providing counselling developed by the editor in 'Narrative approaches to working with adult male survivors of sexual abuse' (Jessica Kingsley, 2000). This earlier book has been reviewed very positively. Although there are differences between sole authored books and edited collections like this one, I consider that Kim Etherington's bold experiments in both books speak eloquently of the value of personal reflexivity, especially where this is not the norm. I hope that this book will not only advance practice but that it will also influence the way we write about counselling practice. I know that I have learnt a great deal from knowing many of the contributors to this book and listening to their experiences. This book provides a welcome opportunity for a much wider dissemination of their experience.

Tim Bond
University of Bristol

Acknowledgements

This book is the result of hard work by the authors who have offered us a glimpse into their worlds, both professional and personal. For some it is the first time they have written about their work in this way, using 'I', placing themselves in the centre of what they write, leaving themselves open to be seen by their clients and fellow professionals. This can sometimes be an act of courage. Clandinin and Connelly (1994) recognise this when writing about research: 'The researcher is always speaking partially naked and is genuinely open to legitimate criticism from participants and from audience. Some researchers are silenced by the invitation to criticism contained in the expression of voice.'

This book is a qualitative, narrative research study. I set out to find people who knew about counselling in health settings who would tell me their stories. I was surprised to find so many interesting voices – all wanting to be heard. In drawing this book together I have been a witness to these stories and now offer others an opportunity to witness them too.

I would therefore thank most sincerely the chapter authors who have responded so willingly and worked with me to produce this book. I particularly want to thank the clients who have contributed their stories, without which only half a story would have been told.

I want to thank all the students at the University of Bristol who have taught me so much during my time as course co-ordinator of the Postgraduate Diploma in Counselling in Primary Care/Health Settings. This book is being prepared just as I hand this role on to Alison Leftwich who has also taught me a great deal about this work.

There are many others I also want to acknowledge; my supervisees, MSc students, clients, my trainers, therapists and friends and family who have all supported my growth in different ways.

My colleague, friend and co-tutor on the above course, Shirley Margerison, has been a special inspiration for me, always creatively questioning and challenging the dominant stories of therapy, as I have done in this book. Our working partnership has brought me a great deal of learning, stimulation, fun and outrageous hysteria at times. I shall miss her.

I would also like to acknowledge and thank other colleagues, Janet May, Tim Bond, Michael Carroll, Penny Henderson and Pete Connor, who have read drafts, made suggestions and encouraged me.

I would like to make special mention of Graham Curtis-Jenkins of the Counselling in Primary Care Trust, who has done so much to help counsellors gain a foothold in the medical world. His energy and enthusiasm has inspired many of our students, my colleagues and myself, especially in the early days of the course.

Once again I have enjoyed working with Jessica Kingsley and her staff in the production of this book. I have especially appreciated my contact with Amy Lankester-Owen, who has always been helpful and encouraging in her role as editor.

Last, I want to thank my husband Dave, who, as ever, has supported me and helped me, cooked dinner more times than was his fair share, watered the plants even though that's my job, and responded to my wail of 'help' whenever the computer went on the blink.

Kim Etherington

Reference

Cladinin, D.J. and Connelly, F.M. (1994) 'Personal experience methods.' in N.K. Denzin and Y.K. Lincoln (eds) *Handbook of Qualitative Research*. London: Sage.

Preface

Epilogue for Paula

She was watching a soap opera that last evening before she stopped living entirely. I interrupted when I called to see her but it didn't matter because she wouldn't see next week's instalment anyway. Soap opera only has meaning if you watch it every week. Real life is lived in the moment. She turned her head slowly, as if reluctant to stop watching, and when she saw who was there, her eyes lit up and a slow smile reached them – when it could. Everything was like that – life lived in slow motion – the effort of being alive – but precious too, because of so much effort.

I sat on the lid of the commode, close beside her, her body too frail now to take the pressure of someone sitting on the edge of the bed. She couldn't say hello with her mouth which didn't work any more. Apart from sucking a sponge that was held to her lips, her mouth had no function. The smile came from somewhere else deep inside, and her eyes held the warmth of greeting. I felt welcomed.

There was little left to say and we both knew it was unnecessary to try to find more words. I stroked her lifeless hand and her eyes smiled again. She knew I loved her. Her skin was very fragile and soft like a baby's; her hair was like the downy covering of a week-old chick. So much similarity between new life and death.

Each time I wiped her coated lips with lemon water or squeezed a drop into her silent mouth I thought of Christ on the cross as He asked for water and was given vinegar on a sponge. Men had nailed his body there, but who had put her where she was? For whose sins did she suffer – what was the meaning of her life and death?

Her eyes never died. I did not see them finally close later that night. Always bright with intelligence and sometimes with tears. I saw her tears because she knew I cared enough; that I could listen to her fears; that they would not frighten me away.

Saddest of all for me was to hear how she had lived her life in the reflection of other people's expectations. Stiff upper lip to the end: 'They don't want to know how I really am – it will scare them away and I need them.' So she played their game: 'I'm fine – oh yes, I'm going to be OK.'

'The Health Visitor says she saves me for her last visit of the week because I always cheer her up.'

They spoke of her dignity in death, of her constant cheerfulness, her popularity: 'The crematorium was packed to the door!'

Too late now for her, but not for me.

I think only of her eyes.

Introduction

Kim Etherington

Background

Paula was my very first counselling client.[1] I had been working as an occupational therapist (OT) for social services for several years when I met her, and she changed my life. I had been asked to assess her needs nine months after she had been diagnosed with motor neurone disease. Her husband Jack opened the door to me when I arrived on the doorstep and he showed me into the sitting room where Paula sat, a tiny neat woman in her late fifties, smartly dressed, and with a bright smile on her face. I asked her to tell me her story so far.

She had first noticed something wrong when she had started falling off her bicycle. Later she had begun to stumble about when she walked. It had taken a long time to be given an appointment at the hospital and eventually she had seen the consultant, undergone tests and then been told: 'You have motor neurone disease – unfortunately there's not much we can do about it. Come back and see us in six months' time.'

She and Jack did not know what this meant but it didn't seem very serious from the manner in which the diagnosis had been given, so they had a cup of tea and went home. Paula was a bit upset that there was nothing that could be done, but she thought she could probably manage without riding her bicycle and she would just have to take more care while walking. On their arrival home they sat down to watch the TV. Coincidentally, the programme they switched on was a documentary about motor neurone disease. She watched in horror as the full meaning of her diagnosis unfolded before her eyes. At the end of the programme the message on the screen was 'Since making this film all six of the people participating have died'.

By the time I met her she was unable to walk without a walking frame indoors and she needed a wheelchair for outdoor use. She had difficulty bathing, dressing and going to the lavatory; she could no longer do the cooking or cleaning. Jack had taken early retirement from the ambulance service, so he was a great help.

I asked about other professional involvement and support. She told me the health visitor came to visit weekly, saying that she saved her for the last visit of the week, as she was always such a pleasure to visit. Her neighbours popped in and always marvelled at how well she looked. Her adult daughters visited from time to time – not knowing the seriousness of their mother's condition. 'What's the point in worrying them?' Paula asked. 'They'll stay away if I'm always miserable.' I asked her if she and Jack talked about their feelings about her illness. 'Oh, no. He's got enough on his plate without that.'

It seemed that there was nobody Paula could talk to about the fears that beset her day and night as she lay trapped inside her failing body – waiting for the disease to take over, waiting for the inevitability of death. I asked her if she *wanted* to talk about what was happening to her and the tears rolled down her cheeks. 'Yes,' she whispered, 'but who is there who wants to listen?'

At this time (1987) I had just begun a diploma in counselling at the University of Bristol – a postgraduate course for people in the helping professions who used an element of counselling in their work. This course has since become a recognised professional counsellor training (BACP accredited); at that time it was the first of its kind at Bristol University.

For some time I had been feeling a great deal of frustration about the limitations of my role as an OT: visiting people in their homes to make an assessment of their needs and providing equipment to help them manage daily living activities. Often I would arrive with a bath board or raised lavatory seat under my arm, only to end up in the bathroom with the client, the door firmly closed against the rest of the family, whilst they told me about their distress. I began to realise that whether it was a simple bathing aid or a complicated stairlift, a housing adaptation or wheelchair that was required, there were other needs that were not being met – or indeed, even acknowledged or assessed. What most people seemed to need was someone to listen to their story, their pain, anger, frustration and fear as illness or disability took its hold over their lives – just as Paula did. But although there was official recognition of the need for mobility aids, holidays, adaptations etc., there was no recognition of the emotional needs (Etherington 1990).

My manager at social services was sympathetic and agreed to my request to offer Paula my services as a counsellor in addition to my role as an OT. I explained to Paula that I was a beginner, a counsellor trainee, that I would need to visit her separately in that role, and that we would have clear boundaries around the counselling work. Paula accepted the offer gratefully, and so our relationship began.

The helper role

At that point in my life I was firmly stuck in the 'helper' role. I had not looked inside myself to discover my own need for help. It was through my work with Paula that I became aware of how my self-esteem was almost entirely dependent on meeting other people's needs whilst ignoring my own. As Paula struggled with similar issues and began to face her own mortality, I too began to feel a kind of pain I had not experienced before. I couldn't understand this – I had worked as an OT with dying people so many times before but this time it was different. Looking back from where I am now I can see clearly that by using the newly acquired counselling skills, reflecting, paraphrasing and empathising, I was opening up a space inside myself that I had not visited before. My own deepest and unacknowledged wounds resonated with Paula's wounds and the defences I had used to keep myself 'safe' were falling away. At this time I began to seek 'counselling supervision'. I needed to talk about the client and, of course, I began to talk about myself. But it was so much easier for me to ask for supervision, focusing on the client, than it would have been to ask for counselling for myself. Fortunately my supervisor was wise enough to realise that this was the case and my supervision led me into therapy as I began to acknowledge my own mortality, in both a physical and an emotional sense.

So this is why I say that Paula changed my life. She led me along a pathway with her and we faced the fear of the unknown together. Jung, in recognising the power of the wounded healer, said that the ideal therapeutic situation was one in which the patient brought the ideal salve for the therapist's wound. Paula brought to me the perfect salve for my wound. Whilst gaining support through my own therapy I was able to stay with her even in the darkest places, and as we watched her life drain away she knew that she was valued as she was. By tuning into her empathically as she lost the ability to speak, I was able to put into words what she was herself unable to say – checking out constantly with her that I was expressing *her* thoughts and feelings rather than my own. Her blinking messages (one blink for yes and two for no) kept me on track. Our sessions were shared with her husband towards the end and he began to communicate with her in the same way.

My last visit was on the night she died. I wrote the epilogue to honour her story and the importance of our relationship.

What this book is about

Paula's is only one story and it would be reassuring to think it was an exception. Sadly it is not. Even now, 13 years later, people are still being given devastating news like this every day in hospitals and there are few opportunities for emotional support. How much kinder it would have been had Paula and Jack been offered a space in which to reflect on what the diagnosis meant to them, been given the opportunity to ask questions and to learn in a caring environment about what they might have to face together. It might not have been appropriate on that first day, but they could have been given an appointment for a future date, a named person to contact when they felt the need to talk.

In this book I have drawn together accounts of how some of the more progressive NHS trusts and voluntary organisations are now using the services of trained counsellors. I wanted to give voice to the stories of clients and counsellors who have experienced working in a range of health settings, and provide an opportunity for us to hear these stories from different perspectives. These are rare stories, written by 'pioneers' in counselling arenas that are relatively undiscovered. I particularly asked contributors to write from a personal, contextualised perspective, because I wanted to give recognition to the value of individual stories and local knowledge and place them alongside 'the posture of authoritative truth' and 'grand narratives' (Gergen 1992). Individual authors have produced stories that are a rich blend of academic and personal; others have used diary format; most have used clients' stories directly or indirectly to create a unique harmony; and clients have told their own stories. All of the chapters add many layers of understanding, knowledge and experience, interwoven in a rich, creative synthesis.

Most of the chapters have been written by qualified counsellors who have previously gained qualifications in other areas, most as members of a caring profession. It is well recognised that people who are drawn to the caring professions have identified in themselves a capacity for empathy with the suffering of others, whilst often denying or ignoring their own suffering. However, it may be that we cannot feel truly empathic towards another unless we are able to be truly empathic with our own wounds (Levasseur and Vance 1993). To deny our own suffering we may be denying our 'selves'. Rogers (1975) described empathy as 'entering the private perceptual world of the other and becoming thoroughly at home in it'; but it is hard for us to feel at home inside the world of another's pain if we are not at home with our own.

Members of medical professions have usually been trained to remain at an emotional distance from their patients – perhaps as a way of protecting themselves from the suffering they observe on a daily basis. It is more common within the medical world to talk about the 'case' rather than the person. However, many medical people begin their training 'with much empathy and genuine love – a real desire to help other people. In medical school however, they learn to mask their feelings, or worse, deny them' (Spiro 1993). I believe the same can be said for most people who train and work in the health services, although nurses feel they have much to teach doctors about empathy and caring, claiming they care for 'the whole person rather than focusing on disease' (Levasseur and Vance 1993). However, in general the culture supports the 'experts' to take an objective view of their patients and provide a 'cure' for their ills. Nurses who present themselves for counselling training frequently state that their reason for doing so is their dissatisfaction with their nursing role in terms of wanting more time, per-mission and skills to help them to be with patients in ways that patients tell them they value – much as I found for myself when I was working as an OT.

The culture of medicine does not encourage staff to reflect on their own thoughts and feelings in their relationship with patients; there are however tiny shifts where provision is currently made for some members of staff to receive supervision and develop reflective practice. (I supervise three members of NHS staff who are in this position.) Other hopeful glimpses of change can also be seen within the medical literature; doctors are beginning to write about the value of listening to patients as the experts on their own stories (Frank 1995; Greenhalgh and Hurwitz 1999; Kleinman 1988; Launer 1999; Spiro et al. 1993) and the need for empathic listening and psy-chological support for both themselves and their patients.

Between two worlds

Working at the interface between the 'two worlds' of counselling and medicine can be a complex and exciting place for counsellors and other team members. There can be clashes between the underlying beliefs and values that are held by those who have been trained in the 'medical model' and those who are more in tune with the psychosocial model.

We seem to speak different languages because we come from different worlds – well, certainly different cultures (Etherington 1998). Counsellors working in traditional health settings have entered the world of the medical model, which has been around for a long time. Towards the mid-to-late eighteenth century medical men were established as leaders in knowledge about health as science took over from religion. Later developments in the field of laboratory science firmly established the biomedical model, which was at its peak in the 1950s.

Within the biomedical approach the patient is seen as a problem to be solved, a disease to be cured, and the solution lies in using a scientific approach. This has been described as the 'modernist' view of illness: 'The *modern* experience of illness begins when popular experience is overtaken by technical expertise, including complex organisations of treatment. Folk no longer go to bed and die, cared for by family members and neighbours who have a talent for healing. Folk now go to paid professionals who reinterpret pain as symptoms, using a specialised language that is unfamiliar and over-whelming' (Frank 1995).

However, a challenge to the biomedical view began to emerge from new professions that had to struggle to find a place within a fairly closed community of medically trained people. As professions such as nursing and occupational therapy developed, there was a growing need for a body of knowledge that challenged the medical model. At the same time the medical model was increasingly incorporating psychological and sociological per-spectives. In turn psychology and sociology were themselves changing and applying these changes to problems in health and social care (Cooper, Stevenson and Hale 1996).

In 1977 Engel proposed an alternative approach to the biomedical model – the biopsychosocial model, which was accepted in both academic and practical circles. It was seen as providing an holistic understanding of the individual's experience of health and disease. This model was further developed by locating it within a framework of general systems theory recognising that biological, social and psychological perspectives exist complementarily, each affecting and being affected by the others.

A growing interest in the biopsychosocial model highlighted the increas-ing unease around the power of biomedicine and its associated models of health and illness. The change in terminology from 'alternative' to 'comple-mentary' almost parallels the way in which the biopsychosocial model has evolved from being an alternative model to being a model which not only complements biomedical approaches but in fact incorporates them (Cooper *et al.* 1996).

Illness stories

Postmodernism challenges the individualistic thinking that has informed traditional therapy and the idea of an autonomous, bounded self, favouring instead the concept of fragmented selves that are constantly reconstructed as we interact with others, and it promotes the idea of ourselves in relation to others and our environment. A postmodern view of the person is that the stories people tell themselves and others create the personal meanings that influence their ways of being, and the ways they might then limit themselves or make use of possibilities hitherto unrecognised (Bruner 1990; Geertz 1978).

In telling and retelling our stories, new selves are formed:

> Telling our story is a way of reclaiming our selves, our history and our experiences; a way of finding our voice. In telling my story to you in the introduction to this book I am also telling it to my 'self' – and my 'self' (who is the audience) is being formed in the process of telling. So there are witnesses to my story, the 'other' to whom I recount my story (which is what clients do with us in therapy), and the self who is growing within me as I hear my story retold as I speak or write it down. (Etherington 2000, p.17)

Frank (1995) said that 'repetition is the medium of becoming' and when we use our own stories, or those of others, as I have done in this book, we give testimony to what we have witnessed; and that testimony creates a voice.

The postmodern experience of illness reflected the growing interest in the recognition of 'local knowledge', the power and importance of individuals' stories, as people began to realise that much more is involved in their experiences than the 'medical story' allows for. People wanted to tell their own stories, have their voices heard – and there was a proliferation of personal accounts as people reclaimed their stories and made them their own again, no longer satisfied with the stories that were told of their experiences from the medical perspective. People had previously told their illness stories during the traditional era, passing on their knowledge from one generation to another. In postmodern times technology, publishing, TV, the internet give us opportunities to disseminate stories and share experiences on a global scale. We are influenced and changed when we tell and listen to stories; through wider contacts with the different cultures that are now available to us, those influences and changes are enriched by a much broader range of ideas.

Perceptions of power

Counsellors in health settings often have to struggle in order for others to understand philosophies that may seem alien to the dominant culture – philosophies that promote ways of being with patients that dispel the notion of 'expert healer' and empower patients to find their own resources and use them.

All of this challenges the power and status of the medical profession as having all the answers. Dr Glin Bennet devotes a major portion of his book *The Wound and the Doctor* (1987) to issues of power which he says 'affect all aspects of medical work'. Bennet has written of the possibility of unconscious motivation of power-seeking, particularly in the role of doctors. I believe this power has become associated with the medical profession more generally although I would agree that doctors have held the greatest power hitherto. Their power is now being challenged by an insistence on greater openness and accountability, ownership of mistakes and an acceptance that in many instances the patient knows best and their stories should be taken into account.

Society has always insisted that doctors should be powerful, and we have given them authority, set them above us as befitting people who are able to save our lives when we are faced with mortal danger. It is easy to see what a burden this power has become for some. We set them apart by projecting our power onto them and in so doing diminish and distance ourselves from them. Paradoxically, it may be that those who have the greatest need for power (perhaps as an unconscious reaction against a sense of inadequacy or powerlessness) feel most powerless when faced with patients whose illnesses they cannot cure, or by the mistakes they have made. Or indeed by a fellow professional whose skills are equally or – dare I say it – even more effective in certain circumstances.

Counsellors too can be the recipients of other people's projections of power much as social workers, police officers and others are at different times. Power, once acknowledged and owned, can be shared and used in ways that promote greater equality, more awareness of an individual's rights, and the responsibilities that power inevitably brings with it.

Health settings

Although we use the phrase 'health settings', we are normally referring to places where people attend when they have a need to improve their state of wellbeing, whether that be in a physical, mental, psychological or even sometimes spiritual sense. Health has sometimes been said to be 'an absence of disease'; I would prefer to call it an absence of dis-ease (a sense that all is not well with the person for whatever reason). Sometimes physical illness can bring with it psychological problems; mental illness and psychological problems can bring about physical symptoms; and spiritual dis-ease can affect both the mind and the body. Illness can be defined as a subjective feeling of being unwell, that may or may not be accompanied by pain or other unpleasant bodily sensations.

However, during the 1980s and 1990s there has been a growing recognition that health is not the prerogative of the NHS. With the growth of alternative and complementary medicine, and the progression of post-modernism, with a movement away from certainty and positivism, voluntary organisations have flourished. This book includes chapters written by counsellors working in several voluntary organisations; the Bristol Cancer Help Centre, the Terrence Higgins Trust and Brook Advisory Clinic.

The first two of these organisations could be seen as a reflection of what Frank (1995), who has himself had the experience of cancer, has called the 'remission society', which he describes as 'all those people who, like me, were effectively well but could never be considered cured. These people are all around, though often invisible.' These are people who would probably have died prior to the achievements of 'modernist medicine': people with heart disease, cancers, HIV/AIDS etc. Modernism took account of people who were either sick or well, people who adopted 'a sick role' for a short or long period. People in remission often have some level of treatment or care that may extend throughout their lives. These are people who learn about the world of medicine from inside their experiences, and they question the place that their stories have been allotted in medical narratives. These are an articulate and sometimes vociferous group, and their voices are included in this book.

Health settings in the context of this book also include places where advice is given to young people about sexual health, and fertility clinics where people attend who are not necessarily 'ill' but may suffer from 'dis-ease' about some aspect of their lives. Again, these situations have arisen out of the success of modernist scientific medicine and a developing society in which people have more choices about how they want to live their lives.

Counselling can help people make choices, or come to terms with their lack of choice as they sort out their thoughts, feelings and behaviours in a safe and confidential setting where their unique and individual stories are honoured with respect.

Loss

This book hardly mentions the word 'loss', but loss runs throughout like an almost invisible thread that links many of the stories. Loss is clearly a central concept in counselling in health settings. People attending health settings are often facing the loss of physical and sometimes mental health, of freedom to choose for themselves, of independence, role, sometimes a relationship with a loved one and, perhaps, loss of life itself. As people face their losses they may begin to question the value and meaning of their lives, past and present relationships with those who are dear to them, what lies beyond death, and the meaning they place upon religion and spirituality. These are often terrifying issues for people to face. Even for those who have spent a lifetime reflecting on these concepts, in facing the actuality of loss they may feel overwhelmed. Clients may wish to mourn their lost opportunities; examine their regrets about choices they might have made differently; they may want to face up to things about themselves that they have chosen not to confront previously, mend fences and heal old wounds, make their goodbyes and let go of the world.

However, loss is also an inevitable part of growth and transition; transition is a natural and normal part of life that repeats until life itself ends. Many people experience loss as an opportunity to move on, providing they can let go and learn from what they leave behind. As we move from adolescence to adulthood we experience loss but also gain, more freedom, autonomy, independence, etc. As we change from single childlessness to 'coupledom' and parenthood we may mourn the loss of freedom while at the same time valuing what we have gained in love and intimacy. As we move into retirement we might mourn the loss of further economic growth and employment whilst gaining in wisdom, maturity, and perhaps even peace. In the transition from health to illness there can also be gains. Many of the people I have spoken with about their experience of illness have said, 'I wouldn't have chosen to do it this way but I know that being ill has given me so much. I am a better and stronger person than I was before.'

Living with uncertainty is part of what postmodernism brings. There are no longer many 'givens' or 'truths'. Many of the old bastions of certainty have been eroded; people depend less on the Church or tradition to supply answers. For many people this can be liberating – letting go of old structures that were imposed from without and had no personal meaning may provide an opportunity to construct more meaningful stories about their existence. However, this throws us back on ourselves, sometimes creating paralysis and fear until different structures take their place and equilibrium is regained – at least for a while. Illness is often a time when a person's outdated view of themselves is challenged – their sense of 'who they have always known themselves to be' has been brought into question. They can no longer be sure of what the future holds. This is the time when new narratives can be constructed, new alternatives examined, new possibilities realised and life can be valued in new and richer ways.

The wounded healer

The concept of the 'wounded healer' is familiar to many of us who work in the caring professions. On looking back on their reasons for becoming a counsellor, many would agree that their motivation was, at the time, at least partly an unconscious way of vicariously seeking self-care.

For some their need is more conscious and derives from a wish to offer to others what they have themselves been given. Heather Goodare realised she wanted to become a counsellor whilst undergoing treatment at the Bristol Cancer Help Centre during the first year after her diagnosis of breast cancer. However, she accepted advice to wait until she had experienced the healing of 'old wounds' and 'unresolved issues from childhood' through undertaking her own therapy. In Chapter 1 she writes about her journey from 'client to counsellor' – a wounded healer who could bring the 'boon' gained by undertaking her own healing journey into her role as a counsellor (Frank 1995). Heather provides us with an insider's view of the political struggle that followed the publication of research into the value of the holistic treatment offered at the Bristol Centre. She herself became involved in the successful fight that followed for recognition of the centre's work. Heather is convinced that people with cancer need to seek and understand the meaning of their illness – an approach the centre encourages. Heather also introduces us to the value of using the arts, alternative therapies and support groups for patients with cancer and their carers. Her richly described experiences are underpinned by the philosophy that welcoming, loving and accompanying the patient throughout the journey is of fundamental importance.

Palliative care

The importance of searching for meaning is also recognised by Kate Kirk and Maria Lever in Chapter 2. Kate and Maria offer us their view of a model of palliative care counselling which has a broad remit to support patients (and those directly involved in caring for them) who have received news of 'a diagnosis of a potentially life-limiting illness', and not only of impending terminal illness. This counselling service was set up in 1994 using Health Improvement Programme money. It was the first service of its kind in the UK to employ counsellors – rather than counselling being offered by nurses or social workers who combine counselling with their primary role. It is a model for the future that could be adopted throughout the NHS. Kate and Maria work in different ways that reflect their background and training – this is one of the many strengths of the service they offer: the 'luxury' of having two counsellors allows clients some choices. Kate's work includes psychodrama and visualisation and Maria's work is informed by cognitive behavioural ideas. However, from their writing it is clear that both are concerned with helping clients make sense of their condition and gain a sense of control. Both workers believe that when people are cared for emotionally, their physical welfare can be greatly enhanced. Mind–body–spirit connections are now well established and increasingly explainable in terms of hard scientific evidence (Damasio 1994; Goleman 1996; Pert 1998). This chapter also gives us an insight into the flexibility required by a counsellor who works in the patient's home, a hospital ward, or wherever suits the client best. Kate and Maria share with us what they have learned about the 'shadow side' of doing this work – 'what they didn't tell us'. Perhaps the important lesson of this chapter is that we cannot tell others what it might be like for them to do this work; we can only say how it is for us.

Somatisation and primary care

In Chapter 3 Sue Santi Ireson picks up the theme of body–mind connections in her writing about the counselling service she offers at a GP surgery. Because there has already been a plethora of recent writing about counselling in general practice (Curtis-Jenkins et al. 1997; East 1995; Einzig, Curtis-Jenkins and Basharan 1995; Henderson 1999; Hudson-Allez 1997; Wiener and Sher 1998) – a growing arena for the employment of counsellors – this book focuses mainly on counsellors who are working in a variety of other health settings that have been less well recognised. Having said that, general practice is a health setting where counsellors are employed and this book would be incomplete without it. Sue's chapter focuses on issues related to how adults who did not receive the kind of emotional support they needed during childhood might express traumatic experiences (such as sexual abuse) through physical manifestations such as chronic or acute illness, self-harm, addiction or disability. Sue's research over an eighteen-month period within her own practice highlighted the GPs' inability to recognise the problems abuse creates for their own patients, whilst preferring to believe that these things only happen on other people's 'patches'. Her chapter particularly helps us understand the needs of clients who self-harm and some of the difficult responses they evoke in those who try to care for them.

Team membership

Traditionally trained counsellors may suffer something of a shock when they enter a culture where they are expected to communicate with other members of the team about their clients. However, being a member of a team, whether a primary or secondary care team, can provide huge benefits to all concerned, the counsellor, other team members and the clients. It can also raise ethical conflicts and dilemmas. In Chapter 4 Julia Segal explores some of these important issues in relation to her membership of a team of people working with patients who have multiple sclerosis in an NHS unit. She describes some of the ways in which she set about establishing the role of counselling and the counsellor within the team. As part of her role she offers consultation not only to patients, but also to other team members who seek support in their work with patients. Confidentiality in these settings is complex and requires mature consideration of underlying ethical principles rather than strict adherence to rules. Julia describes the way she struggles to establish an approach that is ethical, confidential, and takes account of team membership.

Intensive care

An intensive care unit is a place where trauma is a daily occurrence, but is rarely thought of as a place where counsellors may be employed. Nowhere could I imagine greater need for psychological care and emotional support than where people watch and wait anxiously for their loved one's recovery from accident, illness or surgery. When the patient is a child that need is all the greater. As parents we suffer when our child is in pain and distressed; we may feel powerless to help; we would rather suffer ourselves than leave the child to cope. Penny Cook trained originally as a paediatric nurse and later as a counsellor, and in Chapter 5 she writes of how she has helped to create the post of counsellor in a paediatric intensive care unit. She offers us a vivid picture of that environment and the people in it. 'There are continuing and sudden noises from equipment, alarms and seemingly constant ringing of telephones and bleeps. There are the human noises of crying, sometimes wailing and shouting. I have strong memories of a quiet and peaceful morning shattered by the gentle wail of a four-year-old girl: "I don't want my sister to die."' Penny describes the role of counsellor and the issues that a counsellor and client may face, whether the client is the ill child or members of the family.

Sexuality

In our society sexuality is an area of our lives that is often fraught with complications, taboos and conflicts. Many of our health issues are related to sexuality and therefore it is not surprising a book concerning counsellors in health settings should include some of the arenas where sexual health is on the agenda. In Chapter 6 Caroline Stedman describes her work with adolescents in a Brook Advisory Clinic. Young people need a safe and supportive environment to explore their sexual relationships, responsibilities and problems. During adolescence young people try to discover the unique and separate person that they are becoming; there are struggles of sexual identity, orientation, behaviour and reproduction to consider. Caroline gives us an interesting insight into the complexity of this work and brings it alive by allowing us a peep into her work 'diary'.

In Chapter 7 Pete Connor writes about his work in an agency that offers counselling and other support to people with HIV/AIDS and those closely connected with them. His powerful and personal account of living and working with the effects of HIV/AIDS provides us with a blend of his academic and emotional understanding; his use of case examples gives us a glimpse into the diversity of client work. 'HIV infection touches on the most crucial issues in society today. It connects with sex and sexuality, drug-use and addiction, racism, sexism and homophobia, the ethics of medical research and the power of drugs companies, the treatment and rights of the terminally ill and the bereaved, and with the status of the poor and the marginalised.' Pete provides rich insight into the way new treatments have impacted on the experiences of people who become infected with the virus.

Many more people are now learning to live with both the hope and the uncertainty that new medication has brought, whilst there are still those for whom medication does not work. He recognises the limitations of counselling and the need for counsellors to view the client within the context of their whole existence.

Yet another arena concerned with sexuality is that of fertility. In Chapter 8 Gill Woodbridge describes her work as a counsellor in a fertility unit where, uniquely, counselling is mandatory for people who seek assisted conception. She describes how she delicately balances her role to maintain the focus on meeting the client's needs whilst also meeting her responsibility as part of a multidisciplinary team who are assessing whether or not prospective parents should be offered treatment. Counselling in this environment may be to help clients think about the implications of the treatment they are seeking; to provide support for those who are undergoing treatment; or longer-term work for those who have marital or sexual difficulties or who may become seriously depressed during the process.

Clients' stories

A book like this would be incomplete without the clients' stories. In Chapter 9 Helen Boxer (a pseudonym), one of the patients who attended the fertility clinic Gill writes about in the previous chapter, offers us her moving account taken from the diary she kept during her year of treatment in a NHS fertility unit. Helen describes the rollercoaster of emotions she and her husband experienced as their hopes were raised and dashed; a year of anguish during which they struggled for her to become pregnant. She has written this account with her husband's help and encouragement. It is a story with a happy ending and one that clearly shows us the importance of counselling in such circumstances.

Rosie Jeffries is the author of another personal account in Chapter 10. She writes from the perspective of a woman who has been diagnosed with and treated for breast cancer whilst herself working as a counsellor. Rosie therefore offers a uniquely informed insight into the patient's need for counselling and other support. She writes with honest and painful humour about her experiences of diagnosis and treatment, and of what has helped and hindered her along the way. Her cartoons add a touch of wit and lightness to what might otherwise be a dark and humourless reality.

Both of these chapters highlight the fact that health issues do not only affect the individual, they also affect family members, partners, friends and all those people who come into contact with the patient. Patients like Helen and Rosie call our attention to the benefits that counselling can bring for patients with very different needs in health settings. Rosie has a serious illness; Helen was having difficulty conceiving a child. Both were given bad news in a hospital setting, and both had partners sharing the process, who also needed support.

The interface between mental health services and counselling

In Chapter 11 Rachel Freeth, a psychiatrist who has also trained as a person-centred counsellor, draws our attention to the interface between psychiatry and counselling and the possible culture clash when these disciplines meet. She describes the tensions created by having dual roles and how she manages them. She highlights the complex political scene that may affect the future of counsellors within the NHS and helps to separate out the differences between what can be offered by doctors and counsellors, taking into consideration the pressures created by the NHS system:

> As critical as I am of the lack of counselling skills within psychiatric practice, I wish to acknowledge, however, that psychiatrists are only able to listen to the patient as much as the 'system' (e.g. the NHS) enables or allows them to. The psychological and practical demands of the role are very heavy. The responsibilities are great and the volume of patients passing through the ward or outpatient clinic can be overwhelming. As a psychiatrist I am aware of these pressures, many of which are imposed by poorly funded services, and, therefore, insufficient resources and time to meet increasing demand. It can often simply be too emotionally demanding to attempt to listen in a way that the patient experiences as therapeutic.

Rachel draws attention to the advantage for counsellors in receiving supervision and personal counselling – something that is not required of psychiatrists, and is to their disadvantage with such a heavy workload.

The theme of the possible clash of cultures is continued in Chapter 12 where Karl Gregory demonstrates how he has integrated counselling into a mental health setting. Karl gives us a glimpse of how he worked as a counsellor with a client who has been diagnosed as schizophrenic. There are those who say that people with 'psychotic' illness cannot benefit from counselling; Karl shows us otherwise. His use of the client's words, distilled into a beautiful poetic form, demonstrates how a relationship of care and respect can provide for the client an experience of healing love.

What this book tells us about the training and supervision issues for counsellors working in health settings

Finally, in Chapter 13, I have explored some of the training and supervision issues that concern counsellors working in health settings. As a tutor and course co-ordinator of the Diploma in Counselling in Primary Care/Health Settings at the University of Bristol over the last six years I have learned a great deal from my colleagues and our students about those needs. As a supervisor I gain a 'insider's' view of some of the organisational, professional and personal struggles that counsellors experience when working in the NHS or voluntary health settings. So in this final chapter I focus on issues related to training and supervision.

Conclusion

Creating this book has been an interesting and informative journey that has taken me into places that I didn't know existed where I have met people I didn't know before. I have been touched by the willingness of the authors to invite us into their stories, sometimes stories that have been painful for them to revisit, but they have been willing so that others may benefit by the knowledge they have to share. Writing personally and reflexively is exposing and can leave us feeling vulnerable to the judgement of others. However, Miller Mair (1989) rightly points out that 'intimate knowledge is likely to teach us more than distant knowledge. Personal knowledge is likely to change us more than impersonal knowledge.' (p.2) So it is my hope that these stories might change you, the reader, in ways that you will value.

For many people the experience of illness starts them on a journey that becomes a quest story (Frank 1995). Being alongside clients as they make this journey can be painful and exhausting; however, the rewards can far outweigh the costs. Even as I said goodbye to Paula that last time, guessing that I might never see her alive again, I knew that our counselling relationship had helped to make her journey towards death less lonely and fearful. She had also helped to make my own inevitable journey to death seem less frightening and perhaps, when it comes, more manageable. My relationship with her husband continued after her death, through his grieving and on to a wonderful evening concert he had organised in his wife's memory. The funds he raised were given to the Motor Neurone Disease Association – his way of 'putting something back' for what he had received.

Note

1   Throughout the introduction and the final chapter I refer to 'clients' and 'patients'; this reflects how counsellors in health settings often refer to the people they counsel. For ease of narrative I use the pronoun 'him' when meaning client/patient and 'her' when meaning counsellor: I acknowledge that both men and women are counsellors and clients. All clients' names used in this book have been changed to protect their anonymity.

References

Bennet, G. (1987) *The Wound and the Doctor.* London: Secker and Warburg.

Bor, R., Miller, R., Latz, M. and Salt, H. (1998) *Counselling in Health Care Settings.* London: Cassell.

Bruner, J. (1990) *Acts of Meaning.* Cambridge, MA: Harvard University Press.

Cooper, N., Stevenson, C. and Hale, G. (eds) (1996) *Integrating Perspectives on Health.* Milton Keynes: Open University Press.

Curtis-Jenkins, G., Burton, M., Henderson, P., Foster, J. and Inskipp, F. (1997) 'Supplement No. 3 on supervision of counsellors in primary care.' Staines, UK: Counselling in Primary Care Trust.

Damasio, A. (1994) *Descartes' Error: Emotion, Reason and the Human Brain.* New York: Avon.

East, P. (1995) *Counselling in Medical Settings.* Milton Keynes: Open University Press.

Einzig, H., Curtis-Jenkins, G. and Basharan, H. (1995) 'The training needs of counsellors in primary medical care'. *Journal of Mental Health 4*, 205–209.

Etherington, K. (1990) 'The disabled person's act – The need for counselling.' *British Journal of Occupational Therapy 53*, 10.

Etherington, K. (1998) 'Establishing a discourse between GPs and counsellors.' *CMS News – Journal of the Counselling in Medical Settings Division of BACP 55.* Rugby: BACP

Etherington, K. (2000) *Narrative Approaches to Working with Adult Male Survivors of Child Sexual Abuse: The Clients', The Counsellor's and the Researcher's Story.* London: Jessica Kingsley Publishers.

Frank, A. W. (1995) *The Wounded Storyteller.* London: University of Chicago Press.

Geertz, C. (1978) *The Interpretation of Cultures.* New York: Basic Books.

Gergen, K. (1992) 'The post-modern adventure.' *Family Therapy Networker 52*, 56–58.

Goleman, D. (1996) *Emotional Intelligence.* London: Bloomsbury.

Greenhalgh, T. and Hurwitz, B. (1999) 'Why study narrative?' *British Medical Journal 318*, 7175, 48–50.

Henderson, P. (1999) 'Supervision in medical settings.' In M. Carroll and E. Holloway (eds) *Counselling Supervision in Context.* London: Sage.

Hudson-Allez, G. (1997) *Time-Limited Therapy in General Practice.* London: Sage.

Kleinman, A. (1988) *The Illness Narrative.* New York: Basic Books.

Launer, J. (1999) 'A narrative approach to mental health in general practice.' *British Medical Journal 318*, 7176, 117–119.

Levasseur, J. and Vance, D.R. (1993) 'Doctors, nurses and empathy.' In H. Spiro, M.G. McCrea Curnen, E. Peschel and D. St. James (eds) *Empathy and the Practice of Medicine: Beyond Pills and the Scalpel.* London: Yale University Press.

Mair, M. (1989) *Between Psychology and Psychotherapy: A Poetics of Experience.* London: Routledge.

Pert, C.B. (1998) *Molecules of Emotion: Why You Feel the Way You Feel.* London: Simon and Schuster.

Rogers, C. (1975) 'Empathic: an unappreciated way of being.' *Counseling Psychologist 5*, 2, 2–10.

Spiro, H. (1993) 'What is empathy and can it be taught?' in H. Spiro, M.G. McCrea Curnen, E. Peschel and D. St. James (eds) *Empathy and the Practice of Medicine: Beyond Pills and the Scalpel.* London: Yale University Press.

Spiro, H., McCrea Curnen, M.G., Peschel, E. and St. James, D. (eds) (1993) *Empathy and the Practice of Medicine: Beyond Pills and the Scalpel.* London: Yale University Press.

Wiener, J. and Sher, M. (1998) *Counselling and Psychotherapy in Primary Health Care: A Psychodynamic Approach.* London and Basingstoke: Macmillan.

Chapter 1

A wounded healer

From client to counsellor

Heather Goodare

A cancer diagnosis

When I was diagnosed with breast cancer at the age of 55 it seemed highly unlikely that this would lead to a new career. I had been suffering from severe clinical depression for several years but had recently made a full recovery, only to find my breast lump three months later. (I am certain that the two were connected.)

I had been working sporadically as a freelance editor in academic publishing, and on completing my treatment I started work again – in fact I took on too much, and soon regretted it. Gradually I realised that this work was really now not at all fulfilling. Yes, I did make some improvements in some of these manuscripts sent to me, but what about writing my *own* manuscripts, singing my own song for a change?

The theme of 'singing one's own song' was highlighted in Lawrence LeShan's *You Can Fight for Your Life* (1984), which I had read after my visit to the Bristol Cancer Help Centre in January 1987. I heard about the Bristol Centre through an old publishing colleague who had also had breast cancer and spoke highly of the place. Psychological support had not been available at my local hospital (where in those days there was no breast care nurse or Macmillan nurse), and as a person with recent experience of depression I was still vulnerable, and certainly needed counselling. This I found at the Bristol Centre, and in one or two sessions was able to do more healing work than had been possible during the previous several years in my emotional wilderness. My general practitioner had been kind and supportive, but did no more than offer medication and the services of the community psychiatric nurse, who also was kind, but had neither the time nor the training to undertake psychotherapy. The psychiatrist to whom I was later referred, again, did not seem to me to offer what I needed: increased medication was not the answer.

The Bristol Cancer Help Centre

The Bristol Centre offered much: art therapy, medical counselling, dietary advice, biofeedback, relaxation, visualisation and meditation, gentle exercise, and (most important for me) psychological counselling and group therapy. Even during the first year after my diagnosis I realised that what I really wanted to do now was to train as a counsellor myself, but my therapist at Bristol wisely advised caution, saying that I needed at least two years to fully regain my own health before embarking on such an endeavour.

So was it really a good idea to do this? Just before the two years were up I enrolled as a volunteer for Breast Cancer Care, undertaking the brief training programme offered, so as to qualify as a befriender to the newly diagnosed. But more importantly, during those two years I sought therapy myself in my home town, to heal old wounds caused by the break-up of my first marriage. I also needed to deal with unresolved issues from childhood – being separated from my parents and sent to a boarding school at the age of 5: though I had never lost the faith they taught me, I had a lasting resentment at the missionary society that had sent them to West Africa and deprived me of their care during those important years. My mother-substitute had been an unmarried aunt, who had been warm and nurturing in the school holidays (in fact I loved her more than my mother), but I sadly lacked a father-figure.

My first husband, a refugee from Eastern Europe, resembled my father physically, and certainly filled an emotional gap for me. For therapy after my breast cancer I went to a Jungian analyst who was also a priest, and could be the receptacle for all my negative thoughts about God, religion, and men who loved me and left me. Both my father and my husband had been creative, imaginative and charming: my father an artist, poet and writer as well as priest and teacher; my husband a musician, extremely well read in world literature in spite of being brought up under Communism, and finally a good writer on musical subjects in a language that was initially completely foreign to him. My father had died relatively young, of bowel cancer; my husband had left me for a younger woman, and although I had married again, these losses (together with the loss of my health) had to be worked through.

Counselling training

I now felt ready to undertake formal training, and embarked on a counselling skills course to enable me to take on an active role in my local cancer support group. After two years of this training I felt that I needed to explore psychotherapy more seriously, and decided to seek entry to a postgraduate diploma in counselling. I filled in the application form with some trepidation: I would be 59 when the course started – would I be considered too old? Apparently not, in spite of considerable competition for places, so in September 1990 I started the two-year course, which during its life accompanied Brighton Polytechnic in its metamorphosis into Brighton University.

During the preceding years I had become aware that there were many routes I could have taken: cognitive behavioural, transpersonal, humanistic, psychodynamic, Gestalt. I decided that what I had to do was to find a 'mainstream' course that would be widely accepted by orthodox medical practitioners, if I were to be able to build bridges with those very doctors who (it seemed to me) so grossly misunderstood the interaction of mind and body, especially in cancer. The course at Brighton seemed to fill the bill.

The first year provided a syllabus in humanistic, person-centred therapy, based largely on the work of Carl Rogers. We were also introduced to various other approaches – Gestalt, Transactional Analysis, personal construct, cognitive behavioural, rational emotive therapy – and in the second year were invited to formulate our own personal models of counselling. Looking back at the essay I wrote at the time, it seems I was already exploring an existential approach, which seemed to me to be particularly relevant to work with people struggling with a cancer diagnosis. With this philosophical position I combined elements of Gestalt and TA and, when appropriate, the relaxation and visualisation techniques that I had first learnt myself at the Bristol Centre, and which formed part of our course at Brighton. I was also leaning towards psychosynthesis: when working with people faced with life-and-death issues it was important, I felt, not to neglect the spiritual element of their experience, and while psychoanalysis was important, the re-integration of the psyche was also vital, particularly for those who felt broken and in pieces. I ended my essay by saying: 'My personal model of counselling would be both person-centred and holistic, engaging with the client at the levels of body, mind, emotions, and spirit.'

The course at Brighton included several intensive weekends exploring topics such as sexuality, drama therapy, and so on, as well as the different approaches to counselling. We had to submit tapes of our work with clients, with transcripts and detailed process commentaries. We wrote essays, we took part in group work, we attended classes where we worked in pairs and saw the results on video. Finally we had to submit a full-length dissertation. My subject was 'Evaluating the outcome of counselling for people with cancer: some issues of methodology and ethics'. A revised version of this was eventually published in the American journal *Advances* (Goodare 1994).

Embarking on this course meant full-time commitment: even though the course itself was part-time, work with clients, writing essays, analysing tapes, and so on, didn't leave much time for anything else. I had also taken on another assignment: the translation of a book by a Swiss psychiatrist, Patrice Guex, with the title *Psychologie et Cancer* (published by Routledge as *An Intro-duction to Psycho-Oncology* in 1994). I was, moreover, involved with a new cancer support group that I had co-founded earlier the same year. I had enough to do. But in September 1990, just as I had embarked on my coun-selling training, the news broke that a study had been published in *The Lancet* (Bagenal *et al.* 1990) showing that women with breast cancer who attended the Bristol Cancer Help Centre were twice as likely to die and three times as likely to relapse as women who had orthodox therapy only.

The 'Bristol study'

When I read the report I was appalled. I had been one of the 'subjects' of that study, and I knew from the inside that it must be grossly flawed. Indeed, such was eventually shown to be the case, but not before the Bristol Centre nearly had to close down through lack of funding and loss of public confidence.

The story of the women's battle to challenge the study and paint their side of the picture is told in the book *Fighting Spirit* (Goodare 1996). This campaign took its toll of time and energy, but had to be pursued to a satisfac-tory conclusion. We were finally vindicated when the Charity Commission upheld our complaint about the way in which the two big cancer charities, the Imperial Cancer Research Fund (ICRF) and the Cancer Research Campaign (CRC), who had sponsored the research, publicised the results of the study without being sure that they were soundly based.

My experience of this study and its aftermath gave me something of a distrust of medical research. How could such a study have gone so spectacu-larly wrong, and still be published in a reputable medical journal? I began to understand that medical research was not a simple matter of the pursuit of scientific truth. Vested interests were at stake: medical, pharmaceutical, even emotional. Doctors who had given their life's work to a certain avenue of exploration would not be likely to sacrifice it lightly. If in one's biomedical philosophy there is no room for the extra dimension of the influence of the mind on the body (or indeed the body on the mind), the kind of work pioneered at the Bristol Cancer Help Centre is deeply suspect. Further, the idea of viewing the human being holistically, that is, as a whole system of mind–body, or body–mind, may be viewed as strange, incomprehensible, irrational. Any preliminary results from the Bristol study that appeared to show the Bristol women doing worse (ignoring the fact that on average they were younger and had worse prognoses than the controls) had to be published immediately. So began the tragic saga leading to the suicide of one of the authors, Dr Tim McElwain.

Of course, no one can know for certain why Dr McElwain took his own life: he was known to be a caring clinician, and his death was a source of deep regret to everyone who knew him, patients and professionals alike. To the women in the survey it was a setback too: it would have been tasteless to pursue our campaign until a decent interval had elapsed. But pursue it we had to; we needed to right a wrong, and set the record straight.

Cancer politics

In doing this work it became clear that cancer politics often got in the way of patients' interests. While psycho-oncologists were squabbling over whether or not stressful life events had any significance in the development of cancer, whether there was a 'cancer-prone personality', whether 'fighting spirit' should be encouraged, whether those characterised as 'helpless/hopeless' could change and overcome depressive tendencies, I was now working with people in my cancer support group, listening to their stories, and finding much that was fascinating. During my training my tutor had been greatly concerned with 'parallel process', imagining that for me working with cancer clients would be hazardous, since their experience would be too near my own. The opposite was the case. My experience with the Bristol study had given me a strange new strength and confidence. Together with a fellow patient, Isla Bourke, I had challenged the heads of the ICRF and the CRC in a television programme and gained an apology from them on film. After facing the possibility of death from cancer, nothing else seemed very frightening, certainly not sparring with eminent doctors. Cancer was no longer a threat, even though my original prognosis had not been good. (My 'Nottingham Prognostic Index', as I discovered much later, had been 6.)

The search for meaning

What fascinated me about my work with cancer clients was *their* explanations, *their* search for meaning, *their* desire to make sense of it all. Rarely did they have the standard set of risk factors for their particular cancer; almost without exception they were convinced that what lay at the root of their disease was some chronic stress, some feeling of being trapped – looking after an elderly relative or a disabled child; stifled by an unhappy marriage; choked in a dead-end job, or made redundant after years of loyal service. Exploring early years, there had often been abuse. During World War II children had been evacuated, and this was sometimes a terrifying experience, leaving deep scars and resulting in personalities that were lacking in trust and turned inwards. As LeShan observes (LeShan 1989), such people, when subject to similar stresses in adult life, adopt similar patterns of behaviour, bottling up feelings and apparently coping in a self-sufficient manner, to the detriment of creativity, and putting a strain on the immune system.

A psychological explanation of cancer aetiology does not, of course, tell the whole story, but I believe it accounts for part of it in many cases, and my clients certainly thought so (Guex 1994; Walker, Heys and Eremin1999). Cancer had given them the excuse to seek help to resolve issues that had dogged them all their lives, and been dormant for years.

Our cancer support group was able to offer six free sessions to clients (later extended to eight), which was often enough to help them to turn around, make changes, gain self-awareness and move forward. Sometimes, however, particularly when there was a case of childhood sexual abuse now revealed for the first time, there had to be an agreement for further work to be done under a renewed contract.

Ever since Galen, in the second century AD, remarked that women with breast cancer were 'melancholic', physicians had noted the mind–body connection in cancer. This lasted until the twentieth century, when the new biomedical sciences started to dismiss such psychological explanations as mumbo-jumbo. Only now in the twenty-first century are the two sides of medicine coming together again, and even in NHS hospitals the value of counselling and complementary therapies for people with cancer is recognised.

Qualifications of a cancer counsellor

I am sometimes asked: do you have to have had cancer in order to be a cancer counsellor? No: a good counsellor should be able to empathise with others, whatever their experience. But I believe that my cancer experience has informed and enriched my work. Though self-disclosure should, of course, only be used with care in counselling, I have sometimes had clients who were particularly anxious to work with a counsellor who had had such personal experience, and in any case, the fact that I have had cancer is in the public domain. It helps, too, to have knowledge of cancer treatments and their impact on quality of life, to know, for instance, that vaginal dryness causing dyspareunia can be a side effect of tamoxifen; that chemotherapy may give rise to severe depression even in those without a previous history of depression, and so on.

For the last four years I have edited the newsletter of the National Association of Cancer Counsellors, where we have debated similar issues and sought further professional development in our seminars. I have now overcome my feeling of inferiority in having no medical background, unlike many of my colleagues with experience of nursing or radiography. My own experience as a patient was equally valuable, and I could join the ranks of wounded healers with pride. But I also felt that it was important to keep up some private work with clients who did not suffer from cancer, and this I still do. For them the fact that I have had cancer is totally irrelevant, and I never mention it to them.

Group therapy

Much of the work I now do is in groups, as well as with individuals. Initially people contact me through the cancer support group telephone helpline, and in most cases I arrange a meeting one-to-one to assess their needs before suggesting the next step, which may be individual counselling (sometimes with other counsellors working with the group), complementary therapies (also offered by the group), or attendance at group sessions. My initial counselling training included group work, and this was invaluable in making me aware of group dynamics and how to handle them. I was fortunate that during the course at Brighton I met a male colleague who was keen to do some voluntary work with cancer clients, and for five years we jointly facilitated the group sessions in our cancer support charity. This meant that we could give each other feedback on our 'performance'. (We took it in turns to be the 'leader'.) When this colleague decided to move on, by some wonderful chance another male facilitator with a counselling background appeared. To have both male and female facilitators for the group is ideal, since this gives a 'mother' and 'father' figure for the group family. It also gives continuity when one or other is on vacation.

Since our group is a self-help group rather than a therapy group, and is open rather than closed, the opportunities for challenging are limited. The group is usually in the phase of 'forming' and 'norming', and rarely progresses to 'storming' (Tuckman 1965). It is always necessary to remember that newly diagnosed clients are often very vulnerable. There is also the danger that in an open group new clients may encounter people who have relapsed, or who have advanced disease. However, after much thought and discussion with the group itself (which is nothing if not democratic) we decided not to segregate the 'advanced' clients from the newly diagnosed. This was for two reasons: first, it is doubly difficult for people struggling with advanced disease to be 'rejected' by a group they have come to know and trust. Second, the newly diagnosed are inevitably struggling with the same issues as those relapsing – that is, the existential issues of life and death. The first question often asked by people with cancer is: 'Am I going to die?'

Working with groups is constantly challenging, but also energising. The facilitator has to be constantly aware of unspoken feelings, and needs to make sure that everyone has the opportunity to speak if they wish, or to remain silent if that is appropriate for them. But the main task is simply to be there and encourage the sometimes miraculous interactions that take place between people who find strength from each other from merely being 'in the same boat' (Ephraim 1988; Spiegel 1993). Anger and frustration are frequently expressed, and tears shed, but there is often laughter – though sometimes it may be 'gallows' laughter. Tips are exchanged about how to cope with cancer treatments. On one occasion I remember a group member was in despair because she suffered from needle phobia and could not face the idea of having chemotherapy. One by one various group members offered suggestions about how to cope. In the event, when she had her treatment, she was able to visualise the group sitting round in a circle, all offering tips in their different ways, and this enabled her to sail through her treatment. She even gave a newspaper interview afterwards, describing how the group had 'saved her life'. Another member was frightened of having an MRI scan, and similarly found that visualising the group helped her through the experience.

Working with death

The death of a group member can be very distressing, but can also present an opportunity. It is particularly difficult for a group if a young member dies, but this will inevitably happen in a cancer support group at some time. My own experience is that such an event must be worked through, and the appropriate rituals observed. For the sake of the bereaved, the person who dies must be remembered; but for those still living it is also very important to celebrate fully. Some members will want to attend the funeral. The group newsletter (if one exists) must mention the death and celebrate the life. For the sake of those who remain, it is necessary to establish that each person is valued by the group, and the death of any member gives everyone the opportunity to meditate on the eternal verities and to consider how they too would like to be remembered. Such an exercise can be truly creative. The worst thing to do is to sweep the whole thing under the carpet.

Children and cancer

I am very conscious that we can do little to help children with a parent who has cancer unless we can provide specialist therapy for them. In my work I have not yet been able to do this. Children need their own counsellors and their own groups. What we can do, however, is to encourage parents to share with their children, as far as they can, what is going on. Children sense when something is wrong with parents, and fobbing them off with incomplete explanations is not helpful. Worse, not allowing them to attend funerals of close relatives can give rise to problems in later life. I once worked with a woman with breast cancer whose life-long problems stemmed not simply from her father's death when she was ten, but from the fact that she was whisked out of the way during his last illness and not allowed to attend the funeral, from the mistaken belief that she would find it all 'too upsetting'. In this kind of context children tend to imagine things that are far worse than the actual facts of the situation.

Boundaries

The traditional wisdom of counselling training holds that it is not advisable to work with clients simultaneously as individuals and in a group. The way to overcome this with a cancer clientele, I have found, is to offer individual work to people initially, if this seems to be appropriate, and then encourage them to progress on to the group as their ego strength develops. Sometimes people are too vulnerable to face a group straight away, but after individual work and encouragement may well benefit from such a progression, particularly when they realise that they are not alone. I found myself working with several individual men who were supporting women with breast cancer, and they were all saying the same kind of thing: 'When I try to help her she pushes me away, and then when I back off she says, "Why can't you see I need help?"' So the idea came to me that my time would be more economically spent if I could persuade these men to join a group and support each other. So was born the 'Men's Group', with the idea that it would be a therapy group, with commitment to attend regularly. One of them (Keith Fuller) wrote in our group newsletter (July 1998):

> I, like many others in the same position, looked upon the situation as society had educated me with the attitude, 'I haven't got the cancer. I'm a man, not a wimp. I should cope with anything that life can throw at me.' Stiff upper lip and all that. WRONG! I hit rock bottom without realizing it. I needed help.

> [After the first meeting] I felt invigorated and couldn't wait for the next one. I no longer felt alone or unusual. It felt as if I was a member of a large club. These meetings have continued over a number of weeks and we all feel as if we have gleaned a great deal of strength, support and comfort from each other and no longer feel quite so lonely. My personal feelings are that this type of group therapy for the carer works extremely well.

This group evolved into a mixed group for carers; then, as some of the cared-for died, those who were bereaved formed a separate group led by another counsellor who used art therapy in her work, while those still caring continued to meet on a different day. Such groups need to change and adapt to meet the changing needs of clients.

Rules are, however, made to be broken. Irving Yalom, a distinguished practitioner in the field of cancer psychotherapy, found that 'the realities of clinical practice are such that the ideal format for a patient is not always ideal or even feasible for a therapist'. Moreover, 'some patients may go through a severe life crisis that requires considerable individual temporary support in addition to group therapy. Occasionally individual therapy is required in order to enable a patient to use the group' (Yalom 1985). Ideally individual work is carried out with another therapist who is not also facilitating the group, but in a crisis the group leader may be the only one available, and it is also important not to be seen as rejecting the client in his or her hour of need.

Self-help groups are different from closed therapy groups in that members are free to contact each other outside the group, and are in fact encouraged to do so. This may give rise to all kinds of sub-groups, which may or may not affirm group norms. Mostly, however, they are formed for purposive action – fundraising, for instance.

Extramural activities

Some of the most life-enhancing experiences in the life of my own group have been just such activities. As part of our tenth anniversary celebrations, which coincided with the millennium year, we decided to hold a fashion show. All the people taking part would be cancer survivors, or those closely touched by cancer. In the event we had 21 participants: 4 men and 17 women, of whom 19 had had cancer and two had cared for parents with cancer. In our town we have a 10 per cent Asian minority, and we were able to reflect this in our group. The participants included two Indian women, one Iranian, and one Chinese. We were even able to parade some Asian fashions – Punjabi suits that actually stole the show (with Asian background music).

The event was a financial success, making over £1000 for our funds, but more importantly, it was a tremendous bonding exercise: women who had been shy about showing mastectomy scars were thrown together in the dressing rooms, and in the scramble to change outfits forgot any diffidence or shame. They strutted proudly on the catwalk, able to look good and feel good in a variety of beautiful clothes. It did wonders for their self-esteem. The three male cancer survivors who took part derived similar benefit: two had had testicular cancer and one cancer of the prostate, which struck at their masculinity no less than breast cancer struck at the femininity of the women. To demonstrate that they were still attractive was an act of triumphant affirmation.

Using the arts

Was this group therapy? Yes, in a way, it was. Music and the arts can also make for vivid group experiences. I have mentioned art therapy: this can enable expression of emotion when words might seem inadequate or banal. The same goes for music therapy, which I have experienced as a participant at the Bristol Cancer Help Centre and elsewhere, and have recently introduced to our local group (I am an amateur musician). Sometimes the group listens to music, but the main activity is participatory, using simple percussion instruments which need no technical skill. It can be incredibly moving to witness the wordless communication between people in a music therapy group, the sending of gentle, loving messages, and the building up of a group piece in which inhibitions are shed and strong emotions such as anger can be expressed without fear of censure. Such experiences can be cathartic, and can also evoke memories and give rise to the telling of personal stories. The sound of a bell for one will be sad – a reminder of the tolling of a church bell for the dead; for another it will mean something quite different – perhaps a mountain pasture, with cattle. The exploration of the meanings of these sounds can provide material for healing work.

Accompanying the client all the way

Inevitably there are times when people contact a self-help group only on discovering that they have recurrent or 'terminal' disease. This is when they particularly need counselling, and when it may be necessary to be flexible in one's ways of working. The client may be elderly, weak, unable to drive, and cannot attend the counsellor's home or the group's premises. They may have difficulty in concentrating for the traditional hour, and sessions may need to be shorter than usual, or more (or less) frequent than once a week, or take different forms. On one occasion I visited a woman who was in the middle of a course of very toxic chemotherapy, and severely depressed. She was also suffering from sore feet (a side effect of the chemotherapy). Talking was not what she needed most. I offered to massage her feet (wondering what on earth my supervisor would say when I reported this session to her). It seemed that on this occasion such a gesture was entirely appropriate, and the client still remembers it. In fact, this may well have been the turning point in her healing: although she had secondary cancer in the stomach (after primary breast cancer), from which the possibility of remission was remote, she has in fact made a remarkable recovery and is well at the time of writing, three years later.

Sometimes, as Elisabeth Kübler-Ross observes (Kübler-Ross 1970), the most appropriate form of contact with people who are dying is that of touch. Holding a hand can often say more than words. Traditional psychotherapy eschews such contact, but for people with cancer, who often feel stigmatised and untouchable, touch can have a magical effect. I remember feeling welcomed into a warm and loving family when I experienced hugs at the Bristol Cancer Help Centre, and in our group too, after initial formalities, hugs are frequently exchanged between group members. This is in contrast to the norm in clinical settings.

Sometimes it is necessary to refer on to other counsellors in a local hospice, but this needs to be individually negotiated, so that the client does not feel abandoned. At the very least, good liaison with palliative care is essential.

Role conflict

One of the problems often encountered by cancer counsellors, particularly in hospital settings, is that of role conflict. People with cancer may well confide in counsellors their feelings of anger and frustration at delays in diagnosis and treatment, and unhappiness with the way they have been told the 'bad news'. Although many health professionals are aware of such problems, and training in communication skills is now more often provided, under-funding in the NHS will take some time to rectify. Counsellors must listen to the client with genuine empathy, while remaining loyal to their colleagues. This is where supervision is so important; ideally it should be completely independent of the hospital setting. A counsellor like myself, working outside the hospital system, does not have such a problem. However, I have occasionally found myself acting as a patient advocate, or suggesting referral to other agencies such as the Community Health Council, when there was a genuine conflict to be resolved.

Finally, I have to say something about self-care. So far I have been lucky enough to survive breast cancer without relapse for the last fourteen years. If I were to have a recurrence, I would either retire (which at my age would be entirely appropriate) or take two years out before taking up a counselling role again. This is because I believe that in my case emotional issues played a large part in the onset of my disease, and I would therefore have to work on myself again in therapy before feeling able to resume my work with others. Whether the psyche always plays a part in cancer is an unresolved question. I believe that being a 'wounded healer' has been helpful in my work. But the wounds need to be properly healed. To love others one needs first to be able to love oneself.

References

Bagenal, F. S., Easton, D. F., Harris, E., Chilvers, C. E. D. and McElwain, T. J. (1990) 'Survival of patients with breast cancer attending Bristol Cancer Help Centre.' *The Lancet 336*, 606–610.

Ephraim, N. W. (1988) 'Self-help groups.' In M. Aveline and W. Dryden (eds) *Group Therapy in Britain*. Milton Keynes: Open University Press.

Goodare, H. (1994) 'Counselling people with cancer: questions and possibilities.' *Advances: The Journal of Mind–Body Health 10*, 2, 4–17.

Goodare, H. (ed) (1996) *Fighting Spirit: The Stories of Women in the Bristol Breast Cancer Survey*. London: Scarlet Press.

Guex, P. trans. Goodare, H. (1994) *An Introduction to Psycho-Oncology*. London: Routledge.

Kübler-Ross, E. (1970) *On Death and Dying*. London: Tavistock/Routledge.

LeShan, L. (1984) *You Can Fight for Your Life: Emotional Factors in the Treatment of Cancer*. Wellingborough: Thorsons.

LeShan, L. (1989) *Cancer as a Turning Point*. Bath, UK: Gateway Books.

Spiegel, D. (1993) *Living Beyond Limits: New Hope and Help for Facing Life-Threatening Illness*. New York: Random House.

Tuckman, B. (1965) 'Developmental sequences in small groups.' *Psychological Bulletin 63*, 384–399.

Walker, L. G., Heys, S. D. and Eremin, O. (1999) 'Surviving cancer: do psychosocial factors count?' *Journal of Psychosomatic Research 47*, 6, 497–503.

Yalom, I. (1985) *The Theory and Practice of Group Psychotherapy* (third edition). New York: Basic Books.

Further reading

Barasch, M. I. (1995) *The Healing Path*. London: Penguin/Arkana.

Barraclough, J. (1994) *Cancer and Emotion: A Practical Guide to Psycho-Oncology* (second edition). Chichester: Wiley.

Bunt, L. (1994) *Music Therapy: An Art Beyond Words*. London: Routledge.

Burton, M. and Watson, M. (1998) *Counselling People with Cancer*. Chichester: Wiley.

Connell, C. (1998) *Something Understood: Art Therapy in Cancer Care*. London: Wrexham Publications.

De Hennezel, M., trans. Janeway, J. (1997) *Intimate Death*. London: Warner Books.

Goodare, H. (2001) 'Patient heal thyself.' In J. Barraclough (ed) *Integrated Cancer Care: Holistic, Complementary and Creative Approaches*. Oxford: Oxford University Press.

Haber, S. (1997) *Breast Cancer: A Psychological Treatment Manual*. London: Free Association Books.

Jobst, K. (1999) 'Diseases of meaning, manifestations of health, and metaphor.' *Journal of Alternative and Complementary Medicine 5*, 6, 495–502.

Leick, N. and Davidsen-Nielsen, M., trans. Stoner, D. (1991) *Healing Pain: Attachment, Loss and Grief Therapy.* London: Tavistock/Routledge.

Lerner, M. (1994) *Choices in Healing: Integrating the Best of Conventional and Complementary Approaches to Cancer.* Cambridge, Mass.: MIT Press.

Martin, P. (1998) *The Sickening Mind: Brain, Behaviour, Immunity and Disease.* London: Flamingo.

Moorey, S. and Greer, S. (1989) *Psychological Therapy for Patients with Cancer: A New Approach.* London: Heinemann Medical Books.

Moyers, B. (1995) *Healing and the Mind.* London: Aquarian/Thorsons.

Wilber, K. (1991) *Grace and Grit.* Dublin: Gill & Macmillan.

Yalom, I. D. (1980) *Existential Psychotherapy.* New York: Basic Books.

Useful organisations

Association of Counsellors and Psychotherapists in Primary Care
Queensway House, Queensway, Bognor Regis, West Sussex PO21 1QT
Tel. 01243 870701

British Psychosocial Oncology Society
Hon. Secretary Cathy Heaven, Psychological Medicine Group, Christie Hospital NHS Trust, Stanley House, Wilmslow Road, Withington, Manchester M20 4BX
Tel. 0161 446 3689

Bristol Cancer Help Centre
(runs courses for health professionals as well as patients and carers)
Grove House, Cornwallis Grove, Clifton, Bristol BS8 4PG
Tel. 0117 980 9500

CancerBACUP
(cancer information service)
3 Bath Place, Rivington Street, London EC2A 3JR
Tel. 020 7613 2121; freephone 0808 800 1234

CancerLink
(a resource for cancer support groups and individuals)
11–21 Northdown Street, London N1 9BN
Freephone cancer information 0800 132905; Administration 020 7833 2818

Counselling in Primary Care Trust
First Floor, Majestic House, High Street, Staines TW18 4DG
Tel. 01784 441782

Faculty of Healthcare Counsellors and Psychotherapists
(a division of the British Association for Counselling and Psychotherapy)
1 Regent Place, Rugby, Warwickshire CV21 2PJ
Tel. 01788 550899

Chapter 2

Palliative care counselling

Emotional and psychological support from diagnosis to death

Kate Kirk and Maria Lever

'This service is a godsend. I don't know what I'd have done without it! Maria has calmed my troubled mind and given me coping strategies.' (Comment from a client evaluation sheet)

The words of this client express very clearly the disorientation that comes about when a person is either diagnosed with a life-threatening illness, or told that they are dying and there is neither treatment nor hope. This chapter looks at the role and experiences of the counsellor working in a palliative care setting.

Introduction

It is generally understood that palliative care is given to people whose illness may no longer be curable. A traditional definition of palliative care focuses on the 'active, total care of patients whose disease no longer responds to curative treatment, and for whom the goal must be the best quality of life for them and their families' (National Council for Hospice and Specialist Palliative Care Services). As will become apparent, for the purpose of our work we choose a much broader definition: we extend palliative care to include times when a person's life is threatened by a diagnosis of a potentially life-limiting illness, for example cancer, motor neurone disease, HIV and heart disease.

In this chapter we intend to introduce the reader to the Palliative Care Counselling Service run in Salford, England, and then present four case studies relating appropriate theory to the practice of counselling clients with life-threatening illness. We will explore some of the significant and unique factors associated with this type of work and reflect on the impact on ourselves as counsellors.

Whilst we both work as palliative care counsellors, Kate is a psychodrama psychotherapist with a background in health visiting and Maria is a cognitive behavioural psychotherapist with a background in psychology. You will become aware of our very different ways of working, both through the content of our case studies and in our writing styles. We view our differences to be of positive benefit to this service and our clients. Following initial assessment, our differences mean that we can respond appropriately to the client's unique needs.

Background to the service

The Palliative Care Counselling Service is funded by Salford Community Health Care NHS Trust. This service commenced in 1994, using Health Improvement Programme money to employ two full-time counsellors to develop a community-based counselling service providing emotional and psychological support to patients with potentially life-threatening or terminal illness and those directly involved in their care. The post is thought to be the first of its kind in the UK, as most other counselling services in this field are attached to hospices or are provided by nurses or social workers combining counselling with their primary role. Referrals to this service are taken from health care professionals, social services, the voluntary sector, and by self-referral. The counselling sessions are arranged either in the clients' own homes or in local health centres.

Relating theory to practice

In this section we present four case studies, two post-diagnosis and two poor prognosis clients. The case studies are intended to demonstrate both the type of clients referred to our service and our different therapeutic styles and interventions. Following each case study we have added our reflections on the work. We explore some aspects of theory that informed us as we worked, as well as personal and professional dilemmas that may have been present. The first two cases present two very different post-diagnosis scenarios, both for the client and the counsellor involved.

Post-diagnosis: Choices (Maria and Charles)

Charles was a 50-year-old man who had been diagnosed with asbestosis a couple of years previously, and more recently had been diagnosed with cirrhosis. He was referred to our service by his social worker, who felt he would benefit from having the time and space to explore his situation and options with a counsellor experienced in palliative care. Charles had been a client with alcohol services for a couple of years, following a severe bout of depression requiring admission to a psychiatric hospital, and at the time of referral he was staying at a half-way house. This was where I met him and where the counselling sessions took place.

Although we were given the privacy of an interview room, there was an expectation from the staff that they should be privy to any information arising from the sessions, as the counselling sessions were perceived to be part of Charles' care plan. In the light of this, I clarified with him the level of confidentiality I could offer. Charles was happy for his social worker to have access to information, but he was unwilling to extend this to other staff. He agreed to my writing my name and the date of the counselling session in his care plan. The aim of his stay was to try and come to terms with his condition and decide his future. He was under pressure from his family, friends and, to a lesser extent, professionals in the alcohol field to 'dry out' and consequently have a longer life. The professionals involved were concerned that he was depressed and therefore not thinking clearly about his situation.

Charles felt very alone, and that no one really understood him. In the course of the counselling it soon became clear that the issue was less to do with whether he wanted to be 'dry' or not and more to do with how he wanted to die. Charles believed he was perceived as selfish by many who thought he was 'taking the easy way out' by not 'drying out'. Charles felt he was taking control of his life; he knew that if he carried on drinking, even moderately, this would kill him. He preferred this to dying a 'long, lingering death', gradually deteriorating and having to rely on others to care for him. Charles had been a fit, active man; because of his breathing difficulties he found walking arduous and had to use a stick, which he found hard to accept.

Charles had left his wife and children when he felt they were being affected by his drinking; he reasoned that leaving would help them come to terms with eventually living without him and teach them to manage on their own. He was pursuing a claim for compensation for the asbestosis and he knew his family would be well provided for after his death. I suggested that he had been 'putting his affairs in order' for some time and he agreed, but this was not how other people had interpreted his actions. In the course of our work it became obvious that he was not depressed; he had thought clearly about what he wanted and the impact his untimely death would have on his family, and he felt he had prepared them as best as he could. Now that his affairs were in order he just wanted to be left alone to get on with his dying. Ironically, Charles felt his family, friends and even professionals were inadvertently placing more pressure on him by trying to encourage him to be 'dry'. When he was under pressure he drank more and he believed this would ultimately kill him sooner.

COUNSELLOR'S REFLECTIONS

This case illustrates the impact of dual diagnosis. Charles had been coping with his initial diagnosis, but the second diagnosis had given him the choice of how he wanted to die. With the second diagnosis Charles felt it was no longer sufficient just to cope with his diseases; he wanted to take control of his own destiny. Charles felt this distinction was important, but for others this choice was not apparent and the subject had become clouded by the alcohol issue. Charles was under pressure to live a longer life by abstaining from alcohol, but this was not what he wanted.

As a counsellor, I believe it is important for me to be clear about my boundaries and to recognise to whom I am responsible. This was an issue I examined at length in supervision. I concluded I was responsible to the client and felt his wishes were paramount. Barnes (1995) suggests that 'palliative care neither hastens nor postpones death. Its goal is to achieve the best quality of life...' This client was clearly saying that his quality of life would eventually deteriorate to a level that was unacceptable to him and that he preferred to die sooner rather than later. As a society I think we have difficulty in accepting when someone chooses to die; it sometimes seems we value length of life over the quality of life. As a palliative care counsellor I have met people who should have died, according to the medical experts, but inexplicably are still alive. Conversely, I have also met people who should have lived, or even recovered from their condition, but unexpectedly appeared to lose the will to live, and died. I believe my role is to discover what the client wants and to support him in this. Sadly, this case also highlights the diverse and sometimes irreconcilable needs of clients and their families within palliative care.

One final issue connected to balancing the needs of others with those of the client in this case was the belief of the other professionals involved that Charles' experiences were common property. This case highlights the importance of collaborating with the client in the confidentiality agreement and ensuring his needs were met, over and above those of the professionals, for whose records we established a compromise. (For further debate, see Jenkins 1997; Kell 1999.)

Post-diagnosis: Life is more than just numbers (Kate and Jack)

Jack, 53, was referred by his general practitioner. The previous week he had received a diagnosis of a devastating major heart condition, of which he had few symptoms other than 'a bit of angina'. It had been picked up following a routine medical examination for work. He required a quadruple bypass operation within two weeks. The chance of his surviving the operation was poor, only 40 per cent. Without the operation his quality of life would change significantly and deteriorate rapidly. Indeed, 'unexpected' death through sudden heart failure was 75 per cent likely.

Jack came into therapy railing at the fact that his life had been reduced to a statistic. His heartfelt belief was that 'life is more than just numbers'. He felt he had little choice but to go ahead with the operation and the hope it offered of an ordinary life. He felt angry at the injustice that, like his father who had died suddenly at an early age, he was being deprived of the opportunity to achieve all he had set out to. He was looking mortality 'straight in the face'. All this was creating a huge amount of anxiety for him and, he believed, exacerbating the stress on his heart.

Given the imminent operation date, and Jack's sense of urgency, we decided to look at preparing him for theatre in a positive state of mind. To scene-set, I asked him to create an unusual scene – the eve of the sort of death he'd always imagined for himself, when he's fully aware of its importance. Role reversing to become his older self, he lay down on the sofa, and using the present tense in a monologue he set out all that he imagined: 'I'm 76, I've just had a warm drink to settle me down for the night. I know that tonight I'll die in my sleep. This holds no fears for me. I've lived a good life.' Quietly he identifies all the components of his life which have brought him pleasures, challenges and pains. 'All in all they add up fine, I wouldn't be who I am today without these.'

I asked him to imagine his newspaper obituary and read the words used to describe Jack Cox. This was his obituary:

Jack Cox died today at the age of 76. He was a good man and a loving husband who worked hard to provide for his wife and family. He supported his two daughters through university and marvelled in their achievements.

When working, he was a sound businessman who was particularly good in conflict management and negotiating with trades unions. The church and his faith were important to him and in his retirement he became increasingly involved in home prayer groups and supporting people who were vulnerable. He had an unexpected dry sense of humour and was not above playing mild practical jokes on his more pompous friends.

After a few moments of reflective silence, Jack said, 'I've done so much of this already, except retire.' For the remainder of the session we explored how he might use the intervening days to be with his family and what strategies he could use to prepare for theatre and the post-operative period.

He contacted me one month later for a follow-up session. He realised that he had been 'spinning like a top and falling out of control' because of the shock of the diagnosis. He felt that he entered the hospital almost at peace, apart from 'usual pre-op nerves'. He had decided to reduce his working hours and work part-time, wanting to start to enjoy his personal life without the stress and pressure of his professional life. He made a full recovery and is fit and well.

COUNSELLOR'S REFLECTIONS

This post-diagnosis case is unusual. Because of the impending operation and its grave implications there was no need to deal with a debriefing of the diagnosis. The immediate need was to find some degree of equilibrium enabling Jack to be emotionally prepared for theatre.

There were three theoretical ideas that informed this session. The first two were the use of *surplus reality* and of *internal* and *external witness* (see Williams 1989). Surplus reality creates in the present a reality that may or may not ever happen: the scenes in which the enactment took place were surplus reality. So, as his own internal witness, old Jack reflects on his life, reviews his achievements and is prepared to enter death without remorse. The external witness of this life that has been lived is the reader of the obituary.

Often, when faced with a diagnosis of life-threatening illness, clients, whatever their age, face the eighth of Erikson's 'ages of man' (Erikson 1963). The task assigned to the age of 'maturity' is resolution of the conflict in 'ego integrity versus despair'. The lasting and favourable outcomes are renunciation, or letting go of the despair of the life unlived, and wisdom. Jack's despair is apparent in his anger, not only at the injustice of not having finished with living but also at the packaging of his life as statistics; all this was fuelled by the death of his father at an early age. The speedy resolution occurred when he recognised through the therapeutic process that he had achieved all his life goals. Had death come at that time it would have been untimely, but the difference was that he now felt ready to meet it.

The next two cases explore the kinds of creative interventions that may be used in work with clients who have a poor prognosis, and the impact of the work on the counsellor.

Poor prognosis: Blasting the monster in the room (Kate and Claire)

Claire, 43, had had a fairly recent diagnosis of an inoperable lung cancer that occupied 75 per cent of her left lung. In the referral by a specialist nurse from the regional lung cancer unit, Claire expressed a desire to work with 'visualisations' on her cancer; she got the idea from a television programme on mind–body and illness. Despite a poor prognosis, giving her at most two months of life, she was undertaking an intensive course of 'extra strong' chemotherapy as part of a clinical trial. Our first session took place on the hospital ward.

On assessment for our service, Claire presented as physically very fragile, mostly due to the intensity of the chemotherapy and its deleterious effects, particularly vomiting and exhaustion. Claire was determined to live her 'life sentence' to the full. She was frustrated by the weakness of her body and being labelled a 'cancer victim' and wanted to have some control over what was happening to her. She talked about the impact of the TV programme and that she wanted to 'do' something like that about her cancer. We arranged to start therapeutic work following her discharge from hospital.

At home she continued to be frail, so we decided to opt for visualisation rather than anything more strenuous. Having gone through a deep relaxation, Claire identified a powerful symbolic image representing her lung cancer. Inside a large pink room lurked a monster, grey and black; the monster was a cross between the 'honey monster' and the Tasmanian Devil. The difference was that it grew at a phenomenal rate, as in Quatermass. The only thing that would halt its growth and destroy it was to blast the monster in the room with laser rods, like the ones in Star Wars. This she did; on my recommendation she exhaled powerfully, blowing away all the bits of the monster. Soon she became adept at both the relaxation and the visualisation. When we concluded the session her comment, to my relief, was that the experience was just like on the television. As my annual leave was due, I arranged to meet her three weeks later; she promised to visualise as often as possible during our break.

On my return Claire described two important changes, one to her visualisation and the other to her cancer. She had decided that it wasn't enough just to blow away the pieces of the monster, she wanted to remove every trace of it out of the room. So she had visualised brushing up every last piece, leaving the room spotless. The second change was that her cancer had 'miraculously' shrunk, leaving just a small growth nestling behind her heart. She felt that she had been responsible for the changes because she had worked so hard to get rid of the monster.

We decided upon a continuation of the metaphor and, because of her renewed vigour, dramatised the process, a *psychodrama à deux*. She placed the little monster in the room hiding behind a sensitive lifeline (symbolising her heart); she decided that the only person who could use a rapier carefully enough not to destroy the lifeline was to be Xena the Warrior Princess. She then role-reversed and became Xena. Her stance and tone of voice strengthened; she became almost aggressive in her verbal and physical assault on the monster. She, as Xena, 'read the riot act' to the monster, threatening what she would do to it. In response, rather than role reverse and become the monster, Xena reported back to me what the monster said. The dialogue continued until Xena ploughed in with her 'lightning sword' and cut the monster away, leaving the lifeline unharmed. The dead body was dropped into a lead-lined cask and sunk in a well hundreds of feet deep. Claire returned from her battle as Xena exhausted but immeasurably satisfied with what she had achieved.

She spent the intervening week going over the action in her mind. At the same time the consultant reported that the cancer was in remission. I asked Claire what remission meant to her and she compared it to a 'dormant, sleeping volcano'. We then looked at how we could 'kill' the volcano so it would never erupt. She packed ice around the base of a volcano that looked like Mount Fuji. This was to remove any of the residual fire and heat that might alight and cause an eruption.

The subsequent therapeutic process followed a more traditional counselling route. We explored themes that included:

- the delay in diagnosis and Claire's anger at being ignored by the GP until it was too late
- the fear that she would not live to see her daughter's wedding
- her mortality and the cancer stories in her family (her father's death through lung cancer and her mother's through bowel cancer)
- the injustice of never having smoked and yet having lung cancer.

Claire's last visualisation, on the hospital ward, was of a bird in a gilded cage with the door wide open. She felt imprisoned and wanted to fly away to freedom, unrestricted by the physical limits she felt were placed on her, i.e. the treadmill of hospital appointments, having blood tests, X-rays, scans. Almost a year after getting her poor prognosis Claire died, not of lung cancer but of a heart attack.

COUNSELLOR'S REFLECTIONS

One important aspect of our work is to work with clients in their homes. They have so many hospital appointments that fill their weeks that we, more often than not, come to them. Working with clients in a domiciliary setting is challenging; dogs, unexpected callers, toddlers straying in from another room, telephone calls, all disrupt the therapeutic space.

Working in a hospital setting is just as difficult. Hospitals are amazingly noisy places where, as will be seen, there appears to be a hierarchy of roles and responsibilities. Claire was in a single room on the ward for our first contact. This was not as peaceful as I would have hoped. Despite the nurses' sensitivities as to what was going on behind the closed doors, just at that time the cleaner needed to mop the floor, the doctor needed to review some aspect of treatment and the phlebotomist wanted to collect some blood. A subsequent session was even more difficult: Claire was in an open four-bedded ward with flimsy curtains drawn around the bed, offering a poor attempt at intimacy. The intrusions were negligible, but promoting confidentiality was impossible.

Individual psychodrama is called either psychodrama *à deux* or monodrama. Moreno (1965), the founder of psychodrama, stated that 'you can do psychodrama just like you do psychoanalysis. Instead of being on a couch you are on a stage in action, in a series of actions. You can do group psychodrama and individual psychodrama.' Casson (1997) identified a number of reasons for working psychodramatically with individual clients, including vulnerable, antisocial or isolated clients, those not ready for group work, or where scenes from a client's life would be too exposing for group members. My primary reasons for working individually, rather than in a group, are that the clients are often too physically vulnerable to be involved in the 'rough and tumble' of a therapy group, and that time is precious to them. Groups take time to set up.

From a psychodrama perspective, a diagnosis of cancer may push the client into a *restricted role repertoire*, as a cancer victim. The cancer victim is perceived to be powerless at the hands of well-meaning doctors, who know what is good for them and their cancer. Through the process of visualisation, Claire felt empowered; she had some control and say in what happened to her body. Importantly, she found alternative roles with which to fight and survive her cancer. It is unimportant to me what works, whether it is the chemotherapy, radiotherapy, or the processes of engaging the client's spontaneity and creativity to work symbolically with the cancer. There is much research to be done into psychoneuroimmunology – put simply, mind–body connections – and their influence. I believe that our mystery cannot be quantified and that our self-healing is as important as the healing of conventional medicine.

Having said that, there is an issue that is related to my beliefs and those of the client. Two concerns have been expressed to me about these methods: first, that I am implying that a cure is possible and giving the client unrealistic hope; and second, on failure, the danger is in the belief that somehow if they had visualised harder they would have been cured. I work with whatever the client brings; if Claire's cancer had not shrunk we might have worked on what it was like to live with a monster in the room. I try to stay as realistic as possible, though as a result I am more likely to undersell or minimise what I believe to be powerful processes.

A counter-argument is to consider what happens to clients and their families when they have been given a restrictive time limit to their life. Once the limit is in place, and given doctors' power and authority, the patient is in danger of being condemned to live only for the prescribed, allocated time, giving up and dying when due. There is, on the other hand, the patient who dutifully sets their house in order, bestowing gifts on their family in readiness for death, only to outlive the time, stripped of their worldly goods. With this in mind, I believe it was immoral to tell Claire she had two months left to live. She, however, proved the scientists wrong and outlived her death sentence.

Poor prognosis: Walking in the shadows (Maria and Phil)

Phil was a 36-year-old man who had been diagnosed with a hereditary renal condition five years previously. He was referred to our service by one of the nurses from the local renal unit. Phil needed dialysis three times a week, following the removal of both his kidneys, and at first he had coped well, but now he was reluctant to go for his sessions. He was finding dialysis increasingly difficult to handle due to the discomfort of the procedure, as his veins were scarred, the boredom associated with sitting around and waiting for the dialysis to finish and, perhaps most importantly, the very fact that he had to have dialysis at all.

In the beginning our work focused on the 'safe' topic of improving Phil's coping strategies, using cognitive behavioural strategies (Persons 1989). However, Phil and I gradually became more aware of the 'dangerous' issues that he wished to explore. We identified his main fear as being that one day he would just not be able to carry on with the dialysis, which meant he would die. Phil wanted to explore the meaning of his illness and felt that in doing this he would be able to come to terms with it and accept his lot.

As the condition was hereditary, Phil had witnessed the devastation that it had wreaked on his family. His mother and one of his brothers had already died, one sister had gone blind and another sister had been paralysed as a direct result of the disease. Phil was faced with the knowledge and fear that this could happen to him, combined with the guilt that his sisters were in a worse state than he was.

One of the major issues Phil had to face up to was the sheer number and nature of losses he had experienced. There were the two bereavements, but Phil was becoming conscious of other losses he had incurred and he wanted to explore the impact of these on himself and his relationship. Phil had had a successful career and the illness had struck at a time when he was beginning to reap the benefits of all his hard work. He wanted to share his anger, his sadness and his sense of injustice.

Physically, Phil had been an attractive man, but the ravages of the disease and the effects of its treatment had radically changed his body. He was trying to cope with not only his altered body image but also the effect his appearance had on other people. Owing to the removal of his kidneys, the toxicity of Phil's blood supply caused him to itch constantly, and his metabolism had also been affected; as a result, he sweated profusely. In an attempt to counteract these problems Phil wore loose clothing such as baggy tee-shirts and jogging trousers. He felt he had not changed as a person and was angry at the discrimination he perceived he now experienced as a result of his altered image.

Phil was also angry with the hospital staff who had implied he could live a normal life on dialysis. He had not been prepared for the disintegration of his body and his health. He felt resentful, not simply because he had to plan his life around the dialysis sessions, but because the illness dogged him constantly. He had bowel problems and 'when he had to go, he had to go', so Phil lost his spontaneity, as even going to the shops was marred by the thought of 'Is there a toilet nearby?' He had to plan even the shortest outings with the precision of a military general.

As his disease was hereditary, Phil and his wife had chosen not to have children. In addition, as a result of his medication, he had become impotent. Phil was struggling to come to terms with the loss of fatherhood and felt cheated that he was now denied a physical sexual relationship with his wife.

Phil was very clear when we finished working together how important exploring these 'taboo' subjects had been for him. It seemed he had instinctively known what was right for him, but he had also known that he could not do this work alone. All the other health care professionals involved in his care had focused on trying to help him find solutions to his problems, as I had done initially, when what he really wanted was to look into the depths of his issues. It was in acknowledging the grim reality that he was able to find renewed hope for the future. Phil, far from disintegrating, discovered his sense of self through having his experiences validated. The counselling sessions enabled Phil to explore the deepest depths of despair and find something worth living for. I finally realised that I was unable to do this for him; indeed, only Phil could do this. My role was to create a safe therapeutic alliance to enable him to achieve this.

COUNSELLOR'S REFLECTIONS

I hope it will become clear to the reader that the reasons for the 'heartsink' feeling in this work might have less to do with the client than with unresolved issues for the therapist. (For discussion on heartsink clients, see McFadzean 1999.) For me the impact of the work on the therapist is the shadow side of palliative care counselling. In supervision I was able to acknowledge that although the client was ready and wanted to explore the horrendous nature of his situation I was, at first, an unwilling participant. It was in recognising my own reluctance to enter into this work that I was able to identify and own my irrational fears. I felt concerned that I might find this situation too awful to bear and fearful that I might not be able to stay with the client as he deteriorated. I was afraid that I would abandon him when he needed my support most. On the other hand, I was aware that Phil might be overwhelmed and become clinically depressed. Phil was a similar age to myself, with a life-threatening condition. This led me to explore questions for myself, such as: 'How would I cope with his situation?' I did not think I would cope very well. In fact, I thought I would rather die than have to undergo dialysis. I felt impotent, due to my helplessness and the apparent hopelessness of the situation. It became clear that these issues paralleled several of the issues faced by Phil.

These feelings were bound up with my sense of responsibility for the client. I knew I could help Phil explore his worst fears, but in doing so I doubted my ability to help him maintain his hope for the future, especially if I was not feeling hopeful myself. I became aware that in taking responsibility for Phil, I was neither listening to him nor demonstrating that I trusted him to know what his own needs were. I was also underestimating his resourcefulness. My fears were groundless. I was able to be with Phil while he told his story, and although this was heart-rending, it was not intolerable, either for him or myself. I learned to trust the client's resilience and rediscovered confidence in my skills and myself as a therapist.

Finally, what they don't tell you...

There are a number of issues that we believe are significant and for the most part unique to this type of work. The first is probably common to all those who work in medical settings: the task is that of straddling the apparently irreconcilable philosophical divide between the scientific medical model and the humanistic counselling model. Some of the themes which clients bring can be seen either as a direct consequence of their being involved in the medical system (powerlessness and medical arrogance), or as compounding issues related to their illness (hopelessness and lack of a voice). The counsellor's task is to enable the client to get the best out of the system in which they find themselves and to feel sufficiently empowered to have some say in what is happening to their body.

One way in which we do this is to avoid becoming embroiled in medical jargon. The client is propelled into another universe where words like 'chemo', 'bloods', and 'radiotherapy' trip off the tongue. We facilitate clients to become experts on their illness. This will have been apparent in the presentation of the case material, where we avoided the distinctly medical terminology (for example: 'squamous epithelial cell cancer' as in Claire's lung cancer) and continued to work in the language of the client.

It seems a truism to say that illness changes people's bodies. The truth is that sometimes we cannot know just how brutal and destructive certain illnesses are. It is not only the illness that can wreak havoc on the person's body, but also the treatment. Mastectomy and other amputations, facial surgery and chemotherapy all play a part in the visible broadcasting of ill health. If as counsellors we are repulsed by the physical changes wrought through illness, how much worse might it be for the clients, who capture their reflections in the mirror? As we have shown, the truth is that sometimes this work can be shocking.

This leads us to consider the impact of this work on the counsellor. It is hard to work with a caseload comprising only clients who are going to die. It is a heavy burden to enter their despair and hopelessness and be confronted by our own helplessness to rescue and heal. It is often more poignant when the counsellor has worked with clients during the post-diagnosis period; subsequently they can work on issues related to treatment and, after a break, perhaps return in the terminal phase of the illness to face the client's death. There are ways to deal with the impact of this. One is to balance the caseload with a mixture of post-diagnosis clients, poor-prognosis clients, and those who have been bereaved. Another strategy is to be involved in supervision, training and research projects related to palliative care, as well as casework. For us, learning of the tenuous nature of life has led to a significant, positive impact: viewing life as valuable and not to be wasted. This brings about a different way of living with our families and friends – and ourselves.

There are of course times when the strategies we choose become less effective. This might be due to an overlap between our personal world and our professional world. In order to deal with this we may need to negotiate a strategic withdrawal within our workplace, increase our personal counselling and supervision, seek additional support, or, as a final resort, have time out completely to make sense of it all and replenish our resources.

References

Barnes, A. (1995) 'An introduction to hospice and palliative care.' In J. David (ed) *Cancer Care: Prevention, Treatment and Palliation*. London: Chapman & Hall.

Blatner, A. (1997) *Acting-In: Practical Applications of Psychodramatic Technique* (third edition). London: Free Association Books.

Casson, J. (1997) 'Psychodrama in individual therapy.' *The British Journal of Psychodrama and Sociodrama 12*, 1, 3–20.

Erikson, E. (1963) *Childhood and Society*. New York: Norton.

Jenkins, P. (1997) *Counselling, Psychotherapy and the Law*. London: Sage.

Kell, C. (1999) 'Confidentiality and the counsellor in general practice.' *British Journal of Guidance and Counselling 27*, 3, 431–439.

McFadzean, D. (1999) 'Turning heartsinks into heroes.' *Counselling in Medical Settings Journal 60*, 10–12.

Moreno, J. (1965) 'The voice of J. L. Moreno in interview with James Sacks.' Tape available from Marcia Karp, Hoewell, Barnstaple, Devon.

National Council for Hospice and Specialist Palliative Care Services in Directory '98: *Hospice and Palliative Care Services in the United Kingdom and the Republic of Ireland.* Hospice Information Service at St. Christopher's.

Persons, J. B. (1989) *Cognitive Therapy in Practice: A Case Formulation Approach.* London: W. W. Norton & Co.

Wilkins, P. (2000) *Psychodrama.* London: Sage.

Williams, A. (1989) *The Passionate Technique: Strategic Psychodrama with Individuals, Families and Groups.* London: Tavistock/Routledge.

Chapter 3

Working in general practice with somatisation of childhood sexual abuse

Sue Santi Ireson

Introduction

I started my first counselling training as a volunteer youth counsellor in 1976 when person-centred counselling was taught in 10 weeks! Counsellors who needed counselling support for themselves were looked on askance: my first supervisor knew my first client quite well and avidly gossiped about her rather than drawing an appropriate boundary and declining to supervise me. None of this seemed too strange to me. I had always managed without help and unclear boundaries were the norm.

I was then a teacher in a tough school, bringing up two sons on my own after leaving a very violent marriage. Through my 30s I had glandular fever, tonsilitis, continual kidney problems, chronic candida, constant migraines, unexplained aches and pains and several disastrous relationships. I didn't feel too much – didn't even notice how depressed I was or how I 'split' whenever the emotional pressure got too much for me. It didn't occur to me that any of this was out of the ordinary. I didn't even think I was unlucky, I just kept on overworking – teaching and continuing my counselling training. I started to specialise in working with abused women, running short courses and giving talks. No one noticed that I wasn't really there lots of the time, not even me.

Then one evening I watched a television programme about a woman who had gone with her therapist to visit the house in which her father abused her. Inside my body it was as if an electric buzzer was sounding. I had never felt such a sensation before and I started to wonder if my body was trying to speak to me – I started to review the kinds of symptoms presented by sexual abuse survivors and noticed for the first time how many of them I could say 'yes' to. Finally I decided that I would seek counselling for myself. However, I couldn't actually recall being abused and I went along to a counsellor with just a 'feeling'. She seemed to imply that if I couldn't remember it then it didn't happen and it would be better if I confined myself to 'reality'. Not really knowing why, I left.

Then I really got ill. I had hepatitis so badly that my GP told me afterwards that he had been sure I wasn't going to make it. When I felt a bit better I went back to counselling, this time with someone who believed me – who worked with my self-abusive behaviours and tenderly cared for me. It was months before I allowed myself to unlock memories of being abused that I had hidden away, and many more months before I could start to recognise for myself how little I cared about myself. I started to recognise that the catalogue of ailments that I had always accepted as the norm was really somatised aspects of my hidden pain. I began to understand why I had chosen to specialise in working with sexual abuse, and to see that I had been trying to deal with my own issues through my work with others. I finally began connecting the knowledge I had with my internal experience – a slow, often painful task.

I now work with another counsellor in a GP training practice of six doctors with a patient population of about 12,000, located in a prosperous town in the southeast of England. Between us we offer 18 counselling hours a week and see approximately 250 clients a year for short- to medium-term therapy. We manage our own bookings and do not restrict the number of sessions we offer, although statistical returns kept over the past nine years show an average attendance to be about four sessions. This flexibility allows us to see clients for longer if we think this to be beneficial. In our surgery the referrer (usually one of the doctors) gives the patient a counselling referral card and a leaflet about counselling so that they can make their own decision to hand it in for inclusion on the waiting-list. This gives more autonomy in their decision to come for counselling. The doctors have a very positive attitude to counselling and promote it to their patients.

Researching an 18-month period, I found that 28.4 per cent of clients referred by the GPs for counselling disclosed to the counsellor that they were survivors of sexual abuse. Only five of these people had been referred for counselling because they had told the doctor about their past. However, many more (44 women and 9 men) had not disclosed their abuse to their GP, and many of them had not realised that it might have any bearing on their current state. Furthermore, the referring GP had not recognised that there might be any history of sexual abuse in these patients. In those patients who had not been referred as a direct result of disclosing sexual abuse to the GP, the presenting problems tended to be depression, relationship difficulties and eating disorders. Three people had a history of suicide attempts. Three women were patients with whom the GP felt exasperated because there was no obvious cause for their sense of malaise.

In the light of my own history, I wanted to discover what GPs knew and understood about sexual abuse, the way it becomes somatised and its ongoing effect on the life and well-being of the survivor. When I first started to discuss the extent of sexual abuse with the GPs I quoted statistics found in a large randomised survey of adults undertaken by the NSPCC in 1990. They found 12 per cent of the women and 8 per cent of the men had been sexually abused by the age of 15. The GPs were astonished to discover that there might be more than a handful of sexually abused people in their practice. Between them they identified eight people in the entire practice whom they believed to have been sexually abused, and could not believe the NSPCC statistics quoted above. In fact, going by the NSPCC statistics, it is likely that about 670 female and 330 male patients in their practice have been abused.

'Not in this town, surely,' said one GP confidently. Another would not consider asking patients if they even thought they might have been abused because it 'would be like opening a can of worms'. Dr G. said it would be 'putting thoughts into someone's head, which weren't there before'. Some GPs felt that it 'should be left well alone'. Dr E. saw 'the problem of playing the "sexual abuse" card, which can never be proven, as a universal absolution of all subsequent psychopathic behaviour' as a reason for not asking about a history of sexual abuse.

When asked to identify symptoms that might lead them to suspect sexual abuse, one doctor identified a patient who had an extreme reaction to the thought of internal examination, but he had never asked her about this. One thought there might be more episodes of genito-urinary tract infections, and another thought personality disorders or eating disorders might be an indicator, but it was clear that there was little understanding of the wide range of manifestation of somatised emotional pain. It was also clear that asking about patients' early sexual history is almost never considered.

Working with sexual abuse survivors in the GP setting

Throughout this chapter I generally refer to the abuser as 'he' (except when talking about female abusers) and the abuse survivor as 'she' (except when talking about male survivors). This is for ease of reading, and is not in any way intended to deny that males are abused, or to ignore the fact that females also abuse. (Twenty-four per cent of male survivors and 13 per cent of female survivors have been abused by a woman (Finkelhor 1988).) Briere (1992) found that 26 per cent of perpetrators were women, and a UK BBC1 'Panorama' programme in October 1997 reported that 'women commit 25 per cent of all child sexual abuse', and that '250,000 children in the UK have been sexually abused by women'. An in-depth study of 25 men who had been sexually abused in childhood found that 13 of them had been abused by females (Etherington 1995).

I have not referred to those who were sexually abused during childhood as 'victims' but as 'survivors'. I believe the use of the word 'victim' offers an insidious message of helplessness that may confirm internalised beliefs, but which does not help the person to feel able to break free and develop a new and more empowered way of viewing their world. However, for men who have been socialised to believe that a 'proper' man is invulnerable and sexually proactive, it is often necessary to acknowledge their victimisation and powerlessness before moving to their identification as a survivor (Etherington 1995).

What is sexual abuse? Sexual abuse is never 'nothing'

A child has been sexually abused if he/she has been used for the sexual gratification of someone who is more powerful than him/herself. It is an act that is controlled by the perpetrator and which denies the survivor the right to be in control of her own physical and sexual experiencing. Abusers frequently imply that something terrible will happen to the child (or to someone she cares about) if she tells. Abusers coerce or seduce their victims into secrecy. Coercion takes place in a variety of ways: sometimes abusers appear to be offering love and the child is deceived; they may offer bribes such as sweets or money, and the child innocently accepts without realising what she has really accepted. Abusers may use violence, actual or threatened, to frighten their victims into compliance. Others will coerce a child with threats of harm to loved ones or the destruction of a loved object, i.e. a sibling, mother, pet or prized possession. For some children abuse is a 'normal' part of their lives, since they have known nothing else.

I have never found that sexual abuse is the only abuse experienced. Sexual abuse is also psychological abuse, in the breaking of boundaries. Equally it is an abuse of the whole person and is often part of a familial process. The person who somatises her pain will probably also be manifesting it in other ways – maybe overwork, overusing alcohol, abusive relationships. The ramifications of the internalised messages that the survivor may carry can permeate almost every part of her being.

Childhood sexual abuse can include:

- private touching or asking a child to touch
- fondling
- kissing
- rubbing
- intrusive looks
- oral sex
- anal sex
- rape
- making a child look at genitals or have their genitals looked at
- incest
- child pornography
- subjecting a child to any type of pornography
- encouraging a child to behave in sexual ways with self and others
- sexual torture
- making a child watch sexual acts.

In my opinion, all abuse is harmful, but Hall and Lloyd (1989, 1998) suggest that the degree of harm may be related to certain factors that influence the development of trust: for example, very young age of the child when the abuse occurred or started, the closeness of their relationship with the abuser, how long the abuse continued, and the exact nature of the abuse. Hall and Lloyd believe that these factors would create greater problems with trust, which might exacerbate the difficulty for some clients of making a good therapeutic relationship and going on to develop healthier strategies for coping with life. When a survivor has had a loving, trustworthy relationship with at least one person in their past, the counsellor will more easily be able to help the client to recognise their own sense of worth, and thus progress to more successful life choices. In general, clients who have had no such good relationship will need a much longer therapeutic relationship.

What is somatisation? The body speaks, however silently

The emotions a child experiences as a result of being abused are often too difficult (or too unsafe) for the child to express. Disturbing emotions that cannot be accessed and processed verbally remain unformulated because we conceptualise our experience and make sense of it through the use of language. However, the body will speak – and although the emotions can be repressed and blocked from conscious awareness, they do not disappear. Without conceptualised thought to help process these feelings, they may be held in the body or 'somatised'. These unformulated experiences or unresolved traumas may then be expressed in ways over which we seem to have little or no control. The unconscious emotion is transformed into sensations, symptoms or behaviours that have been disconnected from the conditions that produced them. The individual's symptoms are dissociated from the event(s) even though they articulate through the body what the individual cannot say in words.

Emotional pain may be manifested or displaced in almost any form of physical pain, illness, psychiatric disorder, emotional disturbance or behavioural difficulties, and victims may find a variety of ways of coping with this pain. A number of studies have shown that a large percentage of psychiatric inpatients are victims of childhood sexual abuse, but information about this is often neither sought nor considered in psychiatric assessments.

Equally, there is a large and growing body of evidence that those who were sexually abused in childhood suffer biochemical changes which can make them much more susceptible to physical illness and disorders. Dr Vincent Felitti's large study of 9500 people (1998) identified sexual abuse as one of seven adverse emotional experiences in childhood which led to an increased risk of chronic disease and early death later in life. Felitti believes that the effects of childhood abuse may be 'hard-wired' into the brain creating psychological and emotional consequences and long-term neurological consequences.

Physical consequences of childhood sexual abuse

Abuse survivors are up to ten times more likely to suffer from a wide range of illnesses, physical disorders and biomechanical disorders than non-abused adults. These range through cancer, heart disease, irritable bowel syndrome (IBS), high blood pressure, emphysema, obesity, chronic pain, yeast infections, muscular-skeletal problems, genito-urinary tract disorders, gastrointestinal problems, skin complaints, menstrual problems, pregnancy and birthing difficulties. Abuse survivors also tend to have more frequent illness and infections.

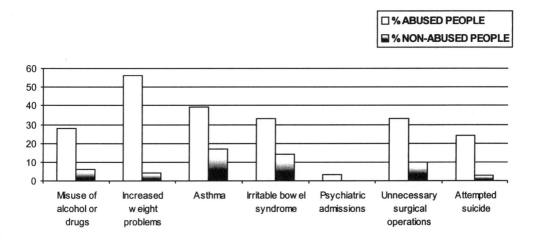

Figure 3.1 Comparative frequency of presentation of symptoms in abused and non-abused people (Smith et al. 1995)

Heim *et al.* (2000), Nemeroff (2000) and Newport (2000) all independently found that abuse survivors had a heightened biological response to stressful situations, and that the degree of their response correlated with the severity of the childhood trauma. Newport (2000) found that those with a history of abuse had marked peaks in cortisol and ACTH, two critical stress response chemicals. These two hormones reflect activity in the corticotropin-releasing factor system, a more basic chemical pathway closely tied to the imprinting of early childhood trauma on stress response in adulthood. Levels of ACTH in abused, depressed women were found to be six times greater than in women of similar ages in the control group. Victims of past abuse also had greater increases in heart rate, a physical marker of anxiety, than did non-abused women. The implication of these changes requires further research, but it seems likely that a consistently higher level of 'stress' chemicals will take its toll on the immune system and thereby make the individual more susceptible to illness and disease.

Table 3.1 Some observations of physical consequences of childhood sexual abuse as manifested in adulthood	
Symptom	Researcher
chronic pain	Radomsky 1995
unwanted pregnancy	Dietz et al. 1999
frequency of physical illness	Felitti 1998
cancer	Felitti 1998
heart disease	Felitti 1998
emphysema/chronic bronchitis	Felitti 1998
genito-urinary tract infections	Dale 1992
heightened reactivity to stress	Nemeroff 2000; Putnam 1990
gastro-intestinal problems	Ali 2000
panic attacks	Santi Ireson 1996
obesity	Felitti 1998
damaged immune system/frequent infections	Kennedy 2000
frequent headaches/migraine	Dale 1992
sleep disturbance	Felitti 1998
skin complaints	Dale 1992
dysmenorrhoea and menstrual problems	Smith 1995
problems during pregnancy and birthing	Smith et al. 1995
irritable bowel syndrome (IBS)	Ali 2000

Mental health consequences of childhood sexual abuse

There is an extremely high incidence of depression amongst abuse survivors; indeed, in the sample I looked at in my practice, I found that all but one were currently suffering from depression and most had a long history of often unrecognised and untreated depression.

As with physical illness, abuse survivors are up to ten times more likely to present with mental health problems than those with no history of abuse

(Felitti 1998). These problems encompass anxiety, panic attacks, low self-esteem, mood disorders, posttraumatic stress disorders, heightened reactivity to stress, dissociative disorders and suicidal ideation. Sixty per cent or more of psychiatric admissions have been found to be of people with histories of sexual abuse (Briere and Runtz 1988; Felitti 1998).

Lewis Herman (1998) found that 'many, or even most, psychiatric patients are survivors of child abuse', and Etherington (2001) quotes a study which found that among patients with severe mental illness, 76 per cent of women and 72 per cent of men had been sexually or physically abused in childhood (Read 1998).

A recent study of 9000 people in the USA (Felitti 1998) found that those who had been exposed to four or more episodes of childhood abuse had between a fourfold and a twelvefold increased health risk for alcoholism, drug abuse, depression and suicide attempts. These people were between twice and four times more likely to smoke, to be generally ill, to have had more than 50 sexual partners, and thus to have sexually transmitted diseases, and up to 1.6 times more likely to be obese.

Table 3.2 Some observations of mental health consequences of childhood sexual abuse as manifested in adulthood	
Symptom	*Researcher*
depression	Briere and Runtz 1988; Newport 2000
anxiety	Mullen *et al.* 1996
post traumatic stress disorder (PTSD)	Silverman, Reinherz and Giaconia 1996
low self-esteem	Gelinas 1983; Romans, Martin and Mullen *et al.* 1996
mood disorder	Nemeroff 2000
frequency of mental health problems	Carmen, Rieker and Mills 1984; Felitti 1998; Mullen *et al.* 1993
heightened reactivity to stress	Nemeroff 2000; Putnam 1990
suicide	Brown 1999; Nemeroff 2000
distorted sense of reality	Fleming 1997
dissociation	Cahill, Llewellyn and Pearson 1991

Developmental disruption is caused by sexual abuse, damaging the child's self-esteem and sense of the world as a sufficiently safe environment. Breaching sexual boundaries can damage a person's capacity for entering trusting, intimate relationships, as well as their developing sexuality, and this may lead in adult life to an increased risk of low self-esteem, social and economic failure, social insecurity and isolation and difficulties with intimacy.

- abusing others
- staying busy
- avoiding intimacy
- creating new personalities
- forgetting
- leaving your body (dissociation)
- staying in control
- gambling
- minimising
- alcoholism
- anorexia/bulimia
- workaholism
- taking care of others
- hiding behind a partner
- sleeping excessively
- not sleeping
- humour
- shoplifting
- denial
- rationalising
- creating chaos
- repeating abuse
- fantasising
- perfectionism
- self-mutilation
- compulsive eating
- compulsive exercising
- dogmatic beliefs
- running away
- suicide attempts
- drug addiction
- compulsive sex
- avoiding sex
- spacing out
- staying super-alert
- getting into dangerous situations

Source: From The Courage to Heal Workbook *by Laura Davis (1990)*

Abuse survivors are more likely to be alcohol or drug users, to smoke, to have eating disorders, to be engaged in sexually risky or other risky behaviours, to be in abusive relationships, to self-harm, to have difficulty raising their own children. They may have difficulty protecting their own children from abuse. They may have more unwanted pregnancies and abortions, have sexual dysfunction and gender identity confusion. They may exhibit a variety of compulsive or obsessive behaviours and have difficulty fitting into groups. They may be in co-dependent relationships. There is also a considerable overlap between physical, emotional and sexual abuse, and children who are subject to one form of abuse are significantly more likely to suffer other forms of abuse (Briere and Runtz 1990; Fergusson, Horwood and Lynskey 1996; Fleming 1997; Mullen et al. 1996). Mullen et al. (1996) found women with histories of child sexual abuse were five times more likely to have experienced physical abuse, and were three times as likely to also report emotional deprivation, than those with no history of childhood sexual abuse. Strategies survivors may use to cope are shown in the box above.

Children who have been sexually abused and adult survivors of sexual abuse may feel many different (and often confusing and overwhelming) emotions, including:

Fear	• of the abuser
	• of causing trouble
	• of losing adults important to them
	• of being taken away from home
	• of being 'different'
Anger	• at the abuser
	• at other adults around them who did not protect them
	• at themselves (feeling as if they caused the trouble)
Isolation	• because they feel different
	• because 'something is wrong with me'
	• because they feel alone in their experience
	• because they have trouble making trustworthy relationships
Sadness	• about having had something taken from them
	• about losing a part of themselves
	• about growing up too fast
	• about being betrayed by someone they trusted

Guilt	• for not being able to stop the abuse
	• for believing they 'consented' to the abuse
	• for 'telling' (if they told)
	• for keeping the secret (if they did not tell)
	• for wishing that a sibling could be abused instead
	• for not being able to protect siblings
Shame	• about being involved in the experience
	• about their body's response to the abuse
Confusion	• because they may still love the abuser
	• because their feelings change all the time

Given this formidable (and probably not comprehensive) list of well-documented consequences of surviving sexual abuse in childhood, survivors' internal belief systems may be full of negative introjections – unconsciously acquired beliefs about themselves and others which are unhelpful or even harmful. These may lead to survivors' being less able to sustain satisfying relationships, less likely to fulfil their potential, and to their lives being likely to be more difficult and less fulfilling than for those who have not been abused.

Some people who have been abused have blocked it from their conscious awareness. Back in 1983 Gelinas wrote that many who do remember their abuse may consider it irrelevant to their current situation and do not mention it; this is, however, less frequently the case in the current climate of awareness. Clients may never have defined what happened to them as a form of abuse. Sexual abuse survivors often exhibit a 'disguised presentation', and this disguised presentation may include symptoms of depression, self-abusive behaviour, confusion, impulsive acts, very low self-esteem and a history of assuming adult responsibilities as a child.

Despite the large and growing body of evidence that childhood sexual abuse has a lasting and profound effect on the survivor, it still seems that it is easier for doctors to focus on somatic (bodily) symptoms rather than discuss what else is going on in the person's life. Without investigating the significance or the symbolism of these symptoms for the patient, the doctor may be prescribing medications or suggesting treatments which do not really address the problem. Although medication may offer temporary relief from symptoms, the underlying problems which have produced the symptoms are not dealt with.

Many doctors and other clinicians feel uncomfortable and helpless when a survivor discloses that he or she is being or has been abused; so they may feel safer by staying within the medical model, searching for an organic cause, sending the patient for multiple investigations, prescribing medications, and offering various surgical interventions. In time, when the symptoms fail to respond to medical treatment, doctors may blame the patient for 'refusing' to be cured, failing to recognise the limitations of the strictly biomedical approach. Moreover, patients themselves may present only the physical or psychological symptoms.

GPs may minimise, rationalise or excuse abuse – indeed, one prominent GP trainer told me that 'almost everyone has had an uncle who fiddled with them, but really people just have to get on with it and stop claiming that abuse is to blame for everything they can't do'.

First sessions

One of the great benefits of working in a GP practice is that patients are easily referred to the counsellor. Often people who would not consider attending for private counselling will willingly see the counsellor who is just another member of the practice team. As I mentioned before, many people who experienced sexual abuse in childhood come for counselling when presenting something else. The most frequently presenting problems I found in my practice were depression and relationship difficulties.

The most important task at the beginning of the counselling relationship is to create a sense of safety for the client. Counsellors need to make clear boundaries and contracts with all clients, but with a sexual abuse survivor the clarity and strength of the boundaries needs to be further reinforced. In maintaining firm boundaries, I demonstrate that it is possible to be close to someone and remain safe. Some clients need boundaries to be clarified many times, and I encourage them to do this for as long as they feel it is important. By doing so I believe I am helping to create a relationship in which the client can go at her own speed and learn that she will be encouraged, rather than punished, for checking out anything about which she is unsure. I am also modelling how to make safe relationships. The boundaries we make can always be renegotiated; however, unless this happens, I keep them firm. I believe that if boundaries are unclear or broken, this will confuse the client and may confirm their belief that all boundaries can be broken.

Confidentiality

When making the initial contract with the client I outline what confidentiality means. This has been discussed with the GPs, and in our surgery they accept that confidentiality is essential for the building of trust. I outline briefly what supervision is, and that I record on the computer the fact that there has been a counselling session. I also make it clear that nothing else is written on the computer screen and that information the client gives me is confidential. This can pose dilemmas in certain situations:

- is confidentiality sacrosanct even if the client is threatening to take her life?

- should I divulge information that the client may not give permission for? What if I know that a child is being abused?

- to whom am I accountable – to the GPs for whom I work or to my client? Who would take responsibility if there were litigation?

The legalities and moral decisions about these issues are carefully explained in Tim Bond's *Standards and Ethics for Counselling in Action* (Bond 2000). As the client is the GP's patient, counsellors need to remember that the duty of care lies with the doctor. GP and counsellors need to have a clear contract that is mutually agreed and shared with the client. If the counsellor feels the need to disclose information, ideally she should have the client's consent. If she opens up her concern with the client and explains why she feels the need to disclose, the client may experience this as a caring act (Smith 1999). Generally in GP practices, the counsellor is not expected to give blanket confidentiality when there are issues of harm or self harm, and counsellors should have considered what their ethical standpoint is on such (rare) matters and have discusseed it with the GPs. If the client were to withhold permission for the counsellor to talk with the GP about the fact that the client intended to harm another person, or to take his or her own life, the counsellor should avoid overreacting and should take time to work through with the client what he or she has said. Sometimes just working with the client to discover what the client expected when making such a disclosure will enable him or her to move forward and develop more insight into his or her pain.

For me, the struggle is between honouring the bond of confidentiality with my client, versus a possible situation of harm or self-harm. In practice, I have found that when clients have talked about harming themselves, they have been willing for me to share this with their GP. I believe this is because we have been able to create a trustworthy relationship and my concern defines a boundary of caring for the client. My supervisor is the first port of call when I am faced with such dilemmas, and often this is where I can formulate how to share my concern with the client more clearly.

Counselling suicidal clients

I believe that it can be very helpful to accept statements about committing suicide calmly and without panic. I encourage the client to explore what she means, and what is too painful to cope with right now. We explore what other options might be available to her – it might be that in-patient care could be helpful, or getting a friend to come and stay for a few days. Sometimes I make a contract that asks her to put off committing suicide until we have had time to talk about it more at her next session. I think this offers a containment of frightening feelings which may feel out of control, and encourages the part of the client that wants to survive to 'hang on in there'. Assessing the client's intention is a delicate and tricky business. It is important that the counsellor knows what facilities are available in the secondary and tertiary services so that the client can be given realistic choices. It may also be very helpful to check who the client can rely on for support and to make sure that he or she has useful phone numbers (e.g. The Samaritans – 0345 909090).

I don't always feel as confident as I might look, however, and even with excellent support and supervision there have been a couple of clients whose state of mind has had me waking up in the night, wondering if I have done the right thing. Over the years since I have been working in the surgery, GPs' attitudes have moved from 'sectioning' anyone who seems suicidal to understanding that this in itself might be abusive, and that the client might do better if she is able to negotiate a planned strategy of contact and support.

Even if the client's material is spilling over, this initial establishment of the counselling process as being safe and trustworthy must not be neglected. Judith Lewis Hermann writes, 'The single most common therapeutic error is avoidance of traumatic material, probably the second most common error is premature or precipitate engagement in exploratory work, without sufficient attention to the tasks of establishing safety and securing a therapeutic alliance' (Lewis Herman 1998).

Kim Etherington (2001) reminds us that clients who have suffered rejection and damaged trust should not be made false promises. Clarity about what is on offer is essential to the development of trust. Trust does not mean that the counsellor will always be there, any more than their trust in their GP depends on him/her always being available, but rather that the counsellor behaves in a consistent and trustworthy manner.

The unfolding story

As the client's story unfolds I may soon develop a sense that abuse might be part of her history, but know that I must allow the client to reach disclosure in her own time. However, she may be describing acts which were, or are, clearly abusive – at which point I can gently observe that I think this was abusive of her. This can enable the client to move from a child's perspective, where she may have had no words for what happened to her, to an adult perspective where she can formulate words in order to begin to process the experience.

The client may have found a variety of ways of holding the memories. She may minimise, rationalise or justify the abuse. She may have dissociated from it – so it is forgotten until something triggers a memory. (Dissociation is defined as failure to integrate different aspects of an experience, with the result that it is difficult to connect with some aspect of the experience explicitly.) For example, Carly, who came with panic attacks and depression, said:

> It never came to actual sex, so surely it doesn't really count [*minimising*]. Anyway, I was such a flirty little girl. I used to prance about in my nightie and it encouraged him [*justifying*]. He was helping me to know the difference between a man touching me who loved me and someone who didn't really love me [*rationalising*].

Another woman, Jenny, said:

> I didn't remember it until I took my daughter for her first riding lesson. As soon as I smelled the stables I remembered what he did. But really I have always known; I just hadn't kept it in a place that my thoughts ever went to. [Jenny was describing her dissociation from memories which were remembered consciously when triggered by her sense of smell.]

As the survivor recovers and/or re-evaluates her memories, I am constantly aware of balancing the need for her to feel safe, and avoid retraumatisation, with her need to face the past. I encourage the client to monitor her somatisation carefully, so that the uncovering work remains within the realm of what is bearable. If symptoms worsen dramatically during active exploration of the abuse, this may be a signal to slow down, and I will take time to explore with the client what these symptoms may mean to her and what has triggered them.

Trisha went back to her home-town for the first time since she had run away from her abusive mother. Her mother was now dead and Trisha had determined that she would seek out her aunt to see if the family had known what was going on. Although the aunt was very welcoming, she said she didn't remember anything about those days, and they were best forgotten. Trisha came home with an acute attack of fibromyalgia. Every joint ached and she couldn't sleep.

It was important to help Trisha to recognise that she was shocked, and for the next two sessions we worked on how she could take care of her body, which was feeling such pain. The GP was very helpful and was able to offer Trisha acupuncture and a short course of sleeping tablets. He emphasised that she needed to rest and take good care of herself. Consideration of the issues raised by the visit began later, when she felt better and was able to sleep again.

The healing journey

When we start out on the client's healing journey, I usually offer her a metaphor of being in convalescence. I think it is helpful to explain that the process can be very hard work, and that she may feel worse before she feels better. Abuse survivors are often so punishing towards themselves that learning how to be kinder can be a difficult process that is painful in itself. Judith Lewis Herman (1998) says, 'Reconstructing the trauma is ambitious work. It requires some slackening of ordinary life demands, some "tolerance for the state of being ill."'

Issues of touch should be made explicit. Some clients will ask for hugs or some other form of physical touch during the session. I am cautious about offering such contact, and might ask: 'In what way would our relationship be different if I hugged you?' or, 'What would it mean to you if I hugged you?' The longing of some clients to be held can be very powerful, and it may be very difficult to resist their request. However, it is worth remembering that the person towards whom the longing is directed is not necessarily the counsellor, but past caretakers who failed in their tasks. When clients are starved of touch it is sometimes very helpful to discuss how they can receive touch safely. Massage, aromatherapy or other bodywork, practised by someone who understands the issues related to abuse, can be a really helpful way of experiencing non-abusive, caring touch. I am probably more cautious than some about touch because I am still anxious that I might be triggered into dissociation if I am touched. However, for those clients who want to be hugged before they leave, I think it is a splendid way for us to celebrate the hard work we have done in the session.

I try to be as transparent and immediate as possible in my relationship with clients, because this helps to encourage them to check out their observations and felt experiences. If the client thinks that I look upset or angry, I encourage him or her to ask about that, so that I can tell the truth about what I am feeling. This is not an invitation to refocus the session on my needs – rather a safe way for the client to start to rely on their own sense of what they see, hear and feel. (This is particularly important for survivors who have been unable to rely on adults to tell them the truth, where secrets and distortions of reality have been the norm.) For example:

Mike: You looked really uncomfortable when I talked about my visits to motorway toilets.

Me: I'm not feeling uncomfortable about that, but I *have* hurt my back. I wonder why you noticed that just now? How do *you* feel about your visit to the motorway services?

The double standards of some abusive families, the lies and hypocrisy, may cause the child terrible confusion which may remain unchallenged in the adult.

'My parents were pillars of our church community,' said Nadia. 'They even used to run parenting groups and we would have to sit there with fixed smiles on our faces while they went on about how we were gifts from God and what wonderful children we were. Everyone thought we were the perfect family and my mother encouraged that belief too. She used to tell us how lucky we were. But she knew about the humiliating punishments my father imposed on us, like having to stand wrapped in a wet bedsheet for hours to teach us not to wet the bed, or being locked in the freezing cold outhouse because we had bad marks for our homework. And I'm sure she knew that he came to my bedroom at night. And then in the morning she'd find some way of telling us how much luckier we were than other children. I still feel awful because I would find ways of getting my sister into trouble and he used to strap her. She still hates me because I used to do that.'

What were Nadia and her sister to believe? How were they to make sense of the messages that came from both their parents? If they were gifts from God, what kind of God was he if religious people could punish and abuse them this way? One way in which Nadia tried to save herself was by trying to refocus her parent's displeasure on her sister. Though her sister feels angry about that now, the responsibility rests with the parents for putting Nadia in such a position. Nadia coped with her confusions by 'splitting' or dissociating. She spent most of her life in a daydream, seldom making conscious decisions, and finding herself in one abusive relationship after another. She would experience asthma attacks if she was ever in a 'group' situation, and would become nauseous if she smelled 'churchy smells'. As we worked together, I encouraged her to notice when she 'split'. Sometimes it was very obvious – she would just look as if she wasn't there. When that happened I would gently ask her what we had been talking about before she 'went', so that we could make sense of what had been unbearable.

A very important part of the healing process is for the client to recognise that this is her history, but that it does not have to be her present and her future. I think my task is to help the client to learn to parent herself in a nourishing, cherishing and respectful way and not to act out the abusive and unboundaried behaviour that she experienced in the past. I believe it is also very helpful to 'normalise' her responses to the experience, i.e. explain to her that others who have been abused may have experienced similar thoughts and feelings and beliefs. If a survivor has never disclosed her abuse before, she may believe that she is 'mad', unhelpable and unreachable. I think it is important to state quite clearly that I believe that what happened was wrong, demonstrating my belief that abuse is unacceptable. Sometimes I will disclose that I am also a survivor, if the client asks why I am doing this kind of work.

Many clients find it very hard to accept that they are completely and absolutely not to blame for their abuse. They have often internalised the abuser's shame – in that the person who should feel ashamed, the abuser, frequently does not, and the client carries all the shame. I think it is important to tell the client that she was not to blame, and to remind her of this whenever it seems appropriate. It can be helpful to ask the client to think about her own children, or to observe children of the age at which she was abused, and perhaps also to bring along photographs of herself as a child, to reinforce the fact that she could not have been responsible.

Helping clients deal with trauma

There are a number of helpful techniques I use, depending on the client and degree of the trauma. For some, speaking to an empty chair, as if their abuser (or maybe even an abusive part of themselves) is sitting in it, can be helpful. For others this would be much too traumatising, and we may have to negotiate how far away the client might need to be before she could look at her abuser without feeling victimised.

When working with traumatised clients it is important to avoid re-traumatisation. It may be helpful to ask the client to go back to a time when things were 'good enough' before the trauma. This way, the trauma can be approached from a time when the client felt resourceful and OK. This can apply both to work on events occurring now (as in the work with Penny – see below), or to work on past events. Sometimes the client feels that there has never been a 'good enough' time in the past, so it is probably better to invite them to distance themselves from the event by observing it from a distance. I like to check out with the client how far away she would have to be from the event before she could feel free enough to describe it without being overwhelmed by feelings. Some people can look down from the ceiling, but some need to be much further away. Trisha has to sit on the top of a nearby church spire before she can 'see' her mother and remain the competent adult that she is.

Often clients have an unrealistic belief that they should have been able to prevent the abuse somehow. They have discounted the power differential in the relationship, and the distortions of boundaries perpetrated by the abuser. Some clients find it impossible to forgive themselves for the fact that their body was stimulated to arousal by sexual encounters. They need to be reassured that this shows only that their body was in good working order, and *not* that they had any choice in the matter. In the whole range of terrible choices that the abused child was forced to make, e.g. offering to be abused so as to avoid a beating, or to protect a sibling, there was nothing that she could have done differently. This message may need to be constantly reinforced. Placing responsibility for the abuse firmly with the abuser is also an issue that has to be revisited many times.

Often, the somatising client will have a long history of similar symptoms, as noted previously. We work together to understand the significance and the symbolism of those symptoms. This can help the client become alert to stressors and bring them into awareness.

> Louise, sexually abused over nine years by her grandfather, suffered considerable arthritic-like pain in her knees. She identified that this pain was more intense when she felt helpless or trapped. As she started to recognise that she was being abused within her current marriage, and to take decisions about it, she became aware that the pain in her knees lessened and was often absent. Awareness of this helped her to start to ask herself questions about

what in particular was stressing her, and what decisions she could make to relieve the situation.

Changes in behaviour, for example eating more compulsively, feeling unable to eat at all, an increase in self-harming, or mood disturbances, could all be useful indicators of a raised stress level.

I feel sure that when I retire, the one word that all my clients will remember me saying is 'breathe!'. During the session I will observe the client's breathing, noting when it becomes more shallow, sometimes matching my own breathing to hers, so that I can get a sense of what it feels like to breathe like that. Teaching the client to breathe well can help her to 'ground' herself, giving her techniques to manage panic attacks and other manifestations of anxiety. Sometimes it is important to remind the client that she is in the present, not in the frightening events of the past. As well as reminding her to breathe, I might ask her to make eye contact with me, and to become aware of her body being supported by the chair, in order to help her ground herself in the present.

If the client is in a relationship, it may be helpful to suggest that the partner reads about sexual abuse and its effects – or that the partner also seeks counselling. It may be that when she was a child the sexual abuse survivor coped by somatising, a way that helped her to survive the abuse. As she begins the healing work, feelings that were held out of awareness may start to be re-experienced, and this can be a difficult time. Support networks and survivors' groups can be a helpful resource during this time.

It may be helpful to suggest that the client read about abuse and its effects on the person. There are many books now readily available, and many of them have cognitive behavioural exercises that the client can do at home. This can work really well alongside the counselling sessions. Working through books helps the client to see that she really can take responsibility for herself and need not remain a victim. Recommending such books can also signal to her that the counsellor is not the only person who can help. Reading about abuse helps the client to normalise her responses and to begin to find resources for herself.

For some the written word can provide an extra dimension of understanding which complements the counselling process. Some clients may greatly benefit from creating a journal. This can be made up of a mixture of writing, poetry, drawings, collage – indeed, whatever helps the client to capture how she is feeling. The journal also provides the client with a reference point to look back over. Kim Etherington (2000) describes in generous detail how the narrative process provided her clients with useful, graphic tools for dealing with their abuse.

Often abuse survivors have unrealistic self-expectations and minimise anything positive about themselves. The following history illustrates how a competent woman survivor lost all sense of her own competence when an external event triggered powerful memories for her.

Penny, now 42 years old, originally came to the doctor with panic attacks and chronically recurring candida. She had been abused by both her father and her brother. Since she started counselling, she had made the decision to leave her physically and emotionally abusive husband. She had managed to get herself and her two children rehoused, had been to the dentist to get her broken teeth fixed, had got herself some smart clothes and a new hairdo, found a job, and had also confided in her sister about her abuse. Then one day she came in for her session with me looking just as she had when she first came for counselling. She was wearing the same shapeless tracksuit she had worn when we first met. She told me, 'It's pointless coming to talk about all this stuff. I feel just as bad as I did before. And I've had panic attacks again.'

After acknowledging that she felt hopeless about it all, I started by asking her when things had changed, as she had been managing well last time I saw her. She said she didn't know, but I persisted: 'Were you OK on Thursday? What about Friday?' Suddenly she sat up. 'I had an invitation to my cousin's wedding. My dad and my brother will be there too.' I noticed that she was holding her breath, and asked her how her body was feeling at that moment.

'I don't feel anything,' said Penny. I wondered aloud if that wasn't a bit surprising when she had received such a shock. I asked if she could feel anything at all: how were her throat and her chest (familiar places where she experienced feelings)? She reported that her chest felt like a plate of old, cold spaghetti. I offered her some paper and pens and asked her if she thought she might draw that spaghetti. For a while she drew furiously, then swore and said she hated feeling like this. I asked her if she remembered when she had felt like that before. The old, cold spaghetti was a familiar feeling she remembered from when she would hear her father coming to her room. I asked her why she thought she might be feeling this right now, and she finally made the connection with the wedding invitation and the anticipation of seeing her abusers.

The session continued with a reminder about how much she had already accomplished, and her strengths. Time, too, to remind her that she could manage her panic attacks, and to revisit the techniques she had learned for dealing with them.

Typically, Penny had completely discounted the enormous steps she had taken and the achievements she had made. Starting from the reminder about her strengths and abilities, we began to explore how she could deal with the wedding invitation. Penny's breathing was an excellent indicator for her of going too fast, or of setting herself goals that were too difficult. When I noticed her holding her breath I gently reminded her, and asked her to go back to the point where she last remembered breathing easily.

An abused child has suffered a terrible loss: the loss of a childhood that could have been free of sexualisation, shame and secrets; maybe the loss of the parents they might have had; the loss of trust and innocence. I think that part of healing can be to help the client identify and mourn these losses. As with any loss, there will be a mixture of feelings, and sometimes I share information about recognised ways in which people grieve, so as to normalise these feelings for the client.

Self-harm

Abuse survivors are sometimes self-abusive. This may manifest itself in a variety of ways. They may overwork, but always feel that they haven't done enough. They may spend their lives trying to make things comfortable for others, perhaps their children, whilst at the same time denying themselves any treats or fun. A useful goal might be to find more cherishing ways to treat themselves. Some clients may be able to engage with their 'inner child' and think about what the neglected, abused child that they once were might have liked. This can be very painful, as they struggle to face the reality of their lives, or even think about being kind to themselves. Often when we embark on this work, the client says the goal is 'to be happy', but cannot actually say what being happy would be like. The task then is to find small, identifiable and realistically achievable goals, so that the client can become accustomed to doing things for him/herself:

John had been treated in the surgery over many years for asthma and eczema. A new doctor thought he was depressed and referred him for counselling. John grew up with a mentally ill mother and was sexually abused, first by his nanny and then by a male neighbour. His life was a treadmill of hard work for an employer who frequently expected him to stay until eight or ten o'clock at night. He had never had an adult sexual relationship. He believed that no one could ever love him, and could not understand why no one could see how much love he had to offer. His home was cold and uncomfortable; he seldom had food in the cupboard, so he would buy a pie and eat it on the way to work for breakfast. Then he would buy another pie and eat it on the way home. He dressed shabbily, with holes in his shoes (although he was not poor), his face looked grey and dry and he suffered from such tension in his shoulders that he seemed to have no neck.

When John said he wanted to be happy he found it extremely difficult to identify anything that would indicate to him that he was happier. He had no concept at all of self-care, seeing himself almost like a garbage heap. Eventually he thought that he might like to have a bubblebath with the radio playing music. It took three weeks before John could allow himself to have that bath, but slowly he began to internalise the concept that he was worth taking care of, and not just an object worthy of abuse.

Clients who act out the abuse done to them by cutting themselves or hurting themselves in other ways can feel daunting to work with.

Stella, who is 38, though she looks a fragile 14, cuts herself as part of her way of keeping herself 'real' in the world. She regularly presents herself to the GP with pains and worries about brain tumours, cancers or meningitis. Her history is of sadistic abuse and abandonment: she remembers being left alone in the house when she was very little while her mother went out to work. Little Stella would be fed sleeping tablets crushed in milky drinks to keep her quiet. Her instruction was to sit still and be good. Terrified to move, she sat all day in her own urine and faeces, and when her mother returned, she would be punished for being bad. Her father, a professional man, abused her sexually from such a young age that Stella can't remember a time when she was not abused.

Stella started cutting herself when she was about 12; any part of her body above her knees and down to her elbows that she can reach is criss-crossed with hundreds of scars. Four years ago, when her son was born, she made the doctors agree to examine her without taking off her voluminous tee-shirt, and totally refused to have any internal examination at all. But nowhere in her records is any reference made to this, nor to the mass of scars that medical staff could not have failed to see.

I believe that denial arises for many of us in working with self-harming clients. Coping with the feelings engendered by someone who is actually prepared to hurt themselves in such a way may be so difficult to deal with that it is easier to collude with whatever story the client tells about the cutting or burning. People who self-harm account for 100,000 admissions annually to casualty departments where they are frequently treated with rejection, anger, disgust, fury and punishment: horrible parallels of the abuse and abandonment so often found in their early history. Many counsellors also find it difficult to know how to work with people who self-harm. It may be truly difficult to give unconditional positive regard to someone who has repeatedly opened up a wound, pulled out her eyelashes, swallowed batteries, sat in bleach, or worse, especially if the client has been improving and then reverts to this behaviour.

I try to offer a careful balance between reacting in a caring and nurturing way, whilst still giving the client a genuine response. I will try to explore with the client the symbolic meaning of her self-harming. If the only way she can feel 'real' is to watch blood run down her arm, then telling her she mustn't hurt herself in this way is to miss the point and to close down an essential communication. I take my shock, fear and judgments to supervision (both internally and with my supervisor) to remind myself that these feelings may in some way echo the client's feelings about herself. It's not always easy to face my sense of disappointment – 'How could she do that after all our work together?' – or maybe self-blame: 'I must have missed something vital.'

Even with clients who do not self-harm in such dramatic ways, I notice that self-harm is very frequently enacted in the counselling session in some kind of ritualised or symbolic form. I might notice the client picking the skin around her fingers, pinching herself, pulling her hair. Of course, these are far less dramatic ways of harming oneself, but they may hold vital information about how the client copes with his or her pain, and should not be ignored. Focusing on such patterns of behaviour in the present can help the client understand how she continues to act out the abuse that was done to her in the past.

Working with the GP

Many clients are very reluctant to tell their GP about their abuse and it may be important to challenge this reluctance, pointing out the parallel process of keeping secrets and not breaking the taboo. It may be extremely helpful for both the GP and the client to talk through the somatised pain. Others in the team may also be helpful, such as the midwife, the health visitor, the practice nurse or the physiotherapist. These clinicians may be in frequent contact with the client, and if she could tell them something about the cause of her problems they may become useful allies. Often the client has a good enough relationship with at least one of the surgery team, and I will usually invite the client to recognise this as an indicator that there are some people in the world who are trustworthy. It may be that this team member is the person the client first trusted with her disclosure.

Occasionally a client will try to get me to take sides with her against the GP or another clinician. It is not helpful for me to collude with this, so I might put forward the idea of a three-way meeting between the client, the GP and myself to help iron out the perceived difficulties. On the rare occasion that this has occurred, I have sat there feeling redundant while the client, who thought she would never be able to tackle the GP, talks eloquently about the difficulty she is having. This offer of a meeting supported by the counsellor allows the client to feel empowered and supported as she faces an authority figure.

Counsellors can provide important information about sexual abuse to the practice team: the subject seems rarely to be acknowledged in the GP's formal training. Over the years I have been able to talk about the consequences of abuse with GPs; this seems to have helped them to deal with patients' somatised distress, and avoid over-reacting to self-harming.

Supervisory issues

Working with sexual abuse survivors can seem a huge and daunting task, and even experienced counsellors may occasionally feel overwhelmed by the nature of the issues brought by some of their clients. The parallel process (an acting-out of the damaged early relationship within the relationship with the counsellor) can be difficult to deal with. A counsellor who does not feel confident about working with issues of abuse can still provide a strong and supportive framework, assisting the client to seek and find appropriate help (Etherington 2001).

In parallel, this work requires strongly supportive supervision with an experienced supervisor, as well as good, reflective use of the 'internal supervisor'. I admit to having a tendency to overwork and forget to take enough time out, so one of my supervisor's main tasks is to monitor this with me. I use my supervision to talk through the range of thoughts and feelings I might have about a client, and to tease out issues of transference and countertransference. Occasionally I am surprised and even ashamed of the intensity of feelings I can experience; dislike, boredom, disgust and even sexual attraction. I know it is not helpful to judge these feelings as wrong – though of course it would be wrong to act them out in the counsellor–client relationship. But that intellectual knowledge doesn't always prevent me from feeling anxious about having certain feelings. I remember feeling really ashamed about the fact that I felt an overwhelming urge to fall asleep when working with a particular client. Together my supervisor and I worked through the transference and how the client put herself to sleep to avoid the pain she was feeling and unconsciously sought to lead me, too, away from her pain.

An issue I have to deal with sometimes in supervision is that of 'rescuing' my client – that is, of becoming 'overhelpful' instead of staying with the client's past as he or she struggles with doing something difficult. Lewis Herman identifies this inclination as the counsellor's 'defence against an unbearable feeling of helplessness'. This old behaviour, deeply ingrained in many abuse survivors, can emerge when I am perhaps not carefully attending to boundaries. Work with abuse survivors can be extremely intense and I find it is better for me to balance my caseload with a mixture of other clients. That said, it is not always possible to anticipate what will unfold when starting work with a client.

I prize highly the peer support I receive from the other counsellor in the practice. In our weekly meeting we are able to give each other support and disentangle some of the complex issues involved in working at the interface between GPs and other clinicians, and counselling. I also prize the fortnightly bodywork or cranio-sacral therapy sessions I have, which help me to unknot from my body the impact of working so closely with somatised pain.

Conclusion

Despite the fact that this work can be difficult, it is an enormous privilege to work with men and women who have the courage to face their deepest pain and then find a way to reject the damaging messages they received from those who abused them in the past. I thank each of those whose stories I have drawn on in the writing of this chapter, and all those others whose process has been intertwined with my own, and who have enriched me in so many ways. I hope that the twenty-first century will see a huge upsurge of understanding in the medical profession about the consequences of childhood abuse and somatised pain.

References

Ainscough, C. and Toon, K. (2000) *Breaking Free Workbook*. London: SPCK.

Ali, A. (2000) 'How early abuse affects an individual's health.' *Psychosomatic Medicine,* January/February.

Bass, E. and Davis, L. (1988) *The Courage to Heal: A Guide for Women Survivors of Sexual Abuse.* New York: Harper & Row.

BBC1 Panorama (1997) *The Sexual Abuse by Women of Children and Teenagers.* London: BBC1 Panorama.

Bean, B. and Bennett, S. (1993) *The Me Nobody Knows – A Guide for Teen Survivors.* New York: Lexington Books.

Bond, T. (2000) *Standards and Ethics for Counselling in Action* (second edition). London: Sage.

Bradshaw, J. (1990) *Healing the Shame that Binds You.* Deerfield Beach, Florida: Health Communications.

Briere, J. N. (1992) *Child Abuse Trauma and Treatment of the Lasting Effects.* California: Sage.

Briere, J. and Runtz, M. (1988) 'Post-sexual abuse trauma.' In G. Wyatt and G. Powell (eds) *Lasting Effects of Child Sexual Abuse.* London: Sage.

Brown, J. (1999) 'Childhood abuse and neglect: specificity of effects on adolescent and young adult depression and suicidality.' *Journal of the American Academy of Child and Adolescent Psychiatry.* Internet.

Cahill, C., Llewellyn, S. and Pearson, C. (1991) 'The long term effects of sexual abuse which occurred in childhood: a review.' *British Journal of Clinical Psychology 30,* 117–130.

Dale, P. (1992) *Counselling Adults who were Abused as Children.* Rugby: British Association for Counselling and Psychotherapy.

Davis, L. (1990) *The Courage to Heal Workbook: A Guide for Women and Men Survivors of Sexual Abuse.* New York: Harper & Row.

Dietz, P., Spitz, A. M., Anda, R. F., Williamson, D. F., McMahon, P. M., Santelli, J. S., Nordenberg, D. F., Felitti, V. J. and Kendrick, J. S. (1999) 'Unintended pregnancy among adult women exposed to abuse or household dysfunction during their childhood.' *Journal of the American Medical Association 282,* 1359–1364.

Eastham, J. (2000) Text from speech given at the International Conference 'Self-Harm – Meeting Clients' Needs Taking Professional Practice Forward.' 6–8th November 2000, Leicester.

Etherington, K. (1995) *Adult Male Survivors of Child Sexual Abuse.* London: Pavilion.

Etherington, K. (2000) *Narrative Approaches to Working with Adult Male Survivors of Child Sexual Abuse.* London: Jessica Kingsley Publishers.

Etherington, K. (2001) 'Working with physical and sexual abuse in primary care.' In T. Bond (ed) *Counselling in Primary Care* (second edition). Oxford: Oxford University Press.

Felitti, V. (1998) 'Relationship of childhood abuse and household dysfunction to many of the leading causes of death in adults: The adverse childhood experiences.' The Adverse Childhood Experiences (ACE) Study. *American Journal of Preventive Medicine 14,* 4, 245–258.

Fergusson, D.M. and Lynskey, M.T. (1995) 'Childhood circumstances, adolescent adjustment and suicide attempts in a New Zealand birth cohort.' *Journal of the American Academy of Child and Adolescent Psychiatry 34,* 612–622.

Fergusson, D. M., Horwood, L. J. and Lynskey, M. T. (1996) 'Childhood sexual abuse and psychiatric disorders in young adulthood. Part II: Psychiatric outcomes of sexual abuse.' *Journal of the American Academy of Child and Adolescent Psychiatry 35*, 1365–1374.

Finkelhor, D. (1988) 'The trauma of child sexual abuse.' In G. Wyatt and G. Powell (eds) *Lasting Effects of Child Sexual Abuse.* London: Sage.

Fleming, J. (1997) 'Prevalence of childhood sexual abuse in a community sample of Australian women.' *Medical Journal of Australia 166*, 65–68.

Gelinas, D. (1983) 'The persisting negative effects of incest.' *Psychiatry 46*, 312–332.

Hall, L. and Lloyd, S. (1993) *Surviving Child Sexual Abuse* (second edition). London: The Falmer Press.

Heim, C., Newport, J. Heit, S., Graham, Y., Wilcox, M., Bonsall, R., Miller, A. and Nemeroff, C. (2000) 'Pituitary-adrenal and autonomic responses to stress in women after sexual and physical abuse in childhood.' *Journal of the American Medical Association 284*, 5, 592–597.

Koss, M. (1990) 'The women's mental health agenda: violence against women.' *American Psychologist 45*, 3.

Levine, P. (1997) *Waking the Tiger – Healing Trauma.* Berkeley, California: North Atlantic Books.

Lew, M. (1993) *Victims No Longer.* London: Mandarin Paperbacks.

Lewis Herman, J. (1998) *Trauma and Recovery.* London: Pandora Books.

Mullen, P.E., Martin, J.L., Anderson, J.C., Romans, S.E. and Herbison, G.P. (1993) 'Childhood sexual abuse and mental health in adult life.' *British Journal of Psychiatry 163*, 721–732.

Mullen, P. E., Martin, J. L., Anderson, J. C., Romans, S. E. and Herbison, G. P. (1996) 'The long-term impact of the physical, emotional and sexual abuse of children: a community study.' *Child Abuse and Neglect 20*, 7–22.

Nemeroff, C. (2000) 'Corticotropin-releasing factor triggers depression.' *Clinical Psychiatry News 28*, 6, 27.

Putnam, F. (1990) 'Disturbances of "self" in victims of childhood sexual abuse.' In R. Kluft (ed) *Incest-Related Syndromes of Adult Psychopathology.* Washington DC: American Psychiatric Press.

Radomsky, N. (1995) 'Lost voices: Women, chronic pain and abuse.' Philadelphia: Harrington Park Press.

Read, J. (1998) 'Child abuse and severity of disturbance among adult psychiatric inpatients.' *Child Abuse and Neglect 22*, 359–368.

Romans, S. E., Martin, J. and Mullen, P. E. (1996) 'Women's self-esteem: a community study of women who report and do not report childhood sexual abuse.' *British Journal of Psychiatry 696*, 696–704.

Santi Ireson, S. (1996) 'The silent scream: an investigation undertaken in one GP practice of the somatic presentation of childhood sexual abuse to the doctor.' Unpublished postgraduate diploma thesis, University of Bristol.

Silverman, A. B., Reinherz, H. Z. and Giaconia, R. M. (1996) 'The long term sequelae of child and adolescent abuse: a longitudinal community study.' *Child Abuse and Neglect 20,* 709–723.

Smith, J. (1999) 'Holding the dance: a flexible approach to boundaries in general practice.' In J. Lees (ed) *Clinical Counselling in Primary Care.* London: Routledge.

Smith, P. (1995) *Childhood Sexual Abuse, Sexuality, Pregnancy and Birthing.* Manchester: PCCS Books.

Further reading
Useful books to recommend to clients

Ainscough, C. and Toon, K. (2000) *Breaking Free Workbook.* London: SPCK.

Bass, E. and Davis, L. (1988) *The Courage to Heal: A Guide for Women Survivors of Sexual Abuse.* New York: Harper & Row.

Bean, B. and Bennett, S. (1993) *The Me Nobody Knows – A Guide for Teen Survivors.* New York: Lexington Books.

Gil, E. (1983) *Outgrowing the Pain.* New York: Dell.

Lew, M. (1993) *Victims No Longer.* London: Mandarin Paperbacks.

Chapter 4

Working as a counsellor in an NHS multidisciplinary team

Julia Segal

Introduction

In 1985 I joined the staff of a research unit in the grounds of the Central Middlesex Hospital, London, as a counsellor. The unit had been set up by a charity run by and for people with multiple sclerosis (MS) and members of their families. At the time little was on offer to most people with MS once they had been diagnosed, unless they needed social services input. The unit was to provide the services which people with MS and members of their families felt they wanted: originally dietary advice and exercise groups, together with research projects to demonstrate the value of these services in the hope of having them adopted by the NHS.

Counselling was seen as important by some members of the organisation who knew its value in terms of the support they needed themselves, either as people with MS or as relatives; counselling was to be made available not only to people with MS but also to members of their families, particularly partners and children. My role was to include persuading other branches of the organisation to employ professional counsellors and writing papers to disseminate knowledge of its value both to potential clients (often members of the charity) and to the professionals who were in a position to provide or fund it. In 1992 the unit was taken over by the hospital, and it continues to function as part of the NHS today.

I had been trained by Marriage Guidance (now Relate) and had been working with people who came seeking help with marital difficulties. I had been introduced to the ideas of the psychoanalyst Melanie Klein several years before and found that in marital counselling I could use Klein's concepts to help people with ordinary difficulties make sense of their situation. I watched anxiety lifting and some problems losing their force. I had become convinced that understanding itself was often sufficient to enable people to sort out their lives. This impression was confirmed in evening seminars I ran for the University of Manchester Extramural Department attended by professional people who were interested in using Klein's ideas in their work. I had written up some of my observations in a book, *Phantasy in Everyday Life* (Segal 1985), in hopes of helping a wider audience, both professional and lay, understand themselves and others better. It seemed that people with MS were also ordinary people facing difficult circumstances and that understanding might help them too. The job offered me the opportunity both to offer counselling and to think and write about the work I would be doing.

Later it emerged that I had a further qualification. Before I was old enough to go to school I had accompanied my mother while she taught in a school for physically handicapped children. I was a bit scared of the 'big boys' in wheelchairs who scooted down the corridor and I literally 'looked up to' them. I also developed an attachment to a boy who lay on a couch all day and (according to his teacher) did little – but he was sometimes allowed to listen to me read and talk; a rare pleasure for a three-year-old with a working mother. Over the years I have learnt to appreciate how different my attitude is from that of some others. I am not frightened by disabilities, have never looked down on people who have them and have no problem seeing 'the person in the wheelchair'. I seem to have more of an inbuilt, automatic respect for people with disabilities than many of my disabled clients do. I do not feel I have to like anyone just because they are disabled, but I do not automatically dismiss them. I also have a strong opposition to the idea that anyone is 'useless'.

Throughout the early years of my work for the unit I was supervised by Isabel Menzies, a Kleinian analyst herself, who helped me to understand the organisational aspects of the work and my place in the team, as well as providing insight into the actual counselling with clients. Her own work and experience was an inspiration (see for example Menzies-Lyth 1959). She encouraged me to think in terms of working with the other staff members and, where possible, supporting and enhancing their capacities to work with clients. She made a strong link between the way staff feel supported and contained emotionally at work, and the way they are able to support and 'hold' patients. This link was frequently the subject of discussion at a fortnightly seminar on consultation to organisations which I attended for a while at the Tavistock Clinic, under the leadership of Anton Obholzer (see Obholzer and Zagier-Roberts 1994). Here we discussed in some detail the effects of client problems on staff in various organisations. For example, primary school teachers could be observed at times relating to their headteacher as if he or she was teacher and they were small children, while staff in adolescent units sometimes behaved, and clearly felt, as if they were adolescents themselves. I became very interested in this aspect of the work and took every opportunity to further my understanding of the impact on professionals of working with people with MS and other disabilities. I discovered that when the MS unit first opened, a lot of the staff found they had MS symptoms for a while. Gradually I found other more significant connections, some of which I describe elsewhere (Segal 1996), and some in this chapter.

In this chapter I describe some of the ways in which I set about establishing the place of counselling and the counsellor within the unit. I describe the staff consultations with other members of the team and discuss the role these played in my relationship with the team as it evolved over time. I link this with the function of the team and its relation to patients. I then describe some of the other groundrules for counselling which had to be established. Finally, I look at some of the issues involved for a counsellor within team discussions.

When I joined the team...

The team when I arrived included two physiotherapists, a nutritionist, a doctor and two secretaries, who spent a lot of time talking to patients and members of their families. Later others joined us. When I arrived I was afraid that I might be resented as an interloper who would want to take over clients who had been confiding in other members of staff. I made it clear that I thought such patients would be unlikely to take kindly to being 'handed over' to me and that I would not do it. Instead I would help any staff involved in such relationships to think about the feelings and thoughts aroused by the client or patient, and to use this to enhance their understanding of the client and the work. I was also aware of the dangers of burn-out for staff, and wanted to offer support to prevent this.

I made appointments with staff members individually to discuss their work, sometimes in general but more commonly focusing on work with one particular client and the interaction with him or her. Usually we were discussing clients I did not know; however, occasionally I did know a client and

I decided I was permitted to share, in a limited way, some of my own ideas about the way the client related to me, though not information given to me by the client. Often there was relief on finding that the other staff member and I had similar feelings and reactions. These discussions were so successful from the beginning that I still offer them now, with 'new' staff members and 'old' ones.

This process enabled each of us to learn from the other. I could learn about MS and the experience of working with it. For example, I learnt of the frustrations of a physiotherapist who said, 'I know it's not her fault, but we have worked so hard, she had made so many improvements, and now I'm furious with her that she's had a relapse and it's all gone!' I observed and was able to discuss many of the distancing mechanisms professionals use with clients. For example, descriptions of patients as 'manipulative' or 'difficult' were sometimes used by professionals outside the unit. Discussion of these concepts led us to a greater understanding of the patient's emotional state, which could provoke them. It also enabled us to look at the professionals' difficulty in coping with their own emotional reactions to the patient.

We also discussed the effect patients could have on staff members: whether to spur them to particular efforts; to get them involved over and above the usual interventions; or to make them feel detached, uninvolved, useless or hopeless – or angry or invaded or sexually threatened. I linked these feelings to the feelings clients with MS had to struggle with daily.

Melanie Klein's concepts of countertransference and projective identification were very useful. (See, for example, Segal 1992.) For example, an occupational therapist discussing a difficult couple we were both seeing suddenly burst out with feelings of impotence and uselessness, saying she thought she ought to leave the unit, she was not doing any good and her work was not being valued. (I had expressed similar thoughts to my supervisor on more than one occasion, and they always turned out to be linked with the particular case I was presenting in supervision.) After a few moments of sympathy I was able to ask if these were feelings which the clients might be feeling, and a moment's thought was sufficient for both of us to recognise that they were. Impotence is a fairly common symptom in MS, and impotence in a husband can lead to a wife feeling impotent too (by a mechanism which I would call projective identification, a form of transference; see Segal 1992). We began to suspect that both of them felt undervalued and I knew they were thinking of separating. The link with the clients made sense to the distressed occupational therapist. This was a huge relief to her, as she no longer felt she had to get out and leave; as she said, she knew she didn't really want to leave, she liked working with us. We were able to continue our discussion of the clients and sort out the management issues involved.

With some members of the team I could explain how people sometimes convey to others feelings they cannot bear in themselves. We could look closely at the professional's feelings (such as a sense of frustration or guilt) in order to take them seriously as a pointer both to the realities of working with MS, and also to a perhaps unrecognised (or even unconscious) emotional response of the patient concerned. Some professionals are taught to put their feelings on one side to such an extent that they find it very difficult to access them at all; using the professionals' emotional response was not possible with everyone. In addition, a few staff members have just not been interested in working in this way with me. Staff varied in their willingness to be involved with patients and their potential for some kind of 'counselling' support. Some went on to study counselling, while others clarified and defined their own role more closely, becoming clearer about their own boundaries. I could sometimes help them to feel less anxious or persecuted or guilty about a particular relationship.

For the most part this process has worked well. However, there have been times when it has seemed to me that discussion with a professional has not led to greater thought about a patient, but to snap judgements and even dismissal of thought. An idea of mine put forward as something to consider has once or twice been used as a defining label for a client, simplifying what seem to me complexities rather than opening up awareness of them. To some extent this may be based on different training and expectations for different professions; to some extent it may be personality-based. It has made me careful about who I talk with, and what I say.

Since clients tend to evoke in professionals precisely those responses which feel most personal and often shameful, I had to be very careful when discussing clients in some depth to avoid the development of a counselling relationship between myself and another member of staff. Where necessary I have suggested that a professional seek counselling elsewhere. This leaves us free to concentrate on the client's contribution to the relationship, while acknowledging that the professional's own psyche also plays an important part. This has, I think, been a significant part of my involvement in the team. The matter-of-fact suggestion that counselling might help difficult relation-ships with patients has had at times a powerful effect on a team member – and on their subsequent work.

One staff member brought to me issues raised by a patient who was making lewd suggestions. She was surprised that I saw it as a problem for team management rather than just her 'fault'. Her insecurities seemed to me to be a reflection of the patient's; he was perhaps attempting to deal with them by bullying and victimising her. We talked sympathetically about his problem and hers. In the discussion it became clear that very serious issues in her own past were contributing to her stress at work far more than she had realised. She (somewhat reluctantly at first) agreed to go for counselling, where she was again surprised to find she could deal with these issues. She visibly changed and grew in confidence during the time we worked together.

As clients were referred directly to me for counselling, the team told me with some considerable relief that my presence meant they 'could do their job properly' – they no longer found themselves caught up in a counselling relationship for which they felt they had neither skill, training, nor real inclination. This worked in several ways. Clients seemed to off-load less to the physiotherapist or nutritionist or receptionist, for example, when they knew they were about to see the counsellor. If clients did stray into talking about their marriage, or their difficult daughter, for example, the staff found it easier to say 'perhaps you should talk about that with the counsellor' and so lead the conversation back to their own area of expertise. There was also a sense that, if they did let a client talk about their emotional or family problems for any reason, I would help them with it afterwards. I suspect that this sometimes enabled them to allow certain clients to talk just long enough, without having to break them off quite as early or perhaps as brusquely as they might have done previously. I think this may contribute to a sense our clients have of being well contained and held by our unit. I also helped some staff to find ways of closing conversations while leaving the client feeling cared for.

Not only did the relationship between staff and patients benefit from these discussions, but the staff gained an appreciation of the task of a counsellor. This meant that they never belittled what I did, nor confused it with 'just listening' as some within the wider charity did. It also meant that they learnt my language and were able, in turn, to support me. When a client had seriously upset me or exhausted me, I could 'off-load' to one of my colleagues, knowing that they would listen constructively and with some understanding of what I was trying to do and how to do it.

All of this work directly with staff gave me insight into the work of the unit and the experience of MS. It helped to develop a mutual respect between myself and other members of the team. It also helped me to under-stand something of the effect of MS on those around the person who has it, including other carers. Carers, I think, 'pick up' emotions from the person they care for, whether they want to or not. I often find it helpful to work with this process as a way of helping a carer to understand their partner, particu-larly if the partner is cognitively affected by the MS. Primitive modes of communicating through projective identification continue to function where words fail. A wife who becomes furious with her paralysed husband may have been provoked by him into feeling anger he can no longer express, partly because she has her own reasons for anger which also have to be acknowledged. Her capacity to express it may be satisfying to him in some ways, even if it is directed at him. Picking up the part played by the husband's anger for a carer partner helps to reduce the burden of guilt (for feeling angry with a disabled man) and to restore understanding and more adult functioning. This understanding can be as significant as understand-ing the ordinary, real reasons the carer has for anger. Professionals who understand this process may feel less vulnerable to displacing their own patient-induced anger onto other team members, and less guilty and over-whelmed by it. As in psychodynamic counselling we sometimes use our own emotions as a guide to understanding the client's emotions, so other profes-sionals can sometimes learn to use this too.

It was only later that I realised how beneficial this consultancy role was (and is) for our relationship and the work of the unit. Menzies-Lyth (1959) found that in a hospital nurses were sometimes envious of their patients' comfort, to the extent that they could undermine it. More recent examples of this can be found in Obholzer and Zagier-Roberts (1994). Just as mothers can sometimes envy their baby's comfort, so too care workers can be jealous of the care lavished on their patients. By offering close attention to colleagues they have less reason to feel jealous of the attention clients receive in the counselling session. By listening seriously to staff members' difficult emotions and concerns about their work, I can contribute to their capacity to listen to clients appropriately in their work.

On one occasion I discovered that a series of appointments had not been entered in the diary, and ongoing work with a client was compromised. On close enquiry the receptionist expressed a strong sense that the client concerned should have had enough; other people needed counselling, and the client could not take all the appointments. I explained the importance of long-term work for my research as well as for the client, but, more important, I also offered her more time to discuss the pressure she was under from people who rang in wanting to talk to her. The problem did not recur.

Over the years as we have worked together there have been several ways in which I have had to draw my colleagues' attention to differences between my requirements and theirs. Physiotherapists, for example, expect other people to pass through the gym while they are working; this may in fact help them to handle the sexual aspects of working in intimate contact with client's bodies. Nutritionists and doctors, in my experience, also do not object to taking a phone call or a message during a consultation. Cleaners regularly assumed that they could knock on my door, however clearly it said 'Do not disturb'. Since no one else seemed to consider that interruptions might affect clients or patients adversely, appealing to this aspect of counselling could have been understood as implying a criticism of other professionals, which I in no way intended. I had to spend some time spelling out to the unit manager exactly why and how it would disturb my own concentration and the work with the client before I could be certain I would not be interrupted by every new cleaner. I unashamedly used the example of a client telling me about suicidal thoughts, or speaking for the first time of their feelings about the loss of a baby through abortion or stillbirth, in order to convey the distress potentially caused to a client by an interruption. I also explained that I had to use my own emotional state as a tool with which to work; my own feelings could often give me important ideas about the client's state of mind. If my concentration was broken, the consequences were serious for the work I was paid to do.

For this reason too, I had to ask people not to tell me something which might affect my emotions just before I saw a client. For example, I had to ask that if there was some upsetting news, it would be told to me at the beginning of a break, so that my mind would be clear to pick up my emotional reactions to the client at the next session.

Confidentiality

Confidentiality issues were – and are – a problem. Other members of staff write in the notes, but I seldom do. I have developed a concept of 'unit-confidential' which differs from 'counsellor-confidential'. 'Unit-confidential' facts I may sometimes write in the notes. This includes information which I know that other members of the unit share. It also includes information which other members of the unit may need to know, such as reports of conversations with social workers; or any serious allegations made by a client which might lead to a later court case; or any threat to life. In addition I keep my own brief notes of each session separately. Supervision notes are not kept at the unit and are not named.

I write to GPs at certain times with brief and generalised information about the counselling, including issues which concern me and/or the client, which I think the GP should know. These letters are copied to the client and to the notes. Where my letter is part of a letter from the whole team clients have not in the past been given copies; though under the new NHS guidelines this is to happen in future. Sometimes I discuss the text with the client beforehand.

Clients have their own opinions on what should be or will be shared in a hospital setting. Some clients clearly expect me to share anything they say with other members of the team, and are surprised to find I have not passed on information. Others are explicit that they do not want other members of the team to be told what they have said. In between there is a large grey area. This is an issue we have not yet fully resolved.

Quite often clients tell me about symptoms which need further professional input but which they did not mention when they saw the relevant team member. Depending on the circumstances I may leave it to them to raise: if they don't, I will discuss their difficulty with them to ease the process. In more pressing situations I may ask if they would like (or allow) me to raise it, and this has occasionally led to joint sessions with other team members in which I as well as the client have learnt more about the issues involved.

As the team has evolved over the years, we now have case discussions involving the whole team and I share some aspects of the counselling in the meeting, mostly in general terms. This has meant that I now generally check that clients do not object to me exchanging information with other members of the team, including their GP. When I introduce myself I say something like: 'I am the counsellor; I am a member of the team and we do discuss some of our work, so if there is anything you don't want me to pass on you need to let me know.' I am working currently on a handout which will say this, but I have found it difficult to integrate into the session.

Partly I accept the argument which says that we present ourselves as a team within the NHS and that the counsellor is clearly a member of that team; therefore clients must expect some sharing of information. In addition, clients may feel comfortably contained by a team which shares information. On the other hand, the current codes of ethics of counselling insist that information is not passed on unless it involves a threat to life (although these codes are under review) and should not provoke action unless explicitly condoned by the client. Unfortunately there is no generally agreed expectation of counsellors in the public domain, as there is for doctors or nurses or priests (though I sometimes wonder if the public are aware of what I have perceived of doctors' actual attitudes towards confidentiality among themselves). A counsellor cannot be expected to explain the whole code of ethics under which they work in a one-hour counselling session, particularly if they believe in allowing the client to lead.

Team meetings allow a pooling of information and thoughts about clients and the process of working with them. At their best they provide a space for thinking about a client as a whole, sharing anxieties and making realistic plans of action which benefit clients and their families. However, they also increase the temptation to share more with colleagues than I feel I really should – and for them to share with me. These meetings can sometimes give me information about a client which is difficult to handle. If a client has not told me how much alcohol they drink, they may assume I have read it in the notes – or they may not. I cannot simply say 'Your GP says X about you' as I would be breaking medical conventions of confidentiality. There is no certainty that the GP has shared their letter of referral with the client.

However, because counselling definitions of confidentiality do not encourage the counsellor to withhold significant information from the client, information the client does not share is even more of a problem. For example, there may be questions of diagnosis which the doctor prefers to keep from the client for the time being. I find this disruptive to the counselling, and argue that the doctor should share such questions with the client before I see them, but the doctor may not see the urgency. These discussions highlight the different assumptions of counselling and the medical profession. Provision of information is basic to empowerment, but it can also raise anxieties in both patient and doctor. There are also issues of timing involved. Doctors and counsellors handle uncertainty in different ways and see their responsibilities differently. In our discussions we gradually influence each other.

Issues of confidentiality are also complicated by the fact that I see partners and carers of people with MS, sometimes on their own. Having been trained by Relate I have clear ideas about what can and cannot be shared when seeing members of a couple, but even so this can raise complex issues of confidentiality with other members of the team. If a wife tells me about a medical problem she sees her husband (the patient) having, and which he has not mentioned to the doctor, I cannot pass it on. Neither the wife nor I are allowed (by the doctor's conventions) to discuss the husband with the doctor unless the patient is present or has explicitly given permission. Even if it involves, for example, the husband being unsafe on the road (and a probable danger to life), all I can do is facilitate more open communication between husband and wife. It is the wife who has to take responsibility for stopping her husband driving and the wife who has to take her husband's blame.

Where cognitive difficulties are involved, confronting a partner with impairments can be particularly frustrating or even frightening. If a man should no longer drive because he cannot react fast enough or safely enough, it may be very difficult for his wife to tell him so. Cognitive difficulties seem generally far harder to address and accept than physical, presumably because the implications are so far-reaching. They can also make people very irritable and apparently unreasonable. This kind of issue can bring into sharp focus the powerful effect of MS on the relationship between partners, and the limits of professional help.

Complaints

Sometimes clients bring to me a complaint about other members of the team. It may be realistic and straightforward, but it may include a hint about me and my relationship with the client, or about the client's relationships with professionals in general. For example, one client complained that a doctor had been more interested in talking to the nurse in the room than in listening to her. I knew she had recently seen me talking to another patient in the waiting room – which I generally avoid – so I took it up in terms of her possibly feeling jealous and neglected by me as well as by him. This linked with feelings of being jealous which she remembered from her past too, and led to some important work.

Normally I make it clear to a client that I will not pass on messages of complaint but will work to empower the client to handle it themselves. Where possible I would take up issues that might be coded complaints against myself; this can of itself help to empower the client, as they see how I react when criticised.

Very occasionally I have taken up complaints. Recently a client complained that his sudden deterioration was not being taken seriously by a new physiotherapist in our team. He had been sent away with no new appointment for a month, and was unable to challenge this. I felt that my relation with the physiotherapist was such that I could and should raise it with her, and we discussed it. I talked with the physiotherapist about the possibility that the client was misperceiving something, or was feeling some dissatisfaction with me which was being attributed to the physiotherapist. We also talked about the difficulties of 'favourites' having to transfer from old to new members of staff. The physiotherapist then went back to the notes and realised that she had misunderstood the situation. She offered the client the intensive work he wanted; she also asked if she could work more intensively with me on her relationships with clients. However, I am still concerned I should have said nothing. What I took up with the client was his fears that his physical deterioration reflected a deterioration in his social relationships, brought about by our failing to take seriously how bad things were for him. I am still afraid that by speaking to the physiotherapist for him I played into some complex scenario about who can say what to whom, which would have benefited more from thinking than from acting.

Such are the tensions of working within a team. By speaking to the physiotherapist, my client got his physiotherapy and the physiotherapist began to work with me; but perhaps something of more lasting benefit for the client in terms of his relationships was sacrificed.

Case discussion

I still work with staff members to help them to understand a particular client. For example, one member of staff complained bitterly to me about the way a client's son was not helping his mother at all. She was clearly angry with him. As she talked it became clear he had in fact brought his mother to her appointment; he clearly was helping in some ways. We talked about the boy's background. He had been left alone as a child to cope with his mother after an acrimonious divorce; her health deteriorated as he grew up and she became more and more distressed by other family matters, including the absence of her current husband, which made her very angry. My colleague told me indignantly that at the age of 21 the boy had given up his college course and was at home, unemployed, spending most of the day in bed. I suggested that he might well feel that his life was in danger of being taken over entirely by his ill and distressed mother; perhaps he had reason to fight off some of his mother's requests. My colleague seemed to be responding passionately to the client's neediness, which appeared insatiable. I drew her attention to the way this might work on the son; if he could never give her what she needed, could never make her better, even if he gave up his own education and stayed at home with her, he might well at times give up in despair and turn his back on the problem. Perhaps he too, like her, belittled the help he did give. My colleague could recognise her sense that helping this client was an enormous task in which much more help was needed. Perhaps, I wondered, the help of a man, not just a 21-year-old boy? My colleague's anger over the son's failure to help faded and she said she couldn't imagine what it must have been like for him.

I think such discussions help the professional not only to consider the point of view of recalcitrant children or carers, but also to tolerate better their own inability to solve all the problems of their most needy patients. Burn-out is less likely when professionals feel more in control of their work, clearer about what they can and cannot do, and more aware of the influence of patients' or clients' emotions on their own.

Conclusion

Working for the past 12 years in a supportive and caring team of professionals has taught me about people who live with MS; about the NHS; about other professionals; and about my own way of working within a team. Newcomers to the team comment on the atmosphere; one said that it was very unusual in her experience of hospitals to see both staff and clients treated with real respect and consideration. This is within a team which has faced constant demands for reduction of expenditure over the past six years. There are issues which are not fully resolved, such as those of confidentiality and the role of the staff meeting, and the unit is constantly changing, but we have developed over the years a way of working which seems to benefit both patients and staff.

Further reading

Menzies-Lyth, I. (1959) 'The functioning of social systems as a defence against anxiety.' In I. Menzies-Lyth (1988) *Containing Anxiety in Institutions: Selected Essays.* London: Free Association Books.

Obholzer, A. and Zagier-Roberts, V. (1994) *The Unconscious at Work: Individual and Organisational Stress in the Human Services.* London and New York: Routledge.

Segal, J.C. (1985) *Phantasy in Everyday Life.* Pelican Books. Reprinted Karnac Books, London, 1995, and Aronson, USA, 1996.

Segal, J.C. (1991a) 'Counselling people with MS, their families and professionals involved with them.' In L. Fallowfield and H. Davies (eds) *Counselling and Communication in Health Care.* London: John Wiley.

Segal, J.C. (1991b) 'The professional perspective. Beyond community care: normalisation and integration work.' In S. Ramon (ed) *Beyond Community Care*. London: Macmillan.

Segal, J.C. (1992) *Melanie Klein: Key Figures in Counselling and Psychotherapy*. London: Sage Publications.

Segal, J.C. (1996) 'Whose disability? Counter-transference in work with people with disabilities.' *Psychodynamic Counselling 2*, 2, 155–166.

Segal, J.C. and Simkins, J. (1996) *Helping Children with Ill or Disabled Parents*. London: Jessica Kingsley Publishers.

Chapter 5

Counselling children and their families in intensive care

Penny Cook

Introduction

I write from many years' experience as a paediatric nurse, and as a counsellor working in a paediatric intensive care unit (PICU), in a large regional hospital. I have also been asked to help children and families with a relative in the other specialised units.

In the UK there are the following categories of intensive care units (ICUs):

- ICU for general adult patients
- Neurosciences critical care unit
- Coronary care unit
- Paediatric ICU for children 0–16 yrs
- Neonatal ICU for premature and sick newborn babies.

I introduced a counselling role into the PICU where I was working as a nurse, because I recognised the need for this kind of support for patients, their family members and the staff working in a highly stressful environment. There is great potential benefit to all these people from having a trained counsellor in the PICU team (Cook 1993). Patients on a PICU and their families are at an increased risk of developing symptoms of post-traumatic stress disorder and have a great need of psychological support (Colville 1998).

The Royal College of Paediatrics and Child Health (formerly the British Paediatric Association) acknowledged:

There is a need for counselling or support staff specifically to provide for the psychological and emotional needs of the child and family. Such staff should be available for all children in the intensive care unit.

The provision of care and support to parents of children in intensive care is an important, time-consuming and stressful part of the work of the PICU medical and nursing staff. It is important to recognise the needs of staff for support from each other, from managers, and, at times, from counselling or support staff. (BPA 1993, p.49)

The Paediatric Intensive Care Unit environment

Most families are ill-prepared for an experience of PICU care; the sights and sounds may be frightening and stressful, and the appearance of their child could be distressing. Generally speaking, intensive care consists of being given fluids and drugs through a vein, feeding via a tube into the stomach, ventilator assistance with breathing, and monitoring of the heart rate and blood pressure, with the vital signs displayed as coloured squiggly lines on a computer screen. Procedures such as dialysis for kidney failure, X-rays, ultrasound scans and cerebral pressure monitoring are also available.

It is helpful for patients and relatives to regard the equipment as positive aids to enhance the care, so good information from staff, and encouragement to ask questions, is important. The counsellor can help parents identify their fears and the questions they need to ask.

Every attempt is made to present a friendly atmosphere for children, with brightly coloured décor and pictures, and facilities for parents. The nurses often wear tabards in children's fabrics and the doctors do not wear white coats. Families are encouraged to bring the child's favourite soft toys and photographs of the child when well.

In a PICU there is usually one nurse for each patient, sometimes more, and a doctor will always be on the unit or nearby. Decisions made in the morning might be changed later in response to the patient's condition. Families may become confused with the constant changing of condition and treatment, so good communication and regular updating of information is essential. Children do not remain in a PICU any longer than is necessary; it is better for the child and family to progress to a ward and a less intensive routine as soon as the child is well enough. The parents usually understand this, although some parents may feel rather scared and lonely after the reassuring constant attention in the PICU.

The PICU patient

Children may become ill or suffer an injury while away from home; they may need to be transferred from a local hospital to a PICU at a regional centre. The unfamiliar hospital and distance from home increases the difficulties for the family. The most common reasons for children being admitted are:

- head and other injuries following a road traffic accident as a pedestrian or in a vehicle, or on a bicycle or horse. Accidents may happen at schools, on farms, sports or activity centres, at the seaside, or in the home or garden, falling from windows, trees and down stairs

- the effects of smoke inhalation, near drowning, severe burns or scalds

- respiratory problems from infections such as bronchiolitis in young babies, bronchitis, croup, pneumonia and severe asthma

- poisoning caused by ingesting chemical substances, drugs or overdose of medication

- severe acute infections such as septicaemia, meningitis and encephalitis

- brain haemorrhages, uncontrollable seizures, prolonged diabetic coma

- major surgery, especially brain, spinal, heart, vascular, organ transplants, surgery for small babies; children may spend a period in a PICU post-operatively.

The majority of PICU patients require assistance with their breathing by means of a ventilator (which is often incorrectly called a life-support machine). Air and oxygen is given by the machine via a tube through the nose or mouth into the lungs. Children and babies are kept free from pain, positioned comfortably and usually asleep. As the patient's condition improves, he is weaned off the sedative drugs and then off the ventilator as he becomes able to breathe adequately for himself. The period on a ventilator is often the time when parents need most support, as they feel separated from their child and helpless to provide for him. It is definitely far from the familiar solution of Mummy or Daddy giving him a big kiss to make him better!

The PICU team members

Patients and families have confidence and trust when the PICU staff, of all grades and disciplines, work closely as an efficient team. Appreciating and supporting each other's roles, and having trust and respect for colleagues, usually increases satisfaction in what can be highly stressful work.

Parents sense good teamwork and need to feel able to trust staff with their child's care. After being in a PICU, one father said that the 'utter professionalism' had been essential and expected; there was no room for doubts in the team, as the parents had enough doubts in their own abilities at that time (Cook 1999). The multidisciplinary team would include:

1. Medical staff – usually led by a consultant in intensive care who may be a paediatrician or an anaesthetist; specialist surgeons; specialists in genetic or metabolic disorders; microbiologists; virologists; public health and community doctors; haematologist; ophthalmologist – all may visit the PICU as required.

2. Nursing staff are usually led by a clinical nurse leader, senior sister or charge nurse. Most of the nurses have additional paediatric, life-support and intensive care qualifications appropriate to their work. Some specialist nurses may visit to give help on specialist topics. Other visiting staff might include a transplant coordinator, liaison health visitor or community nurse.

3. Physiotherapists, dieticians, nutrition team, radiographers, technicians, social workers, psychologist, counsellor, pharmacist.

4. Hospital play specialists and nursery nurses may be attached to some PICUs.

5. Ward clerks, secretaries, ward assistants.

6. Domestic staff.

7. Fundraising coordinator, volunteer supporters of the PICU.

The morning ward round is a good routine, when the appropriate professionals discuss each patient's history, diagnosis and treatment. Parents and visitors are asked to leave the unit to protect the patients' confidentiality. Important information is shared with others in the team if it is in the best interest of the patient. A counsellor in a PICU benefits from the information shared and may have helpful comments to add, although some information would only be shared with prior permission. When I asked one consultant why he found it so helpful to have a counsellor present, he replied that it always reminded the team to consider the psychological and emotional needs of the patient and family, and it ensured they had an advocate. The counsellor is not prescribing or providing the clinical care, but has a unique role to play in observing and reflecting what is going on – for the patient, the family and for the staff.

Other professionals need to understand the counsellor's skills and contribution to the team, so it helps the team members, the patient and family, as well as the counsellor, if she can be present during some ward rounds, psychosocial discussions, team meetings, appropriate teaching sessions and even coffee breaks.

Assessing the need for a counselling role

A survey (Colville 1998) on the psychological support available on all 26 PICUs in the UK indicates that most units regularly involve psychosocial personnel in the care of their patients, although such personnel may not be formally allocated to the units. In total, 21 out of 26 units had at least one formally attached member of the team with specific responsibility for psychosocial aspects of care. This was most commonly a social worker (14 units) or a psychologist (8 units); a psychiatrist was attached to one unit, although 15 units said one was easily available if needed. Seven units had a play therapist attached and 11 could have one when necessary. In 5 units psychological liaison was seen as the role of a specially appointed liaison nurse. I know that some of these nurses are trained counsellors (as I am included in these figures), or have good counselling skills.

Each PICU will be different – in terms of the number of beds available, number of staff, location, and any specialised surgery or treatment offered. Some units specialising, for example, in cardiac or transplant surgery have a specialist nurse whose role is to inform and support the child and family throughout the ordeal. This might involve teaching them about the condition and the possible treatments, liaising with other health professionals, guiding them through decisions and during the surgery, and following their progress. Good counselling skills help the family to explore their feelings and fears at the various stages of this uncertain path.

My own experience shows that it works well to have a trained counsellor who is also a paediatric nurse with PICU nursing experience as part of the team. The counselling training, which is much more than learning counselling skills, prepares and equips the counsellor well for whatever may be happening on the unit. A counsellor with a substantial training would have learnt a good deal about herself and she would have experience of being a client. I appreciate the importance of this, working in an area where there is such a range of emotions and crises. I have explored different styles and methods of counselling and the theories behind them, know the value of peer support and supervision, the discipline of managing my work, and the standards expected of a professional counsellor. I have access to relevant continuing training and study days, research, and networking with other counsellors in health settings. Counsellor survival must not be forgotten at times when others depend on us for their support.

It is probably for each unit to reflect upon what they offer families already, and how this could be improved. Paediatric nurses are trained to provide family-centred care, and so are used to considering sick children and their families, but there are times, particularly when a child is critically ill and the level of nursing care is high, when they are not able to offer the support that they would like to. It may be too hard to manage the child's physical condition and the family's emotions simultaneously. Parents sometimes prefer to share their deepest fears and feelings in confidence, away from the bedside; some admit that they would not tell their child's nurse about their 'bad' feelings in case it jeopardised the child's care in any way. I know that anxious parents do need to feel 'heard' at a time when they feel rather helpless.

A counsellor complements the support role of the nurses at the bedside. It was pointed out to me that it was very reassuring for a nurse to know that she could always refer family members to the counsellor. It enabled her to extend her care by offering specialist help in addition to what she was able to provide herself. In fact, I think medical and nursing staff are more likely to pick up on the family's emotional issues when they can discuss them with the counsellor, who is a constant reminder of their importance.

It is helpful if one particular person is responsible for bereavement care and support, so the frequency of deaths in the unit may be a consideration. This work requires relevant training and knowledge and it is not easy for nurses to include this sensitive work as part of their normal nursing role. I considered this to be an essential part of my role; a high level of emotional and practical support is required for all family members and the staff.

Establishing the counselling post

Having considered the needs of the unit, and after aims and objectives have been agreed, there remains the question of funding the post. One of the advantages of having a nurse counsellor is that the post can be fitted to the nursing pay scales, possibly at the G grade sister level. It is not unusual for new, non-clinical posts to be funded from a particular source, such as a trust or charitable fund, perhaps for an initial period while being accommodated into the unit budget plan.

The workload of the unit and the available funding may determine whether the post is full-time or part-time. I suggest that a full-time post is preferable, with the post-holder able to work flexible hours if, for example, a critically ill child is admitted and the parents are very distressed, or other parents need some time to talk over bad news about their child. I have found that continuity and confidentiality is important for stressed families, so job-sharing may not be satisfactory. However, adequate cover is also necessary when the designated support person is not available. Large units may feel the need to divide the work between two people.

I have found it helpful to be in a role that includes counselling with liaison and support for families and staff, and some teaching. However, it may suit some units to have a 'pure' counsellor available for set sessions.

Understanding the counsellor role

Many health professionals do not understand the value of counselling, although some have attended counselling skills workshops or short courses. It is well worth spending time doing necessary 'groundwork' by talking to key people who will need to understand the boundaries between their work and the counsellor's. In my own case, I am certain that some other profes-sionals were rather wary of me at first, but by having open discussions about my aims from the start, we have enjoyed extremely good working relation-ships and trust in each other. For example, this enabled the transplant coor-dinators to have faith in my skills in talking with a family who were consid-ering donating their dying child's organs, and social workers knew that I would refer appropriate families to their team. I received superb cooperation from the chaplains, mortuary staff, voluntary services and others.

All medical and nursing staff spend time talking to parents, mostly com-municating information, but also listening to their questions and fears. A counsellor can offer time to explore anxieties, be a sounding-board for parents' thoughts and a safe place for them to express negative feelings. Many parents would not like to 'let off steam', show their anger or cry in the more public arena of the unit or in front of their child or the nurses. Parents pick up the emotions of other families on the unit who are going through a similar ordeal; they may need to be given the opportunity to focus only on themselves, the issues that are personal to them, and how they could be helped to manage their lives at this difficult time.

Aims of a counselling role

Lansdown, writing from his experiences as a psychologist working with sick children and families, recognised that 'Counselling can help, immediately and throughout the course of the child's illness, in the following ways:

1. By supporting families emotionally and socially.

2. By enhancing their self esteem, "helping them to feel good about themselves".

3. By increasing their sense of feeling in control. (This applies to children as well as parents.)

4. By helping them to explore their situation so that they will be better able to understand and anticipate events.

5. By enabling parents and children to communicate with each other to maximise the child's psychological well-being.

6. By enabling them to develop coping strategies.

7. By enabling parents to find their own support systems.

8. By enabling families to communicate effectively with professionals.

9. By enabling them to make decisions for themselves.' (Lansdown 1996, p.165)

When a child is critically ill, perhaps suddenly, the family members are thrown into a totally new and frightening situation. Each person, whether mother, father, brother, sister, grandparent or close friend, will have their own way of trying to cope with their emotions and anxieties; their own personalities and past experiences are important contributing factors too. There will be intense feelings, possibly of guilt, anger, fear, panic, separation and loss of control. The child's unpredictable medical condition is in itself a source of stress for the family; living with so much uncertainty – outcome, treatment, timescale – is extremely hard to manage, and people in this situation find the long periods of waiting intolerable. The counsellor plays an important part in enabling individual family members to find their own ways of coping with this seemingly unbearable situation.

Essential qualities for the role

All the personal and professional qualities expected of any counsellor apply to this work, with a few more that I would suggest:

1. Patience – waiting while a parent is talking with a doctor, or a parent wants to stay with the child a bit longer. You may have to wait while another person is using the interview room, or a parent has to take an important telephone call. It should be remembered that families in a PICU may have difficulty being patient; they are always waiting for something. Patience brings its rewards in the counselling too, for both counsellor and client.

2. Tolerance – working in a PICU may be thought intolerable by some, so the counsellor has to be able to tolerate the events, the environment, the people and hospital culture.

3. Flexible, regarding time spent with people, to be able to work with an individual, a couple or several members of a family. Able to feel comfortable at the bedside or in a quiet room, for five minutes or an hour.

4. Adaptable – be able to adapt the counselling styles, models and theories to suit the situation.

5. Intuitive – to know when to intervene or not, feel the right approach and when it is more appropriate to support the nurse supporting the family.

6. Knowledgeable about intensive care and the children's conditions.

7. Good team member with a high level of autonomy.

8. A sense of humour is essential.

What the counsellor should expect

Counsellors need to be 'unshockable' and be able to hear whatever they are told by their clients, but working in critical care areas involves all of the senses. There are continuing and sudden noises from equipment, alarms and seemingly constant ringing of telephones and bleeps. There are the human noises of crying, sometimes wailing and shouting. I have strong memories of a quiet and peaceful morning shattered by the gentle wail of a four-year-old girl: 'I don't want my sister to die.'

Pale, ill and disfigured children, thin babies, wounds, blood, and distressed families are not pleasant sights, particularly hard for the inexperienced to bear. Some people notice particular smells, and the sense of touch may be affected too. Parents find that their child feels different, perhaps by skin temperature or texture, and does not respond normally to being touched or stroked.

Emotions can be extremely powerful in a PICU, especially for parents of critically ill children. Anger is common: parents are angry about what has happened to their child, perhaps someone must be blamed. Hospital staff members are frequent targets for anger and the counsellor is no exception, particularly when the person concerned has the counsellor's undivided attention! I have seen a seemingly insignificant event or gesture provoke inappropriate or antisocial behaviour – a father punching his fist through a glass door panel, and violent threats to a doctor or nurse. Helping individuals acknowledge and manage their anger is a valuable part of a counsellor's role.

Strong guilt feelings are common in parents, probably tied to the responsibility they have for their child. They may feel that they have let the child down, failed to keep him safe or make him better. It all seems to be their fault: 'If only I had taken her to the doctor yesterday', 'I should have taken him to school myself', 'It was my fault the gate was left open.'

Fear is always around, even if not obvious: fear of the unknown; fear of a diagnosis and of their child dying, fear of how they will cope and fear of what others may think. A counsellor can help the family to manage these fears and anxieties, but may need to acknowledge her own as well.

When under stress in unusual and abnormal circumstances, people can behave and react abnormally. Their usual ways of coping may not help in this situation, adding to their confusion. One mother would pace up and down the unit like a caged animal, which was exactly how she described her feelings to the counsellor. When faced with problems at home she would visit or telephone a friend. In the PICU she was too far from friends and extended family and her money did not last long in the payphone, so she did not know what to do. This mother had not realised how much time she spent walking around, or that the nurses and other parents were finding it annoying. When talking in a comfortable room in private she was able to recognise why she was doing it and to find other sources of personal support.

The nurses commented that another mother was listening at the nurses' station when members of staff were on the telephone, standing close to groups of nurses and doctors when they were talking, and standing around other children's beds. This was becoming embarrassing, as other parents spoke of her being nosey, until there was an opportunity to explore this behaviour. The mother was so worried about her child and desperate for any information that anyone could offer her. Even though she was being given continual updates on her progress, she was convinced that the professionals were not telling her everything. The counsellor enabled her to realise that there were other very sick children in the unit, and that staff spoke on the telephone, and to each other, about *all* of the patients. She had become oblivious to anything but herself and her child.

Existing problems of health, work, relationships, money or housing will add to people's new anxieties and fears, and being at the hospital may revive positive or negative memories. All of these could have considerable bearing on how they cope with the PICU experience.

Styles and models of counselling

It is important to remember that counsellors working in this field have as their clients people who would not normally have chosen to seek counselling. They are there because their child is sick and counselling is part of the care and support offered by the hospital. One father admitted to me, 'I wouldn't usually have anything to do with counselling, but in here you've got to talk. It has helped me get my head round things.'

A gentle, friendly and tentative initial approach will make the difference between a good relationship with the family and a hostile one that could perhaps be misinterpreted as intrusion. The first meeting may turn out to be the only one, or it could be the first of many over a long period. It may help the family to feel more at ease if the counsellor can introduce herself as another member of the PICU team who is there to help support them through this difficult time. Otherwise they could think that they must be in a 'bad way' because the counsellor has been sent in!

Any style or model of counselling for helping families in the PICU has to be supportive, enabling individuals to find within themselves the strength and ability to cope with what is happening. I generally use a person-centred approach, being non-threatening, proceeding at the client's pace and offering the genuineness, empathy and acceptance that such vulnerable people need. I sometimes work more psychodynamically, to consider the relevance of past experiences and relationships to the present. I might challenge thoughts and attitudes, set achievable goals, encourage catharsis or work in the here-and-now as appropriate. Counselling is often brief and focused. It will almost certainly be important to consider whatever else is going on in people's lives at this time, but it is not appropriate for psycho-analysis or deep therapy sessions during the present crisis. There are times when very little is actually being said, and body language becomes more significant. Parents sometimes do not know what to say, or how to say it, especially if feeling overwhelmed by the situation or extremely tired.

Much has been written about stages in counselling, and these may be difficult to relate to this sort of work, particularly when it is sudden, unexpected, irregular or perhaps limited to a single meeting. Tschudin (1995) suggests a model I have found helpful in this work, using four questions:

1. What is happening?
2. What is the meaning of it?
3. What is your goal?
4. How are you going to do it?

The counsellor could use these questions to help the client focus on what is important, but many people are in such a distressed state that they cannot think to answer questions. Rather, the questions serve as a good guide for the counsellor in making a quick judgement as to what is going on and how best to help the client.

Counselling supervision

A good supervisor must be chosen carefully, as the counsellor needs to feel able to talk freely about the sad and traumatic parts of her work without needing to protect the supervisor. I have appreciated having a psychologist who is used to working with children and families as my supervisor. In addition to regular counselling supervision it is essential to have other sources of support, perhaps senior nursing and medical staff or the hospital chaplains. It is also beneficial for other counsellors working in the hospital to meet regularly for peer support, and to feel able to share a difficult case.

Even with good supportive supervision, counsellors may feel as if they carry a huge burden of responsibility for the psychological state of the sick child and family members. A great deal of what clients tell us is deeply personal and emotionally traumatic, so we need to be able to bear it. It may not be appropriate for us to do this work during a personal life crisis. Life must be well balanced, so holidays and time away from work are important – as is an understanding partner, family or friend.

The patient's family

Watching a very sick child can be distressing for relatives; they feel helpless and useless, they may not be able to communicate with the patient and are probably in awe of equipment they do not understand. Parents feel a great sense of separation from their children, being unable to cuddle them or get a smile in response. The nurses would encourage them to take part in the child's care in some way, such as changing a nappy, cleaning their eyes and mouth and reading stories to them.

Being resident in hospital, separated from home and other members of the family, adds to parents' stress. They may be worrying about other children at home, wondering who is caring for them and taking them to school. They may have concerns about their work; not all employers understand that parents need to be with their sick child. Self-employed people have worries about how their work will be done or whether they will have any earnings to pay the bills. Parents might be worrying about elderly or sick relatives or their own health problems.

Time with a counsellor gives parents space to consider themselves, when their focus would otherwise be the child's condition. It allows time for other real life issues to be acknowledged and included in the plan of how to manage, adapt or compromise the situation; they may be helped to change the way they view their difficulties.

It is understandable how siblings of the sick child can feel left out and ignored when their parents are so concerned about the child in the PICU. I always enquire after other children – who is caring for them, and are they happy there? Are they going to school and do their teachers know about their seriously ill sister? What do the children know? It is important that everyone tells the same story, to prevent the child becoming confused and mistrustful.

Grandparents often need time to talk over their concerns with staff as they may be trying to 'stay strong' for the parents, who are *their* children and need their support. Other relatives may be involved, as may the child's school friends or those who have witnessed the accident. I remember the manager of a road haulage firm trying to support one of his employees who was unable to drive his truck until he knew that the little girl who ran in front of him would be 'all right'. A mother was helped by a few sessions with me after witnessing her friend's child being knocked over by a car; she felt guilty, and that she should have been able to prevent the accident. With her friend's permission, I prepared her for the child's injuries and care, and took her into the PICU for an emotional reunion at the bedside.

Preparing to visit

Many of the friends and relations who may visit a child in a PICU come to support the parents; some will find it distressing and need to think about what to expect. A recent photograph of the child, taken on a polaroid or digital camera, is often helpful in preparing visitors for what they will see. Some people have phobias about hospitals, making it difficult to come in to see a sick child or their parents. It is not uncommon for a parent, more often a father, to have difficulty coming into the PICU; this may cause resentment, guilt, anger, and feelings of inadequacy and failure.

One young mother could not bear to go into the PICU where her little boy was very ill. However hard the nurses tried to persuade her, she would not go, but her husband spent time by their child and helped with his care. The counsellor heard from the mother how guilty she felt for failing her child and not being able to be in the PICU, and how much she admired her husband.

Nothing could encourage this mother to go in, so it seemed important to help with the feelings of guilt and failure, and to lower her expectations and help her set a few more achievable goals. The counsellor reviewed with her what she *was* achieving already – being at the hospital, even if she stayed in the parents' sittingroom, she was at least near the child and supporting her husband. She was given a polaroid picture of her son, which helped her feel closer to him. The nurse caring for him came out several times a day to give her reports on his condition so that the information did not always come via her husband. The counsellor helped her to feel that she had not deserted her child, and that her husband was happy to sit with him on behalf of them both – good partnerships are all about sharing roles and trusting each other. Her husband did not complain once about his wife, because he understood her. She was always there for him, and made the tea and coffee, and he relayed to her everything that was being done for their son. Gradually the mother was able to make her way nearer the PICU, then to stand at the doorway, and eventually to venture a little way in, far enough to see her child's bed. The pressure of being made to sit by the child had been lifted; she had permission to go at her own pace with help and encouragement.

Talking to children

Staff and families are encouraged to talk to sick children, even when they are receiving sedative drugs. It is important that they are told what is happening, their fears addressed and constant reassurance given. It may be possible to prepare the child and family before admission to a PICU. Children do need to know about any procedures or surgery they may undergo, as their imaginations can create unnecessary fears if they are not told the truth. Hospital play specialists help children through play to understand procedures and treatments. The counsellor can also encourage children to ask questions and express their anxieties. Some children ask, 'Who is going to do my operation? Will I wake up during the operation? Will Mummy be there when I wake up? Can operations kill you?'

Distressed adults may have difficulty talking to children; if the news is not good they will want to protect them from hearing what they really do not want to tell them. Adults often have fears and concerns about who should tell the child, and when, what the child needs to know, and how to say it. Consideration must be given to the child's possible reactions and how the adults will respond to support the child.

Staff support

Staff members often benefit from a counsellor being available to support them individually, during and after a crisis or busy period. A debriefing or support group is often helpful for those involved to reflect on the situation, share their feelings and evaluate their practice. Working in a critical care area requires full concentration. An accessible counsellor can provide staff with support for personal problems that could interfere with their standard of work and increase their vulnerability to emotions.

Conclusion

The role of counsellor in the PICU includes psychological preparation for children and families before surgery and procedures; managing crises; strengthening coping strategies; understanding defence mechanisms; dealing with feelings and emotions; stress management and relaxation; pacing; goal setting; encouraging; supporting staff; and much more. Counsellors working in this highly skilled and stressful setting must also be well supported in a good team. There is a considerable sense of privilege in being able to support an individual or a family when they are at their most vulnerable, feeling helpless and perhaps desperately fearful for the health and future of their sick child.

References

British Paediatric Association (1993) *The Care of Critically Ill Children.* London: BPA (now Royal College of Paediatrics and Child Health).

Colville, G. (1998) 'Psychological support on the paediatric intensive care unit: a UK survey.' *Care of the Critically Ill 14,* 1, 25–28.

Cook, P. (1993) 'The value of family counselling in paediatric intensive care: Abstracts from the Paediatric Intensive Care Society Spring Meeting, March 1993.' *Care of the Critically Ill 9,* 4, 179.

Cook, P. (1999) *Supporting Sick Children and their Families.* London: Baillière Tindall.

Lansdown, R. (1996) *Children in Hospital.* Oxford: Oxford University Press.

Tschudin, V. (1995) *Counselling Skills for Nurses* (fourth edition). London: Baillière Tindall.

Chapter 6

'Awkward' clients and 'awkward' topics

Young people and sexual health

Caroline Stedman

Introduction

Preparing to write this chapter has brought out a lot of adolescent feelings in me! I want to draw your attention to the drama of my situation – teenagers! sex! abortion! (There, that worked, didn't it?) Then suddenly I feel all shy and confused – what if you don't take me seriously? What if you're judging me – after all, I'm constantly watching myself to see how I perform, and checking whether I like the image I project. So one minute I'm all bluster and the next withdrawn into a world of my own, possibly deflated and depressed. Sound like any adolescents you've ever known?

I don't want to overdraw the picture, but there are some strong parallels. The client group, the subject matter, the setting – all make a variety of demands on the counsellor's skill, knowledge and boundaries and leave one feeling the pull of 'identity versus role confusion' that Erikson (1963) ascribes to puberty and adolescence. Counselling adolescents does require an adaptation of one's skills, and an understanding of their developmental needs (Geldard and Geldard 1999). As they are in a transitional stage when a lot of physical, cognitive and emotional changes are happening (Rutter and Rutter 1992), they require the counsellor – in some respects – to be constantly in assessment mode in order to keep up. They may be childlike one minute and adult the next, and chronological age is not necessarily a guide to their maturity – some 13-year-olds may present as more mature than some 16-year-olds. (As I see clients up to age twenty-five, I am also used to having to work with young adults and their concerns.) Added to that are gender differences, cultural variations and high levels of inner-city deprivation and its attendant problems.

Then there's the subject matter. One has to be comfortable with one's own sexuality, and able to talk with other people about theirs without getting embarrassed or seeming voyeuristic. It's important to educate – about anything from basic body parts, through physical and emotional feelings around sex, to its actual and potential consequences – without seeming patronising. Young people may have found sexual activity to be fun, pleasurable and intimate; scary and exploitative; or just plain disappointing. If they are as yet only contemplating sexual activity, they may lack accurate information, or the skills to make a personal decision about whether or not they are ready. Even when the experience was a good one, it can still have unpleasant outcomes, such as pregnancy or sexually transmitted infections.

Then there's law and social policy – a tricky area because teenagers don't always wait for the legal age of consent to begin being sexually active, and they don't always want to inform their parents of their need for contraception or an abortion. Counsellors are asked to use their skills to help in the assessment of young people's understanding and background in order to help doctors apply the guidelines for prescribing them contraception. Reducing teenage pregnancy rates is currently a government target (Command Paper 4342, 1999) and whilst this can provide a helpful climate, under the spotlight is not always a comfortable place to be. Not all parents are supportive of providing a service like this, or aware that young people are entitled to medical confidentiality.

What about pregnancy? This is an enormous event for any girl, woman, couple or family – especially momentous if it is unplanned, unexpected, unprepared for. Making a decision can be extremely complex, involving consideration of the practical aspects of one's own situation, and a vast array of existential issues. Clients confront (or avoid confronting) issues of creativity; power; loss; self-determination; love; control. Counsellors need to be looking out for these underneath the everyday language of the client's story, which will be told against a backdrop of their (more or less articulated) personal, cultural, familial, religious and spiritual beliefs about pregnancy and abortion. At the same time the pregnancy causes physical and hormonal changes that can have an effect on cognitive and emotional functioning (Brien and Fairburn 1996).

Counsellors in a sexual health centre also encounter clients whose issues include miscarriage; rape; sexual abuse; the effects of sexually transmitted infections (including HIV); concerns about fertility and genetic inheritance; sexual orientation. Young people, in common with adults, do not conduct their sex lives in a vacuum, so they may also bring relationship and family problems; bullying; phobias; bereavement; low self-esteem and concerns about body-image; anger management problems; drug, alcohol and other addictive patterns; eating disorders; self-harm and suicidal thoughts and behaviours; depression; school and career issues etc., etc. – up to and including full-blown mental health problems. They may not know where else to take these issues – and it is appropriate to consider counselling them in a sexual health setting because high self-esteem and a sense of control over their lives are two of the factors that influence regular use of contraception in young girls (Rutter and Rutter 1992). Sometimes long-term work is indicated, so appropriate assessment and referral is vital, but this age group can feel very sensitive to being judged or rejected, so taking their concerns seriously in the first place matters enormously if we are to hold them well enough for referral to be achieved.

Is your head spinning yet? I know some days mine does. And all of this in a setting where lots of my contact is with walk-in clients (though not all of that is crisis work), so I have to be ready to respond to new beginnings fairly constantly. Again this can mirror the experience of teenagers who are regularly responding to and trying to assimilate new experiences. All of us have been adolescents, so when working with them it is useful to get in touch with that experience, but it's also important to help find a way out of the muddle by providing some structure. Let me move on and attempt to do just that.

The setting

I work for a branch of Brook, a voluntary organisation which was founded in the Sixties to provide confidential contraceptive advice to young women. It is now a national organisation with affiliated branches that adhere to a central mission, but which adapt to meet local needs within local funding constraints. The remit is now broader than contraceptive services alone, aiming to provide for a range of sexual health needs to *all* young people (not just heterosexual young women). The overall service consists of medical services; education services (both in the clinics and on an outreach basis); reception and administration in and for the clinics; and, of course, the counselling service. The importance of counselling in this setting is backed up by focus group research within the organisation that suggests young people welcome the chance to talk in confidence about the emotional aspects of starting/having a sexual life (Brook Advisory Centres 1998).

Confidentiality in Brook

One of the great advantages of working under the Brook name is its famil-iarity amongst the client group. Whilst promotion of its services remains important, its reputation does go before it, as young people tell their friends what to expect. Brook's commitment to client-confidentiality is one of its most important aspects. If young people know from their friends that 'Brook won't tell your parents' then they are enabled to make the first step of seeking information and advice about safer sex. The greater complexity of confidentiality is explained to them when they register.

For the counselling service, this means 'confidentiality' is already an established expectation that can be built on to establish trust. For instance, we make it explicit that 'counselling-only' notes (that is, when a client elects to see a counsellor for a non-medical matter) are kept separately from medical notes. This helps clients see counselling as an extra safe space in which to explore deeper issues. Clients are given strong assurances about their confidentiality within Brook, and only if there were serious risk of ongoing harm to a client or others would the organisation consider informing appropriate authorities against the client's wishes. This strategy conforms to the Children Act (1989) which allows children's wishes to be considered when assessing their best interests. Protecting confidentiality allows space and time for the client to fully consider the implications and be enabled to disclose of their own volition. If young people cannot be persuaded to agree to disclosure in situations of serious ongoing risk – e.g. if other children are likely to become victims of a sexual abuser – then, after informing the client, the relevant authorities can be notified. Counsellors make this judgement only in consultation with line management, and also have access to a local child protection expert for advice. The likelihood is that if young people have nowhere safe to test out disclosure in this way, they may choose not to disclose at all, with the risk that harm to them or others may continue.

An outline of the work

My task in the clinic consists of three main functions:

1. to offer ongoing contracts of up to twelve sessions to anyone up to age 25 who requests counselling (whether or not they also use the medical services)

2. to see anyone who has had a positive pregnancy test

3. to see anyone under 16 years of age on his or her first visit to Brook.

Whenever possible, clients are seen straight away. Young people express their needs in a very immediate way, and it may have taken a lot of courage to cross the threshold and speak to an adult about a problem they're having. They need a correspondingly immediate response, even if it can only consist of a ten-minute assessment and an appointment for another time. In this way contact is made, the young person feels heard, and is more likely to return to use the counselling service more fully. I may also have to deal with sensitive telephone calls, or respond to visitors who are outside our remit but have an emotional need that requires particularly sensitive handling.

How can I share with you a more vibrant experience of what my working day can be like? Keeping with the spirit of getting in touch with one's 'inner adolescent' (Geldard and Geldard 1999), perhaps you'd like a peep inside my diary. The sharing of intensely personal experience being an important adolescent communication, this seems appropriate. However, one must have some secrets, so all the 'characters' here (except me) are fictitious. They are made up from over five years' experience, so I hope they will be convincingly authentic.

Diary of a young person's sexual health counsellor (age 42 and a half)

I arrive at the centre with a few minutes to settle before my 'counselling only' client. Too early, and I get caught up in clinic business, as the medical session is already running. (When I'm between clients, it's a good thing to be out of my room and visible, as it makes me more approachable for a client group that prefer informality, but before a booked session with an ongoing client I need a little time to prepare myself.)

Tiffany

Tiffany is 19 and it's the fourth session of the six we originally booked. She came with relationship issues, complaining that her current partner, like her previous one, was not being 'serious' about the relationship. She wants to have a baby, but he can't seem to hold down a job, and prefers going out with his mates to spending time at home with her. She avoids my attempts to focus on her, and seems to have little in the way of ambitions or dreams that she could fulfil for herself. We don't seem to be getting anywhere and I've admitted in supervision to feeling irritated, even bored – in the sessions I feel like I'm the teenager and she's a middle-aged nag!

Last week, as I noticed the same feelings near the end of the session, I decided to act on it and make things more interesting. I grabbed some paper and scribbled out the parent–adult–child (PAC) model from Transactional Analysis (TA). It got her interest, and having explained it and a little about transactions, I said she could take it away – use it if she found it useful, or throw it out if she didn't.

Today she is ten minutes late to the session, which has never happened before. She is more subdued than usual and does not launch into a catalogue of this week's failings on the part of her boyfriend. I wait for her to speak and eventually, without making eye-contact, she tells me she has been thinking about the diagram and not only does she recognise that she speaks about and to her boyfriend from 'Parent' most of the time, but that she hears her mother speak about her father (who left the family five years ago) in this way too. I am touched by her change in affect and, using reflection, encourage her to explore more of her own sadness and disappointment about her father's leaving. It has become clear that she has overidentified with her mother's position as a way of protecting herself from the depth of her own 'Child' feelings. Expecting boyfriends to 'be men', stick around and provide for a family at the tender age of 19 or 20 has been her way of trying to heal both her mother's loss of a partner, and her loss of a father. It now seems that there may be scope for extending the counselling contract to give her space to work with some of her grief, and perhaps to start re-examining her hopes and ambitions for her future.

Time and time again I see this kind of rapid response to counselling interventions with this young age group. Providing trust has been established so that they feel safe from being judged, and providing the intervention is not introduced in a way that makes them feel dictated to, they usually respond very positively. TA concepts lend themselves admirably in this context, because they are meant to be shared with clients. This age group also find the

PAC model very useful in sorting out the different moods, thoughts and expectations they are busy dealing with.

Sarah

Sarah is 21, eight weeks pregnant, and has told the doctor she wants a termination. My role is to ensure that Sarah is aware of the procedures and risks of a termination, and to deal with any of her counselling needs. She tells me the reason for her decision is that she has not yet finished university and hasn't known her boyfriend long. She says she feels selfish, but she also doesn't think she is ready to give up her own interests to look after a child. She'd like to tell her mum but is worried about disappointing her. She looks tearful when she says this and I decide to reflect this back to her in case she wants to go into it further.

In one-off counselling like this there are always a number of possible avenues to go down with a client, and it is important to convey that you are available to discuss such things without seeming intrusive. Clients seeking abortion are in a vulnerable state. They may be very sure of their decision, yet still welcome the opportunity to explore some of its emotional side-effects.

For those experiencing any form of ambivalence, I feel it is important to acknowledge the reality of unplanned pregnancy – namely, that it always involves loss. One may choose, on the one hand, to lose the potential of that particular pregnancy – or, on the other, to lose some aspects of the life one had imagined assuming the pregnancy hadn't happened. I sometimes ask them to describe this imagined life so that they can look clearly at the two options. (Much of my counselling is focused specifically on imparting the notion that they have choices – something that is only just beginning to be real for young people as they emerge from family constraints. For clients younger than Sarah, the practical dependency on family may still be very strong, so consideration of this must form part of their decision.) Getting clients to review the resources they have for coping with loss is important too. Some may have had previous, difficult experiences, but for others an unplanned pregnancy may be the first important loss or disappointment they have faced. It is important to impart the knowledge that grief and disappointment are time-limited and survivable, as well as identifying people in their circle that they could get support from. Everyone is also informed that they can return to see their counsellor (or a different one) if they wish.

Sarah's response is to tell me, 'My mum was only 19 when I was born.' Her mother had interrupted her own education because of this. She has only recently returned to studying part-time, and Sarah is proud of her for this.

She doesn't want her mother to think she's made the same mistake. I spend some time gently unpacking the assumptions in this statement, some of which are potentially very painful for Sarah (such as the possibility that she sees herself – or thinks her mother sees her – as a 'mistake'). Sarah grins at this – she actually feels quite secure about herself and her upbringing, but knows it was a struggle for her mother, and through talking about it she has come to feel even more sure of her decision. She does not want to make the sacrifice her mother made, and feels sure her mother would be supportive of her different choice. She now thinks her worries about telling her mother are cleared out of the way, and the session moves on to talking about the practical procedures and a completion of the referral process.

As Sarah leaves the room and I am writing my notes, the receptionist comes in. A nervous-looking young man has come in and, with a crowded waiting room, it's difficult to give him enough privacy to speak. My next booked client has only just gone in to see the doctor so will be at least twenty minutes – she asks if I can see the young man and establish what he wants.

Jason

Jason, who appeared to be in his mid-teens, had dropped into the centre last week with a friend and the friend's girlfriend. He'd picked up one of the cartoon leaflets aimed at young men which gives basic information about their bodies, their feelings, their sexual health. Since then he'd been thinking that he was 'not like other boys'. As Jason was avoiding eye contact, and speaking barely audibly, I decided on a practical approach that might help get past his embarrassment. I got out the leaflet and said, 'It's quite good, isn't it? What did you think? This bit about everyone being different shapes and sizes – the drawings are really funny – and the bit about how to check your "equipment" for changes every month – that's really important. Is it something like that that's worrying you?' Jason made a bit of a face, which was hard to interpret as either a positive or negative response to my question, yet he sat back and seemed a bit more relaxed. I reassured him he'd come to the right place to 'find stuff out' but felt I should still leave him space to check us out in his own time. I made it clear that he could see medical staff, and that he could attend when our male nurse was on duty if he preferred. I also told him about the counselling service and that he could book a longer time to talk over anything that concerned him. As he left, I noticed him looking at a poster depicting two men giving each other a hug, and he looked straight at me for the first time. He smiled and said he'd make an appointment for next week.

Jason may come for more counselling, next week or in a couple of years. He may have questions about his sexual orientation – as seemed possible from some of the clues he gave – or he may not. He may prefer to see a male counsellor (an option not currently available within Brook) – something I would address in a full assessment session. I hope in this brief encounter he has been given some important messages: that he and his concerns will be taken seriously; that he will not be rushed or expected to present confusion as if it was something clear-cut; that he can expect a non-judgemental approach (specifically, for instance, on matters of sexual orientation). People in this age group are often what Jennifer Elton-Wilson (1996) refers to as 'visitors' – those who are checking out what counselling is, and whether it's what they want. The counsellor's role becomes one of helping them find out, even make a decision, but not to begin the counselling until they are ready to enter that contract.

Mary

Mary is 15 years old and 14 weeks pregnant, saying she wants a termination. She has spoken very little apart from this, and staff are concerned – it's hard to assess whether she can understand what's involved. Also she seemed unsure of her address – has she given a false one? She has said she cannot tell her mother about her pregnancy, so it's over to the counsellor to sort it all out. I begin by reassuring her that we are not trying to make it difficult for her to get what she says she wants, but that because of her age it is important for us to make sure that we are helping her in the best way possible. To do this we need to understand her situation a little better. I ask if there is anyone she has felt able to tell – it's a not-too-intrusive question as she decides whether or not to trust me, and lets me know what support she's got, as well as whether she has realised it's a situation she may need help with. She says she has told her best friend, a boy aged 16, and he will help her. I wonder to myself if this is actually her boyfriend but for the time being leave it at that – she may be worried about getting him into trouble as she's under the age of consent.

I decide to explain the procedures for having a termination. Giving practical information does more than merely inform – it gives the message that we trust them to make use of it, which in turn fosters their trust in us by establishing a more balanced power base than is often offered to teenagers by adults. At her stage of pregnancy, an overnight stay in the termination clinic may be necessary. This is the first thing that produces a strong reaction from Mary, who gasps and says, 'I can't do that! They'll find out!'

I ask who 'they' are, and her story comes tumbling out: she has been living with an aunt and the aunt's boyfriend since her parents' marriage broke up four years ago. Aunt is 'always busy' and Mary has to prepare her own meals and do her own laundry. Aunt's partner has a bad temper and gets drunk a lot – she's afraid of him, as he's threatened to hit her. She clearly doesn't feel very cared for. Mum, it turns out, is actually in and out of mental hospital with depression, which is why Mary can't live with her, and doesn't want to worry her. Dad is out of contact. I ask her if her aunt ever allows her to stay out, maybe at her friend's house, and whether she can talk to his parents. She now admits that this friendship has become a sexual relationship too, but that his parents don't know this. There was no coercion involved – she felt ready for this step, and enjoys sex with him, though she's been put off by worry for now. However, she has another close friend – a girl in her class – whose parents have offered to allow her to stay with them in the past, knowing how unhappy she is at her aunt's. The situation is obviously a little precarious, but Mary's story has a strong ring of truth about it. The stubborn, uncommunicative adolescent has had her reasons for keeping quiet – adults have not proved very reliable support so far.

In amongst all this it would be easy to lose sight of Mary's actual decision. Like anyone else, she needs a chance to explore how she feels, or she may have problems adjusting to it in the future. (Clients who attend for post-termination counselling are often those whose decision-making process was rushed, or not entirely voluntary – frequently at an age when others felt they should make the decision for them.) Mary is clear that she does not want a baby yet – couldn't cope; though she is sad that this is so. She's very close to her boyfriend and it would be their baby. She misses her mother and is upset about not living with her. The last thing she wants (she says) is to have a baby and not be able to look after it properly. Mary is expressing several things about her situation, and the pregnancy has symbolic value for her, both in terms of her own lack of mothering, and by expressing to the world the importance of her relationship with her boyfriend. However, she is used to having to manage her own needs, and knows she could not yet do this for a child as well. She is choosing to give up the 'baby' in order to prolong her own childhood a bit – not unreasonable at 15. Witnessing and affirming this decision will help Mary to process it, even if she never analyses it as completely as I have.

Returning to practical matters, I ascertain her home address, but confirm that we will only communicate with her through her friend's address – the one she has already given. Mary has made it clear that she has no intention of informing her aunt, but says she will talk to her friend's mum tonight – she seems relieved by the prospect of not going through all this alone. I make it clear that this person cannot give legal consent to her operation and that the hospital consultant will make the final decision about whether she can have her operation without informing her mum, or without social services becoming involved. However, the fact that she has a caring adult to support her will help her situation. After Mary has gone I ring the senior counsellor and run the details past her – it's an important safety check in these situations in case I've not dealt with all the significant aspects of the assessment.

Tasmin

Tasmin is 14 and came last week with three friends. The education worker saw them as a group and all but Tasmin stayed on to register as clients. She has come back today and is asking for condoms. I make a joke about me having to ask loads of 'nosy' questions – it breaks the ice a bit. Of course clients realise that I am making some kind of assessment before they access the rest of the service, but if it's done in a friendly manner and I demonstrate genuine interest in them as individuals, most seem to find it acceptable. (Teenagers can often have very strong moral codes, and it's possible that many of them actively approve of us not giving them contraception without checking whether they are ready for the step of becoming sexually active. We all know it won't stop them going ahead if they want to, but at least we are ready to engage with them on this difficult subject, and therefore they tolerate the intrusiveness of the process.)

Some of my enquiries are aimed at finding out if they are in a relationship with someone they trust, and that it's not an exploitative relationship. Tasmin says she isn't going out with anyone, but there's a boy in her class who likes her. In fact, with a little more probing, it's clear she's being teased by her schoolmates for 'being frigid' and is on the point of acquiescing to sex to get them to leave her alone. This is part of a wider pattern where she is also teased (bullied?) for doing homework, refusing cigarettes, and for belonging to a church youth-club. Tasmin is clearly hovering between sticking to her own interests and preferences, yet wanting to be accepted as part of the group – she's fed up of being the one who's 'uncool'.

Listening empathically is the most important aspect of the session, as Tasmin has been too embarrassed to confide her situation to anyone else. However, I am also able to bolster her confidence in sticking to her own position by having a discussion with her about physical, mental and emotional readiness for sex and about this being a very personal decision.

Paying attention also to her need to 'belong', I ask if she knows if many of her youth-club friends are sexually active. She says one couple are having sex, but they are slightly older and have been going out for a year. She smiles and gets up to go – discussion over, she's got what she wanted and there's no need to linger. She doesn't want condoms, but knows where to come when the time is right.

I hope this has given a little insight into a typical working day. Suffice to say that no two are alike!

Conclusion (or 'How was it for you?')

As can be seen, only a small part of my day involves working with a traditional counselling contract that operates for a number of sessions. The rest of the time I am using counselling skills to engage with clients to meet an immediate need, and these contacts have to stand alone as pieces of work, although they may lead to clients seeking further counselling in the future. Having worked in the same clinics for five years now, I am able to provide continuity of care myself (i.e. clients come back to see me specifically), but often that continuity is held within the organisation. In other words each counsellor relies on team members – reception, medical, and education/ outreach as well as other Brook counsellors – to provide a consistent 'product' in terms of how we receive and relate to clients. Although the counsellor has a specialist role in offering the more in-depth attention to psychological needs, this would not be enough without a 'young-people-aware' approach from all staff.

Teamwork is vital, although inevitably tensions can arise between the preoccupations and priorities of the different disciplines. The work can be stressful (and repetitive in some ways) for all staff, and not only are counsellors more accustomed to being aware of their own emotional responses and support needs, but because of professional requirements they have the forum of supervision in which to address them. Any organisation engaged in work like this needs to give attention to the whole team's need for debriefing, support and ongoing training aimed at maintaining a healthy atmosphere for continued grappling with the client group and the topic.

Counsellors need a lot of psychological energy for this work – there are so many beginnings and endings, with often very little in between! However, I have found that this age group gives me a lot of energy in return. They are often willing to work very hard, and results can be satisfyingly rapid. As I described with Tiffany, in mid to late teens it becomes natural to re-examine constructs you have grown up with. My role is often to help them distinguish between mere rebellion and constructive reappraisal, to integrate the best of their past with their own hopes for the future. Most of all I try to offer a view that they have and can make choices, but that the choices they make will depend on the meaning they make of what happens to, and around, them. In other words I use a broadly existential approach, mediated through a warm, open and interested manner. (Recent verbal feedback from a user-involvement group confirmed that young people expect adults to react to them judgementally. We therefore have to be extra clear in our responses to them if we are to counteract this.)

Counselling supervision needs to recognise the 'bitty' nature of the work, alongside the fact that some very deep issues are being grappled with. Group supervision is useful: the pooling of experience can be very supportive. Presentation of individual cases is of course appropriate, especially for the ongoing work, but in my own experience it has also been helpful to deal with one-off sessions by discussing themes (such as indecision about pregnancy; assessment of very young clients; dealing with parents' or partner's needs). Much of our work being single session contacts, the purpose of supervision becomes to help us with the next similar case. In this way we address the anxieties and emotions that affect all of us when dealing with these difficult topics. For instance, although in order to do this work it is important to believe in a woman's right to choose, that in itself is not sufficient to deal with all of one's responses to the work. Abortion is a last resort when contraception has failed and a girl or woman makes an honest assessment that she, or her situation, makes it unsuitable for her to become a parent at this stage. The seriousness of this decision does not (and should not) lighten for me just because it is an everyday part of my working life. The pregnancy must be acknowledged to exist before it can be terminated – sometimes it is I who must hold that experience until the client is ready for it. That adds up to an awful lot of uncompleted pregnancies that I have had to hold, however briefly, and therefore a lot of loss to be in touch with. Counsellors and supervisors involved with this work must be able to process that loss.

I do not want to end on a gloomy note. For me the ongoing work and the chance to sit alongside young people as they examine and process issues in their lives, and make plans for their future, is sufficient balance to the loss side of the work. To do only pregnancy counselling would be too much. It is also vital for young clients that counsellors are available in a setting where they already feel at home. If counselling is not easily accessible, the moment passes, and they may lack courage or skills to get help any other way. I regard it as a privilege to be one of the points of contact available to them.

I have sometimes felt anxious as to whether this kind of work is viewed as 'proper' counselling. My own experience (gleaned from over 12 years' experience with adolescents) tells me it is appropriate counselling for the age group and the issues. I have always espoused humanistic theories – integrating elements from TA, Gestalt, existentialism, personal construct theory – as for me the main point has been to engage with the client's own story and find ways of adapting my responses to them in a way that they can understand. However, I am only one counsellor in this setting and the case examples are only intended to reflect my own practice. Looking beneath the 'awkward' surface, I find the same human dilemmas that all counselling is concerned with.

References

Berne, E. (1972) *What Do You Say After You Say Hello?* London: Corgi Books.

Brien, J. and Fairburn, I. (1996) *Pregnancy and Abortion Counselling.* London and New York: Routledge.

Brook Advisory Centres (1998) 'Someone with a smile would be your best bet.' Unpublished report.

Command Paper 4342 (1999) *Teenage Pregnancy.* London: HMSO.

Elton-Wilson, J. (1996) *Time-Conscious Psychological Therapy.* London and New York: Routledge.

Erikson, E. H. (1963) *Childhood and Society.* New York: Norton.

Geldard, K. and Geldard, D. (1999) *Counselling Adolescents.* London: Sage.

Rutter, M. and Rutter, M. (1992) *Developing Minds: Challenge and Continuity across the Life Span.* London: Penguin.

Further reading

Adolescent psychology and counselling

Freed, A. M. (1976) *TA for Teens and Other Important People.* California: Jalmar Press.

Geldard, K. and Geldard, D. (1999) (see references).

Noonan, E. (1983) *Counselling Young People.* London and New York: Methuen.

Pregnancy and abortion

Brien, J. and Fairburn, I. (1996) (see references).

Pipes, M. (1986) *Understanding Abortion*. London: The Women's Press.

Time-limited counselling

Elton-Wilson, J. (1996) (see references).

Talmon, M. (1990) *Single-Session Therapy: Maximising the Effect of the First (and Often Only) Therapeutic Encounter*. San Francisco: Jossey-Bass.

Useful organisation

Brook Central

421 Highgate Studios
53–79 Highgate Road
London NW5 1TL
Tel. 020 7284 6050

For publications (including leaflets and posters) and other information about Brook services nationally.

Chapter 7

Counselling people living with HIV/AIDS

Pete Connor

'Hope' is the thing with feathers
That perches in the soul
And sings the tune without the words
And never stops – at all

And sweetest – in the Gale – is heard
And sore must be the storm
That could abash the little Bird
That kept so many warm

I've heard it in the chillest land
And on the strangest Sea
Yet, never, in Extremity,
It asked a crumb – of Me.

Emily Dickinson (*c.* 1861)

(For David, Katie and Claire and all
those others for whom hope came too late.)

Introduction

I felt very pleased to be asked to write this chapter on counselling people living with HIV (Human Immunodeficiency Virus) since, over the past 15 years, the work has been of great importance to me, both personally and professionally. Counselling in the HIV field has provided me with a career, friendships, personal development and a great sense of satisfaction. HIV infection as a condition, however, has also led to the deaths of my partner, David, in 1990 and, later, of two of my closest friends, Claire and Katie, as well as many other people for whom I felt affection. The work will always have special meaning to me.

AIDS (Acquired Immune Deficiency Syndrome) was first identified as a condition in 1981 and refers to the collection of infections, tumours and other illnesses that can develop when HIV damages the immune system of an infected person. Significant improvements in the medical treatments for HIV/AIDS have occurred since the early 1980s, and I aim to explore how the hope that these advances have brought has affected the counselling needs of people living with the virus. Also, through case examples and quotes, I aim to give a sense of the enormous diversity of people living with HIV in the UK, as well as to mention more general organisational issues connected to the HIV voluntary sector. Finally, I will explore my personal and professional reactions to the work.

I will concentrate on the counselling needs of adults living with the virus and, to a lesser extent, the needs of partners and family members, since this is where most of my practice experience lies. Information specifically concerning children with HIV can be found in Sherr (1999) and Green and McCreaner (1996).

I work from an integrative counselling perspective with person-centred theory informing my understanding of human beings. Excellent descriptions already exist of specific therapeutic approaches to HIV work, including analytic (Burgner 1994), attachment-based (Purnell 1996), existential (Milton 1996) and systemic theory (Bor, Miller and Goldman 1992). Here, however, I aim to explore issues faced by people with HIV in a way accessible to readers from any discipline or counselling approach.

My thanks go to Kim Etherington and to Megan Price for their comments and support during the writing of this chapter.

Background

My experience of HIV counselling comes mainly from working for the Bristol-based voluntary agency, the Aled Richards Trust (ART). ART was formed in 1985 by a group of people appalled at the poor treatment, prejudice and discrimination experienced by Aled Richards, one of the first people in the Southwest to die of AIDS. A helpline providing information and support was soon followed by a range of services including counselling, buddying, home care, health promotion, complementary therapies and support groups. As local and national funding became available, ART employed paid staff and the volunteer force grew to keep up with increasing demand for services.

Until the mid-1990s, few HIV treatments were available and many people became ill and died. However, the arrival in the UK of HAART (highly active anti-retroviral therapy), also known as combination therapy, in 1996 transformed for many, but not all, the experience of living with HIV. Combination therapy drugs directly attack HIV and so diminish its damaging effect on the immune system. Together with improved treatments for illnesses associated with weakened immunity, such as certain infections and cancers, increased hope for a longer and healthier life with HIV began to grow.

The drugs came at a significant financial cost, however, and by the end of the 1990s some voluntary agencies were cutting back on services or closing due to funding problems, money being diverted into the cost of therapies. Mergers between organisations began to occur in order to ensure financial viability, and in April 2000 ART joined the London-based organisation, the Terrence Higgins Trust (THT), to become THT West. Now running six regional centres, and with more mergers likely, THT is becoming a truly national organisation.

Initially a service provided by volunteers and based on an eclectic mix of theoretical approaches, including re-evaluation co-counselling and the work of Elisabeth Kübler-Ross (1969), the counselling service has changed significantly over the past 15 years. Today, as in THT London, counselling is provided by paid staff, and an integrative counselling approach, underpinned by person-centred theory, is adopted. THT West is a member of the British Association for Counselling and Psychotherapy (BACP) and adheres to its code of ethics and practice.

Counselling issues

Initial diagnosis

> 'At that moment, when she said it was positive, I thought two things: that I was going to die and that my partner had been unfaithful' (woman living with HIV).

Despite some easing of the stigma associated with HIV and the increase in treatment options, initial HIV diagnosis, usually at a hospital genito-urinary department via an HIV antibody test, still frequently precipitates a period of emotional crisis. As counsellor I attempt to offer a safe, supportive and empathic environment as the person begins to experience and explore waves of shock and numbness, despair and hopelessness, anger and depression.

In my experience, most newly diagnosed counselling clients have questions concerning medical facts, disease progression and the likelihood of death, as well as concerns regarding sharing their result with others. A double disclosure may be involved, with the person talking for the first time about their sexual orientation, sexual activity, or drug-use history. We often explore the impact of HIV on sexual relationships, body image and self-esteem, as well as working on any distress resulting from the resurfacing of past painful events, including abuse or bereavements. Clients frequently also need help to plan for the future, perhaps concerning drug treatments, employment, and having children, and to reflect on life's current meaning and purpose.

In initial sessions, we often spend time prioritising concerns in order to prevent the sheer number and depth of the issues from overwhelming the client and possibly me as counsellor. I am also watchful for factors that place clients at increased risk of severe anxiety, depression and suicidal thoughts as a result of their diagnosis. These factors include physical symptoms of HIV at the time of testing, low social support, and concurrent stress caused by bereavement or other losses of job, money, and relationships. It is vital to explore the personal meaning of the diagnosis for each individual client.

Living successfully with HIV involves learning to live with uncertainty and the feelings of powerlessness that this can elicit. As a counsellor I can help clients explore, release and understand their emotional reactions to a positive result, decide and prioritise goals, develop action plans, identify resources and strengthen skills for coping with anxiety and depression. Just as important, however, are the times when I can simply be alongside a person as they struggle with their feelings of fear, hopelessness and isolation and eventually find the inner resources to manage those feelings. An obvious issue for me at these times is my own HIV status and personal experience of the virus, about which clients may have questions. I tend to answer these questions directly, whilst also using them to reflect on the meaning of having HIV for that individual.

Taking HAART

'I saw all those pills in front of me and I thought, "I'll never cope." But I have! It's still a real struggle sometimes, though' (man on combination therapies).

HAART treatments can reduce the amount of HIV (viral load) in the blood-stream to barely detectable levels and thereby inhibit its damaging action on the immune system. Many different drugs and drug combinations now exist, each having specific side-effects and regimes for taking. The decision to begin combination therapies is generally regarded as a lifetime commitment, since stopping or even missing doses may lead to the development of strains of HIV resistant to the drugs.

A significant portion of my counselling work now involves helping clients to make informed decisions concerning HAART, alongside advice from the prescribing consultants. We often explore strategies for coping with the recommended drug regimes, most of which require strict timing and/or dietary restrictions. We also usually make preparations for possible side-effects, which can range from unpleasant nausea, diarrhoea and tiredness to much less common but life-threatening side-effects such as pancreatitis.

Beginning combination therapies can be extremely stressful, especially until the individual develops confidence in the drugs. It can be a frightening time for the client and, I confess, sometimes for me as counsellor, as the person embarks on a new treatment, with the initial risks that can entail. A priority is to ensure that my own anxiety does not compromise the containment of client fears that counselling can provide.

Long-term adherence

'I skip a dose occasionally because I just can't face it. Day after day of pills and more side-effects and more pills and I just think, "What's the point, why bother?"' (man on combination therapies)

Long-term, close adherence to the drug regime is vital for the effectiveness of treatments. However, some evidence, including Hecht *et al.* (1998), reflects my own experience of the difficulty that many clients have in maintaining drug regimes over the long term.

Having an accurate knowledge of their drugs and the importance of adherence certainly helps people to remain motivated, and I do see information-giving in this area as an important part of my counselling role. I can also offer clients support to cope with longer-term side-effects of treatments such as peripheral neuropathy and lipidostrophy, which involves changes in fat distribution and body shape and which can seriously affect self-image as well as physical wellbeing. The person's doctor may recommend diet changes or exercise, and again, counselling can support the person to adopt these measures. If side-effects prove to be intolerable, however, or if viral resistance to the drugs develops, a change of combination will be required and here again, I can offer support to cope with possible new side-effects and adherence challenges.

Establishing confidence in and control of combination therapy is vital but difficult, especially since mood changes, including depression, anxiety and suicidal thoughts, have been reported by people taking HAART. Counselling can help people to manage these distressing psychological reactions, all of which will make adherence difficult. Clients also report that treatments act as continual reminders of their HIV status, and together we often need to revisit feelings concerning living with the virus as part of learning to manage HAART.

Julie, a 37-year-old Ugandan woman, was diagnosed four years ago. Her husband died of AIDS three years ago and she has been living in England for the past 18 months with relatives. She misses Uganda and the rest of her family but her health has not been good and she started combination therapies six weeks ago. Despite being well organised and having only minor side-effects, she has missed several doses.

In our initial sessions, Julie and I uncovered how profoundly depressed she has been feeling recently, and how she is torn between staying here and taking medications or returning to Uganda. She talked about her family back home, the hardships endured by those living with HIV, and the death of her husband. She felt guilty about friends who had no access to therapies and continued to become ill and die. Each time she took a tablet, Julie was reminded of her husband and friends.

Recognising and relieving some of the grief and helplessness that Julie felt eased some of the emotional impact of the drugs and facilitated adherence, although this remained a daily struggle for her. Julie also decided to make more links with other African women with HIV via the Trust's women's group and to use the Trust's treatment support project. This is a group of people already using HAART who offer information and advice for those beginning or having difficulties with their treatments.

Working across gender, race, and sexual orientation, as I did with Julie and with many other clients, demands that I confront my own sexism, racism and other preconceptions, prejudices and misinformation. I must also retain sensitivity concerning religious and cultural attitudes towards HIV, the family, relationships, health and medicine, death and bereavement, and towards the theory and practice of counselling and mental health generally.

Sex and safer sex

'Keeping up safer sex can be bloody difficult. I love my partner and sometimes I just want to be really close to him, without worrying about condoms and barriers. But then the idea of him being at risk and going through all this is awful. We've had a few close calls though' (woman living with HIV).

Sometimes humorous and light and at other times deeply painful and distressing, exploring the meaning and practice of safer sex remains a common part of my work with clients. We usually explore strategies for ensuring that sexual activity remains safe and enjoyable, and this applies when both partners are infected, since there is still the possibility of re-infection with a different strain of HIV. If the person is looking for a new sexual partner, we can review ways to approach and negotiate safer sex, perhaps practising communication and assertiveness skills, and to cope with possible rejection. We also often work with the person's negative feelings concerning body image and sexual attractiveness, especially when newly diagnosed, starting drug treatments or recovering from illness.

Tony came to counselling at his GP's suggestion after he approached her for anti-depressants. 24 years old, gay, and diagnosed with HIV for eight months, he was bored with his job and social life (which revolved around the gay scene), had few friends and frequently drank to excess. Initially very sexually provocative and argumentative in sessions, he gradually relaxed, realising after five meetings that ours was the first relationship he had experienced with another gay man that hadn't involved having sex. This both moved and scared him.

Tony began to explore his parents' negative reactions when he came out to them at 14 and how, increasingly alienated from his peers, he drifted into working as a rent boy for a few years. He realised that he had never actually felt close to any of the men he had sex with, and becoming infected with HIV seemed to reinforce the shame he felt about himself and his sexuality. He also explored the guilt he felt when, occasionally very drunk, he had unsafe sex.

We worked together to explore and release the grief and anger Tony carried about his treatment as a gay man. Experiencing acceptance in counselling sessions, he gradually began to feel and act in more authentic ways and his self-esteem and sense of identity became more positive. Eventually, Tony was able to negotiate the safer sex that he wanted and to limit his sexual activity to men to whom he felt truly attracted.

Counselling with Tony reminded me of the importance of regularly working on my own internalised homophobia and also my commitment to using a gay affirmative approach (Davies 1996). Although often friendly and supportive, the gay scene can be a lonely place, involving pressures to look and act in certain ways, and encouraging sex but not other forms of communication. Counselling can help to explore options such as meeting people away from the scene and using support such as helplines and friends when feeling low, instead of turning to drugs and alcohol.

Whatever the client's sexual orientation, counselling can build confidence to meet new sexual partners and to negotiate safer sex, as well as dealing with issues such as past abuse, distress concerning sexuality, or more general self-esteem issues which may interfere with sexual activity.

Implications of a longer life

'I have been diagnosed for over ten years and, as time goes by, new issues arise. Knowing there is someone who will listen to my thoughts and feelings and not condemn me for them has helped to normalise my life. Counselling has helped me to come to terms with myself. I am now living with my illness, not dying from it' (man living with HIV).

HAART has brought improvements in the health of many people, but adjusting to these can be difficult. Much of my work before HAART involved helping people to develop strategies for coping with a drastically reduced life expectancy. Decisions concerning relationships, finances, employment and housing tended to be made on the basis of having a much shorter time to live. Starting combination therapies, regaining good health and possibly having an extended life expectancy means revising these strategies and decisions.

Today it can be very moving for me to explore with some clients the possibility of returning to work, further training or studies, when a few years ago ill health would have made this unrealistic. Those not in relationships may be considering looking for partners, and need support to do so, whilst clients already in partnerships may be reassessing their needs. An increasingly common counselling issue involves working with sexual problems, since improved health sometimes allows sexual desire to return but drug side-effects or psychological problems may interfere with sexual functioning.

The long-term effectiveness of HAART drugs, however, is still unknown and clients increasingly require help to cope with anxiety or depression resulting from this uncertainty. Also, existential issues may often become highlighted and explored as the person struggles to keep to drug regimes, manage side-effects and reinvest in life.

Simon, 45, was diagnosed eight years ago, at the same time as Jim, his partner. Jim died three years later after a slow decline into HIV-related dementia, Simon having given up work to look after him. Two years ago Simon became ill and reluctantly agreed to his consultant's advice to begin HAART, after which his health improved dramatically.

Having lived on sickness benefits for several years, Simon began to feel frustrated with his life and increasingly depressed. The intricacies of the benefits system made returning to work a difficult decision, and equally complex were the feelings Simon experienced resulting from his good health.

'I can carry on, can exist, without him but it's just so unfair that I'm here and he's not. He would still be here if only he'd got it later, if only he'd been more careful, if only... It does no good thinking that way but I can't seem to stop it.

I don't want to just exist. I want to live. But the better I feel physically, the worse I feel in my head. While I was ill, I could at least think that he was well out of it or that I would be dead soon too, but now... Now I just wish he were here again. I seem to miss him more now than ever.'

Continuing good health robbed Simon of the possibility of an early death and an end to his separation from Jim. As Simon became physically healthier, his grief for Jim became more present and intense. Like many others diagnosed before the mid-1990s, Simon had seen HIV destroy his job, his own health and the life of his partner. Combination therapies gave him the opportunity to rebuild a life, but he felt ambivalent and confused.

In counselling, I supported and challenged Simon to mourn openly and deeply and to talk about his more difficult feelings, including his anger towards Jim at becoming infected and then infecting him. Gradually, as he expressed and managed his grief, Simon's desire for life began to return. He held on to his love for and memories of Jim but also took steps to involve himself in life again, including starting voluntary work. He knew that combination therapies held no guarantees but was prepared to take a risk.

Throughout my work with Simon, my thoughts and feelings would occasionally move towards my own partner, David, and my struggles to continue living without him. Today, ten years after his death, he is perhaps more solidly present in my heart and mind than at any time since his death. Having been lucky enough to be able to grieve openly for him and to have that grief acknowledged means that he truly does feel a part of me now and I no longer fear losing his presence, as I did soon after he died. It is a deeply comforting feeling.

Partners and families

'When my son, on a rare visit home, told me he was HIV-antibody positive, I was devastated and thought of all the years we had wasted. As well as lots of information about HIV and treatments, counselling has given me the chance to share my happiness and tears, my hopes and my fears. My relationship with my son is slowly improving and although my battle isn't over yet, I think I am getting there' (mother of man living with HIV).

As well as needing help to adjust to their loved one's diagnosis, partners and children of those with HIV may need to be tested, potentially leaving a family with more than one person with HIV. Several years ago, I worked with the father of a three-year-old HIV-positive boy, diagnosed following several bouts of ill health. Subsequent testing found that both the man and his wife were also HIV-positive, and it was realised that the man had become infected through an earlier sexual relationship. He had passed the virus on to his wife, who later became pregnant with their son, who also became infected. The guilt, self-loathing and grief of this man were almost overwhelming and much of our early work centred on looking at realistic alternatives to suicide.

Couples who experienced living with HIV before HAART may have difficulty adjusting to a better prognosis, with plans for the future and the carer and cared-for roles changing with the new situation. In particular, antiviral therapies and careful birthing procedures have meant a dramatic fall in mother-to-baby HIV transmission to around 2 per cent. This and the increased life expectancy for adults may mean that couples reconsider an earlier decision not to have children. The situation can be complex, however, depending upon factors such as the woman's current immune functioning and any HAART combination being used, which may affect foetal development. If the man is HIV-positive, sperm washing (removing sperm cells from infected seminal fluid) is an option, but it is not 100 per cent safe for the woman and not easily available. Counselling can explore issues connected to starting a family, including looking at the possibility of one or both of the couple dying before the child is grown.

It is important for partners and family members to recognise the dual needs of supporting the person with HIV while also dealing with their own feelings. Families often gain from meeting others in the same situation, and partners' and families' support groups within THT are one way to assist this, encouraging peer support and information sharing.

Treatment failure

HAART is not effective for all people, the reasons including intolerable side-effects, drug sensitivity or viral resistance. Although new combinations are continually being developed, the hope they bring comes too late for some people. Despite significantly improved treatments for HIV-related infections, tumours, and dementia, the virus eventually may cause a breakdown of immune system functioning, continual ill health and death.

Working with people for whom HAART offers little and whose health continues to decline has been extremely challenging for me. The sense of injustice feels enormous, as a decreasing number of people with HIV continue to decline in health and approach death, while watching many of their contemporaries thrive.

Loss is clearly central to counselling at this time, including losses of physical and sometimes mental health, autonomy and independence, role and sometimes relationships, and, as the person approaches death, loss of life itself. Clients frequently question the value of their lives, the way in which they will be remembered, the nature of death, and the importance to them of religion and spirituality. Hugely powerful feelings emerge as people confront these issues and evaluate their lives. Clients may mourn lost opportunities and estranged relationships, tackle issues of self-worth and self-concept, and examine past losses and abuses. They may also experience processes of completing unfinished business, saying goodbye to loved ones and letting go of the material world.

My challenge is to provide the conditions within which each individual can find his or her unique way to approach the end of life. Rogers' (1961) core therapeutic conditions offer me a way to be alongside the person without imposing my needs, fears and desires. However, it is also at this time that creativity, perhaps with spontaneous drawing, making audio or video-tapes, and using photographs, books, poems, metaphor and stories can all help in experiencing and managing the end of life.

Paul came to counselling three years ago, primarily to consider taking HAART. Infected at least ten years previously, his health was deteriorating and counselling supported him to begin medications. He tried one combination after another, only to experience disabling side-effects from some and lack of responsiveness to others. He developed resistance to most combinations and eventually decided to stop treatments, exhausted and feeling that he had no quality of life.

During the next nine months, as his health deteriorated, Paul used counselling to help him to make changes in his life. He managed to reconcile with his mother, who had always disapproved of his gayness, and to make an arduous but worthwhile trip to Rome, his favourite city. He also took great care in making a will and planning his funeral, which beautifully reflected his character. He looked back on his life and his grief for the many loved ones whom he had lost to HIV, including his partner eight years before.

Paul's final month was spent in a local hospice where he could look out onto beautiful grounds, gardening being one of his passions. I then saw him three times a week, the length of sessions varying depending upon his wishes and energy. In his final days, when he spent most of his time sleeping, and then unconscious, I sometimes talked to him but mainly sat close by in silence while looking towards the garden. He died easily with his mother present. I often think of Paul and feel a sense of pride in him and our work together.

Bereavement and grief

Some of my most satisfying work, on a personal and professional level, has involved counselling with those bereaved through HIV. Although generally similar to any other grief work, there are some factors that increase the risk of difficulties when grieving an HIV-related death. These include the enormous stress often involved in caring for someone dying of HIV-related conditions, which can be complex and numerous, the frequently young age of the carer, who also may be HIV-positive, and the possibility of multiple bereavements through HIV. Also, the continuing stigma associated with the condition may lead some people to feel enormous shame about the deceased, especially true for families who disapproved of the deceased's lifestyle or sexual orientation.

Societal homophobic attitudes can lead to a lack of recognition of the relationship and the grief being experienced by bereaved gay partners. The bereaved may be robbed of their place in rituals and experience the consequences of the lack of legal sanction of their relationship, especially if no will was made and shared possessions are claimed by the deceased's genetic family. Internalised homophobia carried by the bereaved may also resurface, involving feelings of self-hate and possibly excess alcohol and drug-use to numb the pain.

As a part of grief counselling, acknowledging feelings of shame concerning HIV or ambivalent feelings towards the deceased can be both extremely painful and also very liberating for the bereaved. I also emphasise the importance of recognising and validating the relationship, love and grief of a bereaved gay partner within counselling, in order to counter the insidious effects of a still homophobic environment. As well as examining support systems that can assist with the isolating effects of grief, I have found that encouraging ritual can also be very healing, especially if the person was denied his or her role as mourner during the funeral.

The future

At the time of writing, the search for a vaccine against HIV slowly advances while the global situation continues to worsen at a terrifying rate. Reporting on the International Conference on AIDS in Durban, South Africa, this year, the *Guardian* newspaper (8 July 2000) states that in Africa as a whole, AIDS now kills 2 million people a year. Four million people were infected with HIV in 1999 alone, and most will die within 10 to 15 years without treatment. Today around 34 million people around the world are living with HIV and an estimated 16 million have died so far from AIDS.

HIV transmission is preventable but stigma, poverty and politics constantly undermine prevention programmes. HAART drugs remain too expensive for the majority of individuals and governments in developing countries to afford, and even in the European Union alarm is being raised concerning the future financial burden of treatments.

As the number of people with HIV in the UK continues to rise, and as the estimated cost of drugs per person on HAART is now £10,000 per year, resources will become ever more scarce. Treatments are continuing to improve, resulting in a wider range of drugs with decreased toxicity, fewer side-effects and simpler regimes, as well as specific drug formulations for children. Increasing numbers of men and women are now alive who were infected as children, and more information is becoming available concerning the emotional, neurological, cognitive and physical implications of the virus in babies and children.

Medical advances bring both hope and new dilemmas and choices. Improved life expectancy means a greater focus on quality of life issues, including housing, employment, economic security, relationships, sex and mental wellbeing. Those doing well on HAART will need psychological support to adhere to drug regimes and adapt to new lifestyles. Those not responding to treatments will continue to need regular support to cope with periods of ill health, possible physical decline and terminal illness.

HIV services, including counselling, will have the challenges of working in an uncertain and changing environment, with reduced resources, larger numbers of people living with the virus, and of working with an increasingly diverse group of people with differing needs.

The HIV voluntary sector is in a period of enormous change structurally, financially and culturally. For some, the process of agency closures, mergers and alliances is a necessary part of the maturing of the HIV field, ensuring the overall survival and effectiveness of services. For others, this process eventually will rob the sector of creativity and originality, with centralised control becoming more important than responsiveness to local needs.

The uncertainty of living with HIV is currently being mirrored in the uncertain future of many HIV organisations. Some workers in the sector report experiencing similar, although much less intense, feelings of loss, anxiety and powerlessness commonly associated with an HIV diagnosis. A phase of consolidation and stability within organisations will soon be vital and the government's national strategy for HIV should assist in this. The strategy is badly needed in order to ensure equal access across the country to high quality HIV health promotion, treatment and care services.

Personal reflections

In writing this chapter I have had the opportunity to reflect on what motivates and helps me to remain in HIV counselling. Within ART, and now THT West, supportive colleagues and a great sense of camaraderie have been vital motivating forces. There have been times of enormous sadness and grief over the past 15 years, most especially when David died and life for me seemed totally meaningless. It was the love of friends that helped me to survive and to learn how to receive as well as give support.

Honest and effective working relationships with other professionals have also been important but not always easy to establish and maintain. I have experienced the sort of rivalry amongst HIV workers described in studies such as Barbour (1995) and Miller (2000), a competitiveness usually under-pinned by lack of knowledge of or trust in other professions.

I work either directly or indirectly alongside hospital consultants and GPs, nurses, health advisers, pharmacists, social workers, home care workers and other voluntary sector staff such as housing and benefits workers. Views concerning the nature, function and limitations of counselling vary enor-mously and an educative process is constantly necessary, especially concern-ing the place of counselling alongside clinical psychology, psychiatry and pharmacological interventions such as anti-depressants.

It has been important for me to be realistic concerning the limits of coun-selling. A person's needs for sufficient finances, adequate housing and accurate information have to be met alongside emotional and psychological needs. Counselling is one of a series of THT West services, including a drop-in and meal service, support groups, buddying/befriending, comple-mentary therapies, small grants, advice and advocacy. Users of the organisa-tion are encouraged to draw on an integrated mix of services that suits their needs at a particular time.

Counselling can offer a safe and secure base (Purnell 1996) as an individ-ual attempts to manage the uncertainties of living with HIV. Boundaries, including timing of sessions, setting, contact with clients outside of sessions, and physical contact, have traditionally offered containment and safety. Through visiting clients in hospital and at home, working with the same client from good health to the point of death, and through having close identification with many client issues, I have had the opportunity to confront and question these boundary issues many times.

Supervision has been a vital space for considering how a particular thera-peutic boundary assists an individual client at a specific stage of her or his life, the aim being to ensure continuity whilst also recognising practical and human needs. I agree with the psychoanalytic practitioner Burgner (1994) that there is no reason to behave differently as a therapist with clients with HIV than with any other clients, and so I would apply a questioning approach to boundaries, whatever the counselling issue. However, factors such as unpredictable health may increase the likelihood that questions concerning boundaries, including timing and setting, are raised when working with people with HIV.

Supervision with practitioners from a wide range of theoretical backgrounds has helped to keep my counselling focused, intentional and fresh. Personal therapy has given me the chance to explore, accept and challenge my own needs, fears, patterns and blindspots, as well as to identify my strengths and skills. Working as a counselling trainer and supervisor has allowed me to review regularly my personal theory and practice through the teaching of others and exposed me to a range of counsellors working in very different settings. Supervision, personal therapy and work outside of HIV, therefore, have all increased my therapeutic effectiveness and been vital in preventing burnout, a common phenomenon in the HIV sector (Miller 2000).

Conclusion

HIV counselling has allowed me to work in both the short and the long term with an enormously diverse group of people and a wide range of issues: Tim, a white, English, middle-aged gay man, living with HIV for over ten years; 22-year-old Paula from Portugal, an ex-prostitute and heroin user who stayed on in the UK after attending a drug treatment centre where she was diagnosed HIV positive; Celia, a mother of two from Zimbabwe, struggling to rebuild her life here after her husband and several of her relatives died of AIDS; Stephen, a wealthy businessman, trying to come to terms with his own recent diagnosis as well as that of his wife. Each person uses counselling to find ways to live with HIV infection, and each challenges my ability to set aside preconceptions, judgements, prejudices and misinformation.

HIV infection touches on the most crucial issues in society today. It connects with sex and sexuality, drug-use and addiction, racism, sexism and homophobia, the ethics of medical research and the power of drugs companies, the treatment and rights of the terminally ill and the bereaved, and with the status of the poor and the marginalised. It is a terrible medical condition for many and a vital social issue for all people. It is, for me, an intellectual, emotional, spiritual and constantly evolving challenge.

Along with intense joy, pride, sense of achievement and a great deal of laughter, I accept that grief and sadness form a significant part of this work. If I did not experience such feelings when a client dies, or another young person is newly diagnosed, or a mother is distraught with pain as she mourns her dead son, then it would mean that it was time for me to leave the work. The important need is to find ways to use those feelings for the therapeutic benefit of the client.

To be truly present with someone as they attempt to make sense of life and its meaning is a challenge and a privilege. It is healing for the client and, ultimately, healing also for me. Part of the meaning and purpose of my life has been derived from the work I have done with people living with HIV, complementing the fulfilment and love I have felt through my personal life. I have tried to learn from the strength and courage of so many clients and I know that my most important lesson is also the most obvious: to appreciate how precious and how delicate life and love can be and, as Emily Dickinson said, that hope is indeed a resilient bird with the sweetest of songs.

FROM 'AUGURIES OF INNOCENCE'

> To see a World in a grain of sand,
>   And a Heaven in a wild flower,
> Hold Infinity in the palm of your hand,
>   And Eternity in an hour.

William Blake (1863)

VITAE SUMMA BREVIS SPEM NOS VETAT INCOHARE LONGAM

> They are not long, the weeping and the laughter,
>   Love and desire and hate:
> I think they have no portion in us after
>   We pass the gate.
>
> They are not long, the days of wine and roses:
>   Out of a misty dream
> Our path emerges for a while, then closes
>   Within a dream.

Ernest Dowson (1896)

References

Barbour, R. (1995) 'The implications of HIV/AIDS for a range of workers in the Scottish context.' *AIDS Care* 7, 4, 521–535.

Bor, R., Miller, R. and Goldman, E. (1992) *Theory and Practice of HIV Counselling: A Systemic Approach.* London: Cassell.

Burgner, M. (1994) 'Working with the HIV patient: a psychoanalytic approach.' *Psychoanalytic Psychotherapy 8*, 3, 201–213.

Davies, D. (1996) 'Towards a model of gay affirmative therapy.' In D. Davies and C. Neal (eds) *Pink Therapy*. Buckingham: Open University Press.

Green, J. and McCreaner, A. (eds) (1996, second edition) *Counselling in HIV Infection and AIDS*. Oxford: Blackwell.

Hecht, F., Colfax, G., Swanson, M. and Chesney, M. (1998) 'Adherence and effectiveness of protease inhibitors in clinical practice.' Paper presented at the Fifth Conference on Retroviruses and Opportunistic Infections, Chicago, Ill., 2–6 February.

Kubler-Ross, E. (1969) *On Death and Dying*. New York: Macmillan.

Miller, D. (2000) *Dying to Care? Work, Stress and Burnout in HIV/AIDS*. London: Routledge.

Milton, M. (1996) 'An existential approach to HIV related psychotherapy.' *Journal of the Society for Existential Analysis 9*, 35–57.

Purnell, C. (1996) 'An attachment-based approach to working with clients affected by HIV and AIDS.' *British Journal of Psychotherapy 12*, 4, 521–531.

Rogers, C. (1961) *On Becoming a Person*. London: Constable.

Sherr, L. (1999) 'HIV disease and its impact on the mental health of children.' In J. Catalan (ed) *Mental Health and HIV Infection*. London: University College London (UCL) Press.

Further reading

Catalan, J. (ed) (1999) *Mental Health and HIV Infection: Psychological and Psychiatric Aspects*. London: University College London (UCL) Press.

Davies, D. and Neal, C. (eds) (1996) *Pink Therapy*. Buckingham: Open University Press.

Green, J. and McCreaner, A. (eds) (1996, second edition) *Counselling in HIV Infection and AIDS*. Oxford: Blackwell.

Johnson, M. and Johnstone, F. (eds) (1993) *HIV Infection in Women*. London: Churchill Livingstone.

Kramer, L. (1995) *Reports from the Holocaust: The Story of an AIDS Activist*. London: Cassell.

Lucas, I. (1995) *Growing Up Positive: Stories from a Generation of Young People Affected by AIDS*. London: Cassell.

Monette, P. (1988) *Borrowed Time*. London: Collins Harvill.

National AIDS Manual. London: NAM Publications. (Regularly updated manual including a treatments directory, factsheets and directory of AIDS organisations.)

Pratt, R. (1995) *AIDS: A Strategy for Nursing Care*. London: Edward Arnold.

Sherr, L. (ed) (1995) *Grief and AIDS*. London: John Wiley and Sons.

The Terrence Higgins Trust also provides a range of booklets covering all aspects of living with HIV infection. These can be obtained by telephoning the THT Information Centre on 020 7831 0330.

Useful websites

www.aegis.com – American HIV/AIDS site and the largest in the world

www.aidsmap.com – website of the National AIDS Manual (NAM)

www.tht.org.uk – website of the Terrence Higgins Trust

Useful organisations

Blackliners
Counselling and support for people of African, Caribbean or Asian descent living with HIV.
Office: 020 7738 7468; Helpline: 020 7738 5274

Body and Soul
Support for heterosexual men, women and their children.
Office: 020 7833 4929

Positively Women
Counselling and support for women living with HIV.
Office: 020 7713 0444; Client Services: 020 7713 0222

Terrence Higgins Trust
52–54 Grays Inn Road, London WC1X 8JU
Counselling and support for all people living with HIV.
Office: 020 7831 0330; Helpline: 020 7242 1010
Details of local organisations can be obtained via THT London office.

Chapter 8

Working with people with fertility problems

A counsellor's personal experience

Gill Woodbridge

Introduction

I had been working for several years in a district general hospital as a counsellor within a social services team, employed on a part-time basis to help women and/or couples with an unplanned pregnancy to decide on the best outcome from what was often a frightening and confusing situation, when the hospital appointed a new consultant to draw together the infertility service. It was the late 1980s, the early days of in vitro fertilisation (IVF), and some hospitals were beginning to offer this new treatment. The consultant had gained his IVF expertise in Australia and wanted to set up a unit here. Meanwhile I was invited to work alongside him as a counsellor in his NHS clinic. This was something else he had become used to in Australia, so I was fortunate not to have to convince him of the value of counselling.

In our hospital I was discovering what special patients these were. Extremely knowledgeable long before today's widespread Internet use, they were hungry for information about new treatments from the newspapers, women's magazines and TV. The infertility clinic felt like a very co-operative place: patients and the medical team worked together in a way I had not previously encountered in the hospital setting. Elsewhere the Department of Health (DoH) was working on the Human Fertilisation and Embryology Act (HF and E Act 1990) and a voluntary code was in place to guide those units already up and running. Although a local IVF unit was not yet established, an outline agreement had been made, and I was still working in infertility within the NHS. I joined a new counselling group, the British Infertility Counselling Association (BICA), which was being set up by counsellors, social workers, psychologists, nurses and others with an interest in infertility, to address the fact that by May 1988

> the consultation process about assisted conception had reached White Paper stage and policy was being formulated without adequate reference to a professional [counselling] body of expertise…with [an] interest in the needs of infertile people. (BICA newsletter No. 1, Spring 1989, Chairperson's Report)

This organisation continues to support and lobby for the emotional and psychological needs of patients and to provide a forum for counsellors in the field of infertility. It is largely because of their hard work with the DoH in the early days that licensed clinics (i.e. those providing IVF or treatment using donated gametes) are uniquely obliged by the Act to provide 'a suitable opportunity to receive proper counselling about the implications of taking the proposed steps before they consent' (HFEA Code of Practice, Part 6: Counselling).

Initially, the provision of counselling was variable; sometimes the requirement was fulfilled by nurses or doctors who interpreted 'counselling' very differently from professional counsellors. However, more than ten years on, infertility counselling has become increasingly recognised as a specific expertise, and BICA is currently involved in the first NVQ Level 4 training for those offering counselling in the field of infertility.

It took a further five years for our unit to be launched, after an agreement had been reached between the NHS trust and the local private hospital to co-fund a small unit which would treat both NHS patients, who constitute the majority, and private patients seeking licensed infertility treatment. It had been a long process from dream to reality, but we arrived on the scene in April 1994 and I was appointed to provide counselling to both NHS and private patients alike. Five years on the medical team is twice the size, with most of the original members still in post. I am fortunate in having the freedom to offer as much or as little help to all patients and their partners as they need, and feel like a valued member of the clinical team.

The Human Fertilisation and Embryology Authority (HFEA) provides licences to those clinics offering assisted conception, which are renewed annually after an inspection that takes place on site and involves all the members of the core team, including counsellors and administrators, as well as medical staff. As new techniques appear and are accepted by the DoH the

HFEA extends licences to those clinics that provide evidence of required expertise. We are just beginning to convince inspection teams that counselling should play a more important part in the inspection process.

Counselling provision and the welfare of the child

With the directive to clinics to make 'proper counselling' (Code of Practice 1990, Section 2.10) available to all patients seeking licensed treatment (i.e. IVF and related technologies, use and storage of donated gametes (eggs and sperm) and of embryos) the HFEA was instigating a unique practice within the medical world. Although many counsellors work in medical settings, it is still only in assisted conception clinics that counselling provision is mandatory. Unfortunately, in the past, both clinics and the HFEA have sometimes not accorded this directive its full significance: counselling has been provided by other clinic staff acting in dual roles and qualified only to provide the most basic of counselling skills; patients have perhaps been deterred from accessing the service by the extra cost where it has not been built in to the overall cost of treatment; in a few centres counsellors have not felt fully accepted as members of the team, excluded from meetings, etc. Slowly, this is changing. With BICA's new professional training under way, and the proposed higher profile of counselling in annual licence inspections, counselling is at last beginning to fulfil the intentions of those who worked to develop the Act in 1990.

I have been fortunate in being regarded as a full member of the core team from the outset. This has enabled me to influence the development of the work, so that now we consider offering donated sperm to single women and lesbian couples, and carry out requests for surrogacy. All such requests are considered on an individual basis and discussed at a team meeting where representatives of all disciplines are invited to share any personal doubts or anxieties. The patients are made fully aware of the process and always, where applicable, given reasons for refusal, and the opportunity to have further discussions with the director and/or myself. For the most difficult of cases we have resort to an independent ethics committee.

The HFEA also directs clinics to take into account, when deciding to treat couples or individuals, 'the welfare of any child who may be born as a result of treatment (including the need of that child for a father) and of any other child who may be affected by the birth' (HF and E Act 1990, s.13(s)). The HF and E Act applies to licensed centres, but if the centre also offers unlicensed treatment (the treatment usually offered by the NHS, which includes diagnosis of both male and female fertility problems, ovulation induction and corrective surgery), the centre must apply the same standards to that category. In practice, patients are always referred by a GP, who will be asked whether he/she knows of any non-medical reasons why the patient/s should not be treated. The medical team will take all reasonable steps to ascertain who will be the legal parents of the child, and who will be bringing up the child. This is particularly important when patients have come from abroad for treatment and may be returning with a child to a country where the law differs from that of the UK and the child's status may be doubtful.

Other factors for an individual or a couple seeking treatment will also be taken into account: the commitment of both parties to having a child; their ages and medical histories, and those of their families; the likelihood of the child's needs being met, especially in the case of multiple births; and the effect of a new baby on any existing children. Further considerations are made in cases where donated gametes or embryos are used, as will be discussed below.

Assessment

Assessment, which may take one or two sessions, is problematic within the world of infertility counselling. Counsellors are expected to be non-judgemental, but the HFEA Code of Practice has a section entitled 'multidisciplinary assessment', which requires that the views of all those who are involved with prospective parents should be taken into account when deciding whether or not to offer treatment. The views of prospective parents are also to be considered here. In our unit this routinely takes place if single women, same sex couples, use of donor gametes, embryos or surrogacy are under consideration, and occasionally if particular problems have come to light during diagnosis. The team may decide whether or not to treat on medical grounds, and consider whether treatment would be in the best interests of any child so conceived, or in the best interests of existing children, or if sufficient information is forthcoming to reach a proper conclusion.

To a counsellor who is to be part of this process, if there is a requirement that the counsellor will be involved as part of the multidisciplinary team, it is clear that making assessments and judgements runs contrary to the ethos of counselling, so some sort of accommodation must be made. In order to be part of this process myself, I need to make it very clear to couples and individuals from the outset that the session they are attending with me is not only an occasion for counselling, but an opportunity for them to put forward their arguments as to why they should be offered treatment. I explain that if I have doubts or anxieties about their decisions and whether they have fully explored them, I can help them towards a better understanding of what they are embarking on. For example: a couple may attend seeking donated sperm, as the man has no sperm of his own. They may have received this diagnosis the previous week, or several months ago. The clinic doctor will have suggested donor insemination (DI) as one way in which they might achieve a pregnancy and have the family they long for. The diagnosis is likely to be quite devastating for them both, particularly if there is no past history to indicate lack of sperm. Often the quality of masculinity seems to reside in the ability to produce sperm; fertility and potency seem inextricably linked, and a man's sexual self-confidence frequently plummets when semen analyses are seen to fail. Other aspects of his life may be suddenly questioned: he may have previous children whose paternity he now begins to doubt; he feels shame at being abnormal, feels different from other men, including his father and his brothers – these are just some of the considerations that he needs to acknowledge. Donor insemination may help make him a father, but he will remain infertile. Add to this anxieties about the unknown: what sort of father will he be if he is a first-time parent? If he has previous children, how differently will he feel about this DI child? Will he be able to love a child that is genetically unrelated to him? Does his wife or partner want a child at any cost, and is he going along this route to please her, through his own guilt, or for fear of losing her?

This couple may have considered all or some of the above, but their grief process, especially the man's, is often incomplete, and he may not be prepared to work further on it. It is vital, however, for both the couple and their prospective children, to be aware that these questions need to be considered by both of them. Couples are often afraid to discuss such painful subjects alone with each other, and counselling sessions may provide that initial safe space to begin to look at such potentially dangerous feelings. Without the team's demand for my input into treatment decisions, such patients might go unsupported. Sometimes the experience of this very short-term counselling enables patients to have sufficient trust to become clients engaging in longer-term work with me.

Gilly and Stephen had been referred to me by the nurse who ran the DI programme, as she was concerned that Stephen had not dealt with his feelings about his infertility. I had previously seen them for one assessment session, and had felt that they had left long enough to grieve between diagnosis and treatment. Stephen had seemed fine and they planned to tell the child about his/her origins. When they next came to see me Gilly was three to four months pregnant, happy, but upset because Stephen was now saying he would tell no one about the DI – including the child. He admitted he knew it would always be a problem for him, which was why he wanted to leave telling their families until the pregnancy was secure. Despite three counselling sessions he would not change his mind, which effectively prevented Gilly from telling anyone except her widowed mother who had known from the outset. They gave up counselling and as the pregnancy advanced they grew away from the clinic.

We heard from the doctor who delivered her that they had had a boy. We ask all our patients to let us have baby photos for our baby record book, and some weeks later Gilly came in with them and the baby. She told us that within an hour of the baby's birth her husband was proudly introducing him around the ward as their new DI baby to parents and staff alike. She had only a vague idea why he had changed his mind but it had something to do with his having decided, during labour, that he must tell his own father immediately about the baby's conception.

Counselling relationships

The HF and E Act 1990 identifies three distinct categories of counselling that may be offered within clinics. These are:

- implications counselling
- support counselling
- therapeutic counselling.

Implications and support counselling must be provided by the clinic for those clients who want it; therapeutic counselling may also be provided if the counsellor is professionally qualified to do so (and is not a member of the team, offering counselling as a secondary role to nursing, etc.). If the counsellor does not offer therapeutic counselling a suitable referral system must be in place. These three counselling categories fall quite neatly into:

- brief counselling – 1 to 3 sessions
- medium-term counselling – up to 6 or 8 sessions
- long-term counselling – more than 8 sessions.

Implications counselling

Implications counselling offers clients the opportunity to express their feelings of sadness, of being out-of-control of their sexual and procreative processes, and frequently their anger at feeling different from normal. Sub-fertility or infertility can have a devastating effect on the way an individual or couple is able to function, not just within their relationship but also socially and at work. Often there is no one with whom to share these feelings in a world where it often seems to the sub-fertile that everyone else is pregnant or has children. Even the couple's own parents are often perceived as being unable to comprehend their plight, having been successful in procreating. Sometimes just a couple of sessions can normalise their situation, helping couples to understand that most other infertile couples have similar feelings, that they are not mad or bad for feeling envious of siblings and friends, that they are not, in some strange way, being punished for previous actions such as termination of pregnancy years before. Often knowing how to get in touch with others with similar problems can provide the ongoing support that they need.

Jane came to see me alone. She had had five miscarriages and there were communication difficulties between her and her husband. She was very distressed throughout the interview. Her husband, Edward, was experiencing stress at work and was therefore unable to cope with Jane's emotions as well. This meant that Jane was unable to share her fears of never successfully carrying a baby to full term. She also feared that by continuing to express her grief to Edward she would damage their relationship. None of her own family were local and she found that friends could not understand the depth of her sadness, as these were babies that no one had ever seen.

> We discussed other resources: she could come to me for ongoing counselling, or she could contact the support group run by patients, as they had a contact line which introduced people with similar problems to each other. I have seen strong friendships arise from these introductions. Jane saw the consultant the following week and arranged a further appointment with me the week after.
>
> Jane told me that she had started talking to her husband again, both about her feelings and his problems at work, and they were both feeling better for that. The support group had put her in touch with another woman who had also had multiple miscarriages, and they planned to meet for coffee soon. After seeing the doctor she was also feeling that she could face trying for another pregnancy with increased help from the unit.

Being able to spend time with a non-judgemental, non-directive counsellor can help couples and individuals look at what their infertility means to them. Some couples are so desperate to be parents that it seems they will grasp at any new technology or alternative therapy at whatever cost, financial or emotional, to themselves. At the other end of the spectrum are those who have a clear picture of how far they will go within the range of choices available. This may be for financial reasons, for religious or belief reasons, or may be self-protective against the stress of more intrusive treatment. Counselling provides them with an opportunity to check these decisions out and either change or confirm them, having looked at what other treatments may mean to them or how they may be affected. In this setting the counsellor may take on an educative role whilst remaining non-directive and non-judgemental.

> Vivienne and Robert had been treated by another clinic before moving to our area. Vivienne had unexplained infertility, which is one of the most difficult diagnoses for clients to cope with, as there is no obvious reason for the lack of pregnancy. Robert had low sperm motility and they had been told that IVF would optimise their chances of a pregnancy.

Vivienne felt reluctant to contemplate IVF, as she felt it was unnatural – which it is – and she hated being 'prodded and poked about'. Both of them felt that they had been given inadequate information about the procedure by their previous clinic, and that they could not make a decision until they knew what they were letting themselves in for. I asked a nurse to join us to give detailed information about IVF, and I gave them information about the support group, which holds monthly meetings for talks on various aspects of infertility and provides a social forum for patients. I offered further meetings if they wished, but I did not see them again. However, I later learned they had had a baby girl through IVF.

Support counselling

Support counselling constitutes the larger part of my caseload at any time, since clients agree to meet with me for up to six to eight sessions and may then continue in a more open-ended way for as long as they need. Clients may attend at the beginning or the end of, or during, the treatment process, often encouraged by other members of the team who perceive that they are becoming over-anxious, depressed or stressed by their experiences of treatment. Increasingly frequently, people self-refer, a reflection perhaps that counselling in general is becoming more acceptable in the outside world.

The HFEA Code of Practice requires that centres 'should take all practicable steps' to provide 'further opportunities' for counselling regarding implications of treatment, donation, or storage of gametes or embryos after consent is given and throughout the period of treatment. In addition, centres are required to offer support counselling to those who have been refused treatment for any reason and those whose treatment has failed to help them come to terms with their situation.

The vast majority of clients who seek support counselling in my unit do so either during the process of deciding which route to pursue within treatment, or during the treatment process itself, both of which put clients under a good deal of stress. There is evidence that undue stress can prevent pregnancy from occurring. Such stress may manifest itself either at home or in the workplace and it is not unusual to hear that clients have been 'signed off' by GPs for stress associated with treatment. Women experience difficulties when they feel unable to tell anyone at work that they are undergoing treatment, if employers make it hard for them to take time off, or when they feel guilty about increasing colleagues' workload by their absence. If work is an environment where other women are becoming pregnant or even contemplating starting a family, or where work colleagues appear insensitive about infertility, stress levels quickly rise to insupportable levels and clients find themselves unable to remain at work.

Marital problems also arise. Couples may be fearful of communicating their feelings to each other for fear of making a bad situation worse. One partner may feel unsupported or let down by the other, or there may be unexpressed anger or blame which leads to discord. Sexual difficulties such as loss of libido, viewing sex as 'useless' when it does not lead to procreation, and minor sexual dysfunctions, particularly erectile problems, all occur as a result of involvement with fertility treatment.

In the wider world of friends and families, patients feel isolated and different, often abnormal, in what seems a very fertile environment, and this can lead to anger and despair. And always there is the underlying fear that they will remain childless despite advancing medical techniques.

Sally had had investigations for infertility which indicated that IVF gave the best hope of a pregnancy. She first came to see me just before she was due to have her eggs collected. She was feeling very nervous and asked for some ongoing support. As she and her partner were going away immediately afterwards, I arranged to see her after she had done the pregnancy test.

That first test was negative, and although Sally had never believed that conception would happen the first time, and felt she was coping with the disappointment, she was finding it hard to cope with her mother and sister, who were very close but didn't seem to understand what she was going through. She was also very anxious about a planned holiday with her husband's sister and brother-in-law and their small child. We discussed how her husband, Will, could negotiate some ground rules with his sister to allow them some privacy to grieve. This seemed to work, and the holiday went well. Sally met an old friend with a baby and felt fine about being with the child. As we continued to meet, however, jealous feelings began to creep in and she hated herself for having them.

After another transfer of frozen embryos had failed to implant, Sally became more and more upset and tearful. We discussed taking a break from treatment, how to keep in touch with the unit whilst she did so, continuing to see me, and doing something about her work stress, either by working part-time or by giving up work altogether.

Three months later Sally was ready to start treatment again and had changed her job to a part-time one, working for a friend who was aware of the treatment. After the next frozen embryo transfer she had a positive pregnancy test, though not a strong one. She had a blood test which was also inconclusive, but had to wait a week for a scan. This waiting was very hard for her, especially as her worst fears were subsequently confirmed by the scan.

We continued to meet and she made slow progress but was set back by her sister announcing her third pregnancy. Sally's next attempt at a frozen transfer was deferred, as her cycle did not coincide with a working weekend for the unit. When it finally happened this too was unsuccessful, and she found it hard to visit her sister and the new baby. She chose to take time off from both treatment and counselling. I saw her next several months later, by which time she and her partner had decided to end treatment and pursue adoption.

One of the most difficult aspects of infertility treatment for both client and practitioner is to keep the balance between reality and hope – hope that something will be diagnosed as wrong which can then be put right. As many as one third of patients are diagnosed with 'unexplained infertility' where neither partner is seen as having a problem. Such a diagnosis causes great frustration and unhappiness, as there is no clear 'cure' that can be applied. Even when a diagnosis suggests a treatment route, it may not be effective. Yet it would seem pointless to go through treatment without some hope of success. Nationally, centres have a successful pregnancy rate that averages about 17 per cent, though the better centres may reach about 28 per cent. With such results it is sometimes difficult to be optimistic.

Therapeutic counselling

It is comparatively rare for me to offer long-term counselling to infertility clients, but it does happen occasionally. When it does occur, I usually see the client(s) on a weekly basis for a few weeks and then reduce the meetings to fortnightly. With only six sessions available per week I have to be parsimonious with weekly appointments. In general, long-term work is available for those with critical marital or sexual problems or for patients who become clinically depressed.

Working with people in an infertility clinic setting presents me with a range of clients and problems that is infinitely variable. Unlike many counselling settings, here it is vital that I have a sound, if layman's, knowledge of the procedures that my clients are experiencing and that I have some understanding of what my medical colleagues are talking about. I also work as a counsellor in primary care, and do not feel the same pressure to understand my clients' medical conditions there. I am not sure where the difference lies, whether it is within me or comes out of the work setting.

Lorna and Mike had been married for 11 years. During this time Lorna had had eight miscarriages and they were beginning to despair of ever having a baby. I met Lorna and Mike together the first time, though Mike did not seem to want to be there and took little part in the discussion. It was the only time I met him. Lorna was in a very distressed state, having had another miscarriage recently following treatment. They agreed that this next attempt at assisted conception would be their last, for both practical and emotional reasons; besides, the consultant had said that he had tried everything he could.

Lorna talked about her childhood: her mother was psychotic and she was taken into care, where she was abused. Her father was now elderly and dependent on her, but ungrateful for her help. There was no support from her siblings: Lorna had always been the backbone of the family. Given the case history I was not supprised to find that she worked in a caring capacity with elderly people. We discussed the idea of her taking a few months off treatment to get herself better. She agreed to see her GP and to come for regular counselling. She was giving less help to her father and he was being 'horrible' to her. We had several sessions when we focused largely on her childhood and she began to make some progress.

Lorna arrived for the seventh session in a very stressed state, unable to stop crying. She had broken down at work the previous week, and felt very exposed and embarrassed. She and Mike were not getting on: he was very stressed at work and angry that she wasn't able to support him. I suggested that she might ask her GP for sick leave so that she and Mike could go away. The following week things were improving; she had been off work and had talked with Mike. They planned a long weekend away. Both of them were going through a hard time, but Mike would not come to counselling. He talked about looking for a new job and Lorna decided to give up work and go to university, which she had always longed to do.

A week later she was distraught again. Mike had told her that he had never wanted children and had refused to pursue adoption in the future. Lorna was faced with a difficult decision: was she to continue in the marriage or seek another relationship where she might be able to become a mother somehow? A good deal of repair work would be needed to get this marriage back on track, but it needed to be done elsewhere. She had been my client for too long for her husband to feel comfortable joining us, and couple counselling can take a very long time, so I suggested they approach either Relate or a private counsellor. First, Lorna had to decide whether or not her relationship was important enough for her to give up the idea of having a child, then she had to forgive Mike and understand his wish not to be a parent. Both needed to deal with their work stress and with other difficult relationships. Lorna began to grieve for her lost fertility and her dream babies, and this was well under way when we agreed that she was strong enough to continue alone. She wrote to me several months later to tell me she had started her university course and was loving it. She and Mike were also seeing a Relate counsellor.

In contrast to many fertility counsellors, my interest in this work does not arise out of my personal experience. Looking back over my career, it seems to have evolved in an almost organic way. When I started my diploma in counselling, I was asked why I was not doing a diploma in primary care/health settings; I replied that that was not how I saw my career. In retrospect this seems strange, since I spend two thirds of my week working within the NHS! I have a special affection for the work I do in the unit: this is thanks partly to the other members of the team that I work with, who are dedicated and hardworking, but who also know how to have fun together, and partly to my clients, who are, as I said, at the beginning of this chapter, very special people, from whom I have learned so much.

Further reading

HFEA *Code of Practice* (fourth edition). Available from: HFEA, Paxton House, 30 Artillery Lane, London E1 7LS.

Blyth, E. (1995) *Infertility and Assisted Conception – Practice Issues for Counsellors.* Birmingham: BASW Publications.

Blyth, E., Crawshaw, M. and Speirs, J. (eds) (1999) *Truth and the Child Ten Years On.* Birmingham: BASW Publications.

Jennings, S. E. (1995) *Infertility Counselling.* Oxford: Blackwell Science.

Mason, M.-C. (1993) *Male Infertility – Men Talking.* London: Routledge.

Read, J. (1995) *Counselling for Fertility Problems.* London: Sage.

Snowden, R. and Snowden, E. (1993) *The Gift of a Child: A Guide to Donor Insemination.* Exeter: University of Exeter Press.

Chapter 9

Riding the rollercoaster

A personal account of being counselled about fertility

Helen Boxer

When Gill, our counsellor, asked me if I'd be willing to write about our experience of counselling whilst undergoing fertility treatment I agreed, primarily because we thought it was a good way of thanking her for all her support and kindness. However, there was also a desire to write our story as a sort of catharsis and a way of putting it all behind us. It was a desire to acknowledge what had happened. I did miss being counselled and sometimes still do. It was a time when I could take stock of my feelings and a way of helping me stay in touch with myself. Maybe this writing was a way of expressing something that I no longer touch on very much but which is still very much part of my past and an experience which makes me what I am now. I also wanted to write our story in the hope that others going through a stressful period in their lives may be offered this help. This story describes how counselling helped us cope with the rollercoaster of fertility treatment and contains extracts of a diary I kept at the time.

We started thinking about having a child in the early nineties when I was in my early thirties. 'Trying for a family' is what I wanted to say, but through counselling I came to realise that this can be a negative term!

George and I had been living together for several years and enjoyed a very full life. We both had interesting careers. I ran my own business and George was a vet. Our main interests were walking, cycling, dancing and travelling. We got married in 1992 with a family in mind. The months turned to years and still no pregnancy. There was something missing in our lives – a child.

By 1994 our GP started to test my progesterone levels through monthly blood tests and I was put on Clomid for a year. As nothing happened, even though the Clomid was clearly working and sending my progesterone levels soaring, I was finally referred to the fertility clinic. The clinic was a mixture of NHS and private. In vitro fertilisation (IVF) was paid for by the patient and cost £3000 for each attempt.

In June 1995 I was offered an HSG (Hysterosalpingogram) to test whether there were any blockages in my Fallopian tubes. The operation is carried out when the patient is fully awake and is very painful. Dye is passed through the tubes and an X-ray is taken to ascertain whether it has passed through or not. Four weeks later, on returning from a cycling holiday in France, we were told in a very cold and clinical manner that both of my tubes were blocked and that IVF was the only way for me to conceive.

The clinic offered free counselling and it was then that I first met our counsellor, Gill. I had been told about Gill several months previously, but had not felt a pressing need to see her at that time, even though the pressures of being in my mid-thirties and not conceiving were beginning to tell.

I did know about the value of counselling. Several years previously, before getting married, I had explored areas of my childhood with a shiatsu practitioner and had found this emotionally draining but tremendously therapeutic. Also, both George and I had attended a weekend seminar where our relationships with our parents and others close to us were explored. We had found this a very enriching and moving experience and it had enabled us to truly touch our emotions. It had also greatly altered, for the better, our relationships with each other, our friends and families, as well as the way we perceived many things.

Prior to referring us to the clinic our GP had recommended counselling, which we paid for. We had several sessions each. It was a mixed experience for me. I did not feel the empathy and safety I had in previous counselling situations and I experienced the counsellor as sometimes slightly aggressive and unsympathetic. We had one session as a couple, which was a very negative experience and made us argue for the whole weekend afterwards. However, the one-to-one sessions did teach me how to relax and think positive thoughts through breathing, music and visualisation. We were therefore essentially positive about our experiences in counselling generally and felt open to it before meeting Gill.

I was devastated by the diagnosis of blocked tubes and Gill let me cry and listened to my grief. She enabled me to come to terms with the news. I felt angry that my GP had not investigated sooner and felt empowered to confront him. Once the blame had gone and the GP was able to explain his reasons, I felt in a more positive frame of mind to move on to the next stage.

We saw Gill regularly after this and built up a very trusting relationship with her. I always felt that she was listening to everything we said and she made me feel that I had a right to my feelings, suggesting other more positive approaches if she felt it was helpful. Also, I never felt rushed or that I had to watch the clock, even though I knew she was often very busy. Counselling greatly helped George and me to cope with the stresses, disappointments and anguishes of fertility treatment. It helped us to keep positive and to maintain a sense of humour, even when the going got tough. It helped us to communicate with each other and to explore our feelings, enabling us to go forward together as a couple through an experience which tested our relationship to its limits. As counselling progressed we became more in tune with each other's pain and perspective.

Talking things through with a sympathetic, trained counsellor could change my feelings of despair into calm acceptance and at the same time give me a renewed desire to fight on – a trusted person who could suggest that sometimes it was better to do nothing for a while rather than just plough on, and who could just offer a shoulder to cry on; someone who could make me feel that I was not a failure, give me the space to explore my true feelings and empower me to tackle many very difficult situations.

Not only was Gill an experienced counsellor but someone with extensive knowledge and understanding of the causes of and treatments for infertility. This meant that it was not necessary to interrupt the flow of the session to explain medical terms to her. We did get very close to Gill and she felt like a true friend and supporter.

The following extracts are taken from my diary of the twelve months from July 1995 to July 1996.

July 1995

The Consultant has at last agreed that I should be offered a laparoscopy to confirm whether my tubes are blocked. I asked at the hospital reception whether I could be fitted in if there was a cancellation as the waiting is affecting me psychologically.

Have at last got a date for the operation.

August 1995

Am feeling a lot more positive. After a rather unpleasant laparoscopy, which took me more than a week to recover from, my left tube was found to be completely intact and there was some slight scarring on the right tube. That means that I can conceive naturally. What a relief! Why was a false diagnosis given after the horrible and very painful HSG?

I had found the news hard to take on returning from our cycling holiday in France. It was also delivered in a very matter-of-fact manner and I was very relieved when we were invited to sit in Gill's room and tell her about it. This was the first time we had met Gill, the clinic counsellor.

September 1995

Have set a date for our IVF. Feels very exciting.

October 1995

Had a fantastic holiday in Greece. We had a lovely time walking, eating lovely food, relaxing, making love. Am hoping that I might have conceived on holiday. I've been told countless times that people get pregnant on holiday when they're relaxed! It's hard not to play mind games. I've also been told to take Clomid tablets this month for one last try!

Beginning to feel nervous about IVF, the drugs and the intervention but am fed up with waiting. Went hot and cold on the idea a few times but I want a baby.

November 1995

One try at IVF, they say! It hasn't been one try. It's been a pumping full of drugs only to have it all cruelly taken away – to watch my 14 eggs die in my mind's eye – potential babies that never lived.

I had been very excited about starting IVF and finally doing something positive. I started on the Hay diet, which made me feel well and in control. Starting the nasal spray helped me to feel we were working towards our goal. I had resolve and felt all aglow. Even the injections didn't worry me. Granted, I felt anxious about mixing the ampoules. I felt relieved when Sheila told me how to do it – felt proud that I could actually bear the pain and say to myself 'Yes, I want a baby' as the slow-release injection fired into my leg.

Strangely, even the feeling of being bloated and the fear that the eggs were going to drop out after the final injection felt positive. George helped me put the needle into the fleshy part of my leg. Didn't sleep very well the night before the eggs were taken out but woke with a feeling of excitement. Arrived ten minutes early at the clinic and got ready for the egg retrieval. Getting used to operations now.

George watched as the eggs were removed. He's a bit squeamish. He had already asked the Sister, Debby, if he could produce a sample at home and she said 'no'.

In a semi-conscious state I remember Vera, another member of staff, saying to George, 'It's your turn now.' He didn't come back for half an hour. They started to worry about him and asked me to go and talk to him. In a very drowsy state after the anaesthetic, I called through the door of the men's room to ask how he was. He went home and I had to get out of bed and go and sit in Gill's room to wait for him. The time ticked on; I began to feel tearful and worried. It had not really sunk in that there may be no sample. I was drowsy and overconfident – not aware of the possible consequences.

George phoned – my heart lifted – had he got a sample? 'No,' said Vera, 'he'll come and pick you up and take you home.' Susan, the embryologist, and Vera advised a drink. We went to the Merry Duck, a nearby pub. Had phoned Jane and Rachel in floods of tears.

'It's not George's fault,' snapped Jane.

'Go out for a meal,' said Rachel.

How the hell could I as my eggs slowly died?

Horrible drink. Feeling of tiredness and pain. I always feel in agony when I have instruments shoved up the vagina.

'Go and get a video,' I urged.

'No, Jane's behind the counter,' retorted George. 'I'd be too embarrassed.' I went from tears to calm, to panic throughout the whole night. We tried everything. On the bed, in the hall, trying to get George aroused to produce this very precious sample. George ran round the garden naked, we danced, watched 'Baywatch', tried to sleep with the alarm set for one hour's time. 'Ring me in the middle of the night,' Susan, the embryologist, had said. I wish we could have. Nothing worked.

In the morning phoned Vera in floods of tears. 'Keep trying,' she said. George disappeared into the garden shed. No sample. He talked to Gill and still nothing. At three o'clock in the afternoon we had to give up. What sadness, what loss and what a devastating experience for George.

Friends came round with a plant. George phoned my Mum and told her what had happened. I felt suicidal. She calmed me down and told me to care for George. Went to see some friends the next day but felt so wretched. They didn't know what to say.

The next few weeks were a blur. When we saw the consultant all he could say was, 'Shame we didn't have any donor sperm ready!'

I had been expecting some sympathy – not for someone to suggest nominating another father for our child!

We discussed starting again in January. I would have to go through the whole process again to get the eggs and they would try to freeze a sperm sample this time.

December 1995

George still couldn't get an erection. When it came to the next ovulation we couldn't make love. We felt as if we were reliving the whole scene. Gill advised not making love until she told us it was permissible to do so.

We threw ourselves into the social scene. Stopped doing everything healthy like shiatsu but still went to yoga. Everything felt empty and trite.

The support group Christmas party was dreadful. As an active member I thought that we would get a lot of sympathy. Felt so sick that I had to go outside for some fresh air as nobody wanted to talk about what had happened. I told Gill about winning the raffle three times and the consultant, who was giving out the prizes, agreeing that a committee member wasn't entitled to more than one prize. Under normal circumstances I would have agreed, but I felt completely rejected; Gill helped me to analyse my feelings.

I felt that everyone wanted to hide me away. I was shoved into a room at the clinic so that nobody could see my tears. The bill for my second IVF treatment came through in January before we had even managed to get a sample to freeze. They apologised, everyone felt so uncomfortable with the situation. My Dad wrote a wonderful letter to George and myself expressing how sorry he was about what had happened and so did my brother, James.

At home for Christmas with the family. Nobody wanted to talk about what had happened. One sentence would have been enough! I felt really low.

1 January 1996

Woke up worrying about a lump in my breast, discovered just before Christmas. Plucked up the courage to ask George to check and he confirmed that there was one.

Must go to the doctor when I get home.

Had a terrible New Year's Eve party at a friend's house. We had thought we were going to a cosy meal for six, but on arrival quickly realised they had changed their plans and it was going to be a children's party! As we had driven 100 miles to get there and were staying the night, there was no escape! We sneaked out to the pub for half an hour when it became unbearable, feeling really miserable. Our friends apologised the next day.

Still feel a bit shell-shocked by my sister Jane's news of Friday – she is pregnant! I'm very pleased for her but for me the upset of the past few months makes it hard to bear.

I still feel bouts of anger and frustration about what happened before Christmas and our first attempt at IVF. I sometimes take it out on George, but know in my heart that he is suffering terribly from the blow to his manhood. He feels a strong need to make it up to me. He wants children just as much as I do and my anger and upset just make him feel even more of a failure.

2 January 1996

Writing this I feel very sad and upset. I have just been to the doctor who confirmed that there was a lump in my breast and found a second one. I feel a sense of panic and also the need to be strong. Fighting anything, especially cancer, needs strength of will and character. It needs rest and exercise, patience and above all optimism. Health is important – more than the desire to have children. Please God, let it be benign!

4 January 1996

Still feel numb. Gill was good therapy yesterday – a chance to talk and let everything out. Was beginning to feel like a walking disaster but Gill was able to make me feel more optimistic. We talked about taking one step at a time. That little bit of good luck must be round the corner. It's strange but fertility treatment almost seems irrelevant at the moment compared to health. Getting involved in my work today helped. It always helps getting sorted and doing jobs.

Also, talking to friends has been of enormous help. Talking to Gill empowered me to phone Jane today to discuss her baby – hope it's well, happy and healthy. I'm looking forward to becoming an Aunt.

21 January 1996

At the moment things are so strange that I feel very stressed and disorientated. Also very worried about the future. Thursday went to the One Stop Breast Clinic – appointment at 9.45am and it was all over by 3.00pm. George came with me. I had a mammogram, an ultrasound and then the most painful needle you could imagine in each lump. The side lump was very painful and the consultant couldn't draw any fluid or tissue from it.

After a long wait was told that will need to get the lump removed surgically as they were not able to get any conclusive results.

Have started to take sperm samples to the clinic. George produced a sample which we were very pleased about. He handed it down to me ready waiting in coat and gloves. I then dashed into the car and drove through the snow and ice to the clinic, with the sample stuffed down my bra! Susan was ready waiting for me at the clinic so that she could freeze it! The quality of the sperm isn't very good so we'll have to keep on trying. Susan is going to take the best sperm out of each sample and mix them together until she has got enough for another try at IVF.

Feel very sad for Jane. She lost her baby and I feel guilty at my initial reaction. I really wanted her to have a baby and just wish that I lived closer.

February 1996

Got a cancellation for the operation to remove the breast lump. Trying to continue as normal. Went to my niece's christening the day before going into hospital and drove to Birmingham on my own and back in one day. It felt very strange. My parents were there but my sister Jane felt too upset to come. It was hard to cope with all the small-talk as I felt nervous about the following day. I would have rather not been there, but I felt it was important to honour my niece.

The operation went well. The surgeon only had to remove one lump instead of two, as the other had disappeared when lanced with a needle. My breast felt very sore for several days and I wasn't very keen on looking at the wound or bathing it. I went in at 8.30am and was out at 3.00pm. Just have to wait for the results of the lump biopsy. Fingers crossed!

March 1996

Great news! After three long weeks of very anxious waiting, was told casually by the consultant that the breast lump removed was merely fibrous tissue. I wish they could have told me sooner but was very relieved by the news. Felt very emotional when I found out, as had been trying so hard to be optimistic. Had a good cry.

April 1996

Everything feels so terribly sad at the moment. George has had another panic attack, which can be quite terrifying. It happened during the night and I took him to *casualty, as he thought he was dying. Gill has seen George on his own to talk about the stresses that he is undergoing. It has helped him a lot.*

What a year! I can feel motivation and enthusiasm slipping away and a feeling of unwellness coming over me.

As I'm writing this I'm crying for the loss of the child that could have been, for George's upset at not being able to make love to me at the time of ovulation, at the need to pretend to the world that everything is OK, at the desire to have a meaning in my life – my own child. The ban on sex is still on. It will take the pressure off George. Having sex to make a baby becomes so perfunctory that I won't miss it.

1 May 1996

Am feeling positive. The last few months have been hard, driving across town, with samples to be delivered to the clinic within ten minutes. Susan is still trying to get a good sample before we can try IVF again.

We all managed to find the funny side of the situation as a sample appeared wrapped up in a sock.

Relations between George and I are back to normal, just as Gill had intended. We felt guilty telling her that we had made love, despite the ban, like naughty schoolchildren. One thing that this treatment has taught me is that I really love George and that at the moment I really feel the pain that he is going through. I still desperately want a child and feel that it would sandwich our relationship.

A great pressure is on us. I watch George's consumption of alcohol like a hawk! Don't want it to affect the sperm! Got really upset at a party in February when he downed several glasses of spirit as part of a dare! Didn't help that my Mum was staying, as I felt so mad! Gill helped get things into perspective, enabling me to see things from George's point of view. His need to just blot it all out!

I try to draw hope from our experience of buying our house. Having fallen in love with it, as the house where we would bring up a family, we lost it several times. We were very persistent in phoning the vendors when losing it to somebody else, insisting that if anything went wrong with their buyers, we were more than interested. We had got on very well with them and they phoned us a month later to say we could have it. We were overjoyed. We then lost it again on the day of exchange, as they had unforeseen legal problems with the property they were buying. We waited for three long weeks and eureka – got it in the end! Must have been the wish we made up Glastonbury Tor! Hope our second wish is fulfilled!

Going to work and running my own business possibly gives me the strength to feel normal – to block out treatments, clinics, the treadmill of investigations. The support of family and friends has been tremendous. Counselling with Gill has helped me focus on this and to avoid negative attitudes like, 'You don't know what it's like!' It doesn't work. Everyone has problems. It still hurts, however, when yet another friend announces they are pregnant!

5 May 1996

Day 10 of injections and the second IVF attempt. Everyone is willing me to get pregnant.

My parents gave us a very generous donation towards the treatment so feel that the pressure to succeed is on.

Went for a scan this morning – things are developing and going well. About 8 eggs on the left ovary and 7 on the right – almost the same as last time. There was a debate as to when the eggs would be at their best: collection on Wednesday or Thursday? In the end Thursday was decided upon.

Susan was there and had a chat to her. Felt the ice had been broken as other members of staff were there and at last George's failure to produce a sample after egg collection was discussed.

We all felt positive because after several months of racing across town with weekly samples, a back-up was ready in the freezer if needed.

A much more sensitive approach was adopted. George would not have to pore over dirty magazines in the 'blue room' but could produce the sperm at home and bring it in.

It's much better now that we're actually in the middle of treatment. We've jumped right into it and there is no return. Deciding when to start is more difficult. I wanted to feel positive and healthy before starting again.

Gill was great in helping us make the decision about when to start. Six months had elapsed since our previous attempt at IVF due to the breast lump, a period of impotency and the difficulty in getting a sample with good quality sperm. We discussed our mental state and agreed that we felt positive and ready.

The last stage of the treatment is the hardest. The Synarel nasal spray at the beginning does make me feel slightly aggressive and moody but the daily injections are fine once I mastered breaking and mixing the vials and finding the chunkiest part of my leg. However, the feeling of being bloated at the end is very uncomfortable. I'm just aiming to feel relaxed and positive at the moment.

Yesterday was an emotional day as a friend had a little girl – a successful IVF – fourth attempt. I cried for joy when they phoned me – a miracle baby.

31 May 1996

What a day! Went into egg collection yesterday. Broke the record – 29 eggs in 30 minutes! They were just pouring out and all, according to Susan, of excellent quality. I think that the staff were very worried about hyperstimulation as they consider anything above 30 eggs too dangerous to put any embryos back. I will need to look out for the signs of hyperstimulation.

George produced a sample on Wednesday – took the morning off work to do it and he felt like a big hurdle had been crossed. I had felt anxious too as fresh sperm is better than frozen.

Wednesday, I felt dreadful. Had to get up at 1.00am Tuesday night for the final injection to release the eggs. Dozed beforehand as worried that wouldn't get the timing right. George helped me do it and it all felt very weird!

Had been for a massage on Wednesday – feeling very bloated. The massage helped me a bit and helped calm me down. The scan on Tuesday showed that I was likely to produce at least 20 eggs! A friend, who had undergone IVF, reminded me it was the quality, not the number, of eggs that was important.

Everything seemed to be going very well on Thursday. The staff were very relaxed and George produced a sample which had lots of strong, mobile sperm swimming around. He had a look down the microscope – the best one he'd ever produced.

Great – I'd produced 29 eggs, George had a frozen sample in the freezer plus a fresh sample. There was a very jovial atmosphere. Gill came to see us and gave us both a hug. Twins were discussed and obviously frozen embryos would enable us to have another try. We went home feeling elated.

9.15am on Friday the embryologist phoned to give us the bad news. One embryo had resulted out of all those eggs and seemed of only reasonable quality. At first I felt sheer disbelief, followed by anger, then upset, then tiredness and a realisation that action re-play had started yet again. The warm loving feelings I had experienced the day before towards everyone turned to disbelief and upset – why us?

Apparently the diagnosis was that the sperm can't attach itself to the eggs – something very uncommon and only treatable by ICSI (Intra Cellular Sperm Injection). This is a very specialised process only carried out in a few centres in the country. The sperm must be injected into the egg and this treatment is expensive and its success rate not as good as IVF.

I couldn't get my mind round ICSI at that moment. Having pumped my body full of urine from menopausal nuns, having spent £6000, time off work, unthinkable stress, I could not even bear to think about starting again.

Must keep positive for this one embryo I thought. Will it still be alive tomorrow – who knows! No one knows.

George phoned the embryologist – is there anything we could do? We even asked about the possibility of adding donor sperm.

Apart from the obvious reasons of not knowing who the father was – George or donor – this was not an option. The 'killer' sperm would kill the newly introduced sperm. Also donor sperm must be matched to the recipient, ordered, and counselling given.

Gill came round to the house that afternoon. It felt good to talk. She was very kind and sympathetic. I almost felt positive when she left.

I talked to a friend on the phone who was very upset for us. Mum was kind but what can she say? What can anyone say? Others search for the positive – they're one step ahead. I am still in pain with an extended stomach; an immense tiredness is creeping over me and destroying all the good intention and positive thinking. It's back to the upset, the frustration, the realisation that we'll have to keep on trying and that we've got to face up to it. Accept and forget or not accept and fight. I'm tired of fighting.

1 June 1996

Today's another day. Woke up about 7 o'clock feeling tired but having slept well. Still feeling numb but that the embryo needs a home.

We got to the clinic about 9.30am. Another embryo had divided with the help of some frozen sperm and another had just divided. The embryologist proposed inserting the three embryos without knowing the quality of the third. I would have to have an amniocentesis if pregnancy should occur. The other eggs were Grade 2, not brilliant, but not awful either. Felt excited. Went to the theatre and had the catheter inserted. Didn't even feel it. Susan feels that the chances of success are slim but that there is still a chance. She looked upset.

So, as I'm writing this, I have three embryos inside me. It makes me nervous to go to the loo or indeed to do anything. Keep thinking of Jean who was told that an embryo was of poor quality and had baby Alexandra as a result!

4 June 1996

Had a fight with Mum on the phone. She started lecturing me about the drugs used for treatment. Why didn't I give up, she said. Stop being so obsessive. Use donor sperm. I don't feel that I am being obsessive about having a baby – it does require a certain drive – maybe in years to come I'll look back and view it differently.

As I'm writing this I can hear the children in the playground. Summer is here and the world seems beautiful.

Had a meeting with Gill yesterday at the clinic. I felt calm and composed, a time to gather up energies. Spoke to friends who were very kind. Mum phoned to make her peace. Told her that I would be making my own decisions about treatment in future. She agreed and offered her support.

Last weekend George was very sweet and insisted that we went away for the weekend. We had a lovely calm weekend, not without its anxieties though. Have been hanging on to Susan's philosophy that more people get pregnant when they go away and forget about everything. Forget about it! How? Being away from home often makes it come more to the fore.

The first week after implantation was easy. I saw friends, went out with George, even spent the day with a friend who was expecting triplets any day, and visited the friend who had just had her baby through IVF. She looked totally different from the worried person I had known throughout treatment. Those looks of pain, anxiety, bitterness and frustration have all gone and instead there is a contented mother with a beautiful, sweet baby. In a few days the embryos will decide whether they are staying or not. This has been the hard bit – waiting at the end and dreading going to the toilet in case there is blood.

A friend phoned to say she was pregnant.

14 June 1996

Feel very tired and sad today. We got up at 5 o'clock yesterday – the big day to test. All summed up in a line. Waited three minutes – no line. We stared in disbelief. Had really felt pregnant – swollen breasts, a continual need to go to the loo. Must have been the drugs or all in my mind. George had also been excited even though he doesn't usually let himself.

I cried tears of disbelief and belief. I was now able to express feelings that I knew I would have after two weeks of hanging onto the positive and our three possible babies. Looking back, I can pinpoint when I lost them. I had a slight brown-coloured discharge. I'm mourning for the loss of my three embryos. I wonder what they would have been like. Were they girls or boys?

I phoned the clinic. It gave me something to hold on to. I asked them if they would retest. Come down and we'll do another test. Negative. They were very sweet. Had a cry with Susan and Vera who advised us to forget treatment for six months – have a holiday, spend some money, enjoy life together. They seemed to think that it had all been too much. Felt much better when I got home. A neighbour came round with a crystal for me to hold and I felt its inner strength and power. It was very thoughtful of her.

Arranged to meet George at lunchtime. We bought sandwiches and sat in the sun. Bought another tester – thought we would retest in a couple of days' time to be absolutely sure that it was a negative result.

It feels much better than the first IVF failure. This time there is no one to blame. Thankfully, with Gill's help, we are still very much together as a couple. George's ability to express his feelings in the counselling sessions has helped us through a very difficult time.

28 June 1996

It's been an odd week. My hormones are beginning to come down now that I'm not using the pessaries. My breasts are still very swollen. I feel very numb.

I had a vision today of George holding our baby.

At our session with Gill felt numb and practical. Gill said she didn't sense much grieving. I am grieving – I just feel too exhausted, run-down and upset. Don't feel like talking to anyone at the moment.

2 July 1996

My ovaries are throbbing. I feel nauseous, empty, sad and unwell. Had a shiatsu treatment which left me feeling very sick.

George went to France on a cycling trip with work last weekend. Jane came to stay for the weekend and we had a lovely time talking. Cooked lots of food over a bottle of wine for our parents' ruby wedding party at the end of the month and had a few lovely walks.

Went to see Mum for the day in London yesterday. Felt very emotional and misunderstood. Had been reading The Bridges of Madison County *in the coach and it touched a raw nerve. I cried all the way home on the bus. Arrived home feeling emotionally drained.*

6 July 1996

Feeling exhausted. George and I have booked a flight to Morocco. Fed up of planning our lives around possible pregnancies.

Saw the adoption social worker and felt that it was not a path that we wanted to pursue. She was very pleasant but painted a very black picture about the shortage of children to adopt. She has asked us to think very carefully about whether we would want to attend an introductory weekend course.

Had a lovely day with some good friends – they've all got children but were very sensitive.

23 July 1996

I can hardly believe it. I'm pregnant! I've just plucked up the courage to do a second pregnancy test and it's positive! There is a very clear blue line. It's an added bonus that I conceived naturally and only one month after being told that this was not possible!

George couldn't believe it when I did the first test. I had been to aerobics, gone running, but felt very tired. My period was very late and I really did not expect a positive result!

Told my family at my parents' ruby wedding weekend. Everyone was delighted, if not slightly cautious, as it is still early days. Wonderful news – I'm so excited.

Everyone was thrilled at the clinic. We saw the embryo on a scan and it looks very well placed and healthy.

I continued to write my diary throughout my pregnancy. It came as a big shock to jump from fertility treatment into expecting a baby.

Gill continued to counsel George and me for the first twelve weeks of pregnancy. I felt very nervous about anything going wrong and it was lovely to express this to somebody. I just seemed to sleep a lot during this time and really enjoyed the pregnancy for the last six months. It was a very special time and felt like a true miracle.

The pregnancy went very well and my beautiful daughter was born ten days late by emergency Caesarian section after a very long labour. We were extremely lucky to conceive a second child when my daughter was only nine months old, despite the fact that I was still breastfeeding and had had a postnatal thyroid problem! The thyroid problem did sort itself out and our second child was born naturally eighteen months after our daughter.

Our experience of counselling has been very positive. For me Gill was a person who helped me feel secure. She was a person who helped me feel that I had a right to be there and that all my emotions were valid. It should be possible to explore your vulnerability with a counsellor with the knowledge that it will not be discussed elsewhere and that it is strictly confidential. Gill was a very good listener who sometimes commented, but never in a damaging way, and who helped us come to our own conclusions. It was easier to discuss our intimate emotions with someone outside our family or our circle of friends.

I also found being actively involved in the support group helped me enormously. I formed very close friendships with others who were having similar experiences. This helped us to feel 'normal' and less alone. Acting as editor of the newsletter made me feel active and in control – a huge contrast to the lack of control I was experiencing in other areas of our lives. Part of the concern of the support group was to convince our local trust that IVF treatment should be available on the NHS for all who need it, not just for those who happen to live in certain areas. In the current system many people could not possibly afford the cost of such treatment, and even for those who managed to find the money, this added to the stress of not knowing if it would succeed or fail.

We were very lucky in that we had a very supportive group of friends and family who listened to our problems. I would like to acknowledge their support and continued interest.

Reliving this period in my life through writing this chapter has been like opening a closed door. It has been upsetting to revisit events that have been shut out for so long, as life with children is so busy that there is little time for thoughtful reflection. Life has moved on and writing this has only reinforced how special our lives are now, and how very lucky we are to have our two children. It has made me realise how driven we were, but also, having succeeded in having a family, I know why the desire to have children is so strong.

Fertility treatment feels a world away from the world of children. Our two girls have given me a feeling of wholeness, and life with them now feels complete. They are two adorable, very lively little people who make each day a delight. Amy is nearly four and does ballet, gym and loves her nursery. Samantha is two and loves playing with her older sister, and her dance class.

If we had not had children I doubt whether I would have wanted to write this story. It would have seemed like a personal tragedy. I hope we would have come to terms with life without children, as many people have to – probably with the help of counselling.

However, it turned out like a fairy story and we are both so thankful.

Chapter 10

Cut, burn and poison
A personal account of breast cancer
Rosie Jeffries

Love and thanks to J. for all her help with this chapter

The lump

I found a lump in my breast in September 1994. It was the size of an olive and hard as a nut. I wasn't worried because I am not someone to whom dramatic things happen. However, it was a bit alarming that the receptionist at the health centre offered me an appointment quite so quickly. My GP agreed that there was a lump. I had half expected that she would tell me I was imagining it. Instead I found myself fast-tracked to a consultation at the hospital.

The solemn surgeon stuck a long thin needle into the lump to get some cells for testing. A few days later I went for a mammogram, where my breasts were squashed flat first horizontally and then vertically. They seemed to want a view from every angle.

Now I take a deep breath before continuing.

All right, here goes: A week later my partner J. and I went back for the results. Another surgeon (accompanied by a shadowy student presence) told us, 'The lump is non-benign.'

'You mean it's malignant, and I've got breast cancer?'

'Yes.'

I remember that there were only two chairs and that they stood while J. and I sat. I started to shake and giggle.

'But I'm not the sort of person this happens to!'

J. murmured and stroked my back.

The surgeon got out a huge diary and scheduled me in for surgery to remove the lump. I asked for a week to organise things. Then I went back to work. I knew this was mad. I couldn't think of anything else that I wanted to do. Anyway, I am a counsellor and I had clients to see!

Apparently, on this occasion, a nurse gave me a little pink (for girls) card with the name and number of the breast care nurse specialist: I could phone her if I had any questions. This failed to register with me at all, although J. remembers it. A state of shock is not a good one in which to receive information. Perhaps a follow-up letter would have been helpful. It would have been a good moment to make counselling available, too, and to present it as ordinary and routine, rather than something for patients who are 'not coping'. Apart from anything else, this might serve to prevent people from retreating into dysfunctional survival strategies which could lead to long-term difficulties. It would also have helped others in my life who were affected by my diagnosis in various ways, and this would have eased the responsibility I felt towards them in their distress.

The cut: Surgery

The first time I cried was when, a couple of days after diagnosis, I went down with a vicious throat infection. My temperature soared and it was agony to swallow. Finally, sleepless in the early hours, I wept and wailed and gulped and hiccuped. J., relieved that I had at last succumbed to my body's manifestation of distress, ministered to me with tissues, tea and paracetamol. Antibiotics sorted me out and I was well enough to go into hospital five days later for the scheduled surgery.

I had to check in at 2pm. We went out for a delicious lunch first. The reception area in the huge hospital was chaotic. They couldn't find me on their lists and I had to shout my details and my reason for admission repeatedly across a cluster of people at the busy desk. Finally I went up to the surgical ward where I was put in a small end room with three other women. We were all having operations the next day.

By the evening my breasts had been examined by a dozen male medical students. They had to feel both breasts so they could tell the difference. I had answered the same set of questions a dozen times and generally done my bit for their education. Before she had to go, J. and I sat in the huge deserted hospital reception area and drank limp coffee from the vending machine: a strange peace.

Back on the ward an immediate warmth and camaraderie sprang up between the four of us. There was even another lesbian. What a bonus! We all sneaked down to the dingy smoking room late in the evening, although I think only one person was a 'real' smoker. The rest of us just enjoyed feeling rebellious.

I was in hospital for four days. It felt as though there was a cricket ball stuck under my arm where they had taken a sample of lymph nodes from my armpit. It was hard and swollen. This had sounded like such a minor aspect of the procedure but was actually much more sore than the breast. However, having to sit still and do nothing was a novelty. I was attached to two bottles, into which drained bloody fluid from my breast and underarm. Eventually a nurse gave me a pillowcase to put them in, as it wasn't a nice sight for my visitors. J. came before and after work, with the newspaper and letters and cards. Friends came with flowers and fruit, tapes and magazines. My wonderful mum brought me brandy disguised in a brown medicine bottle. Even the breast care nurse came once.

After leaving hospital, the next excitement was an appointment ten days later to hear the results of tests on the lump and the samples from my underarm: the histology. It was the solemn surgeon again. He told me that only one of the nodes he had removed was cancerous. There was a good chance that the cancer had not 'seeded' in other parts of my body. However, they had failed to take out a sufficient margin of healthy tissue around the tumour. In view of this, would I like to have a full mastectomy? Well, not really, since you ask!

This was the first time I felt the absurdity of being invited to make such a choice. What did I know? How can a person make a decision in such a situation? Before this, we thought we had got a grip. We had read voraciously and armed ourselves awesomely with research and statistics! (I say 'we' because J. and I have been a unit in this whole adventure: 'our' cancer, 'our' treatment.)

The burn: Radiotherapy

Our first meeting with the oncologist was a difficult one, partly, perhaps, because we arrived 'armed' with information. My brother is a doctor and had helped us find our way around the literature. Being informed was our attempt to feel more in control of the decisions that would have to be made about the treatment and management of my cancer. It seemed that our knowledge, and the questions this enabled us to ask, put the oncologist on the defensive, which in turn led to us feeling under attack.

Despite the difficulties, we accepted her advice that radiotherapy, together with a regular dose of the preventative drug tamoxifen, would be adequate to deal with any lurking cancer cells.

Preparing for radiotherapy involves being marked with tattoos which ensure that the right bits get zapped each time. Before I started the treatment I came down with a throat infection again, as bad as the last time. I struggled to avoid taking antibiotics this time and tried to be patient while a homeopathic remedy took effect. I didn't hold out! It was just too painful: a swab confirmed a streptococcal infection and I gobbled the allopathic medication like manna from heaven itself. Even so, I started radiotherapy a week later than planned.

Five days a week for seven weeks I went into a windowless room where a series of friendly women would wait while I stripped to the waist and then 'arrange' me on a trolley under the huge and looming machinery. I had to lie exactly right and keep absolutely still. They would put some music on (nice touch!) and then leave the room. They would turn the switches and zap me from a safe distance, watching on a TV monitor.

ROSIE RESOLVED THE PROBLEM OF BEING PRONE TO INFECTION....

.... BUT FOUND HERSELF RATHER A WALLFLOWER AT PARTIES

There were lots of us. Quiet, polite, anxious, we sat upstairs in the oncology centre reception. First we were called downstairs, by name, to sit in radio-therapy reception. Then we were called, by name, to sit outside the door of the room we would be treated in. It was a tedious process at best, though the staff were friendly and comforting. At worst it was exposing physically and emotionally to lie there half naked every day. It was distressing, day after day, to see a stream of very sick people coming and going on foot, on trolleys, in wheelchairs, and worst of all, children in their parents' arms.

Next comes another point at which it would be appropriate for counsel-ling to be offered. The first stage of treatment was over and this one was longer and drearier: less painful but also without the satisfaction of seeing anything happen. It was a time when the fuss had died down and difficult thoughts and feelings had ample space to expand.

It was when I was sitting there one morning that someone I recognised as a lesbian approached me with a letter. She was running a cancer support network, and was seeing if there was any interest in a lesbian group. Yes! Soon after that a group of eight of us started meeting fortnightly. We were sisters, daughters, and partners of people with cancer, and a couple of us had it ourselves. Joining the group was the best thing to happen in months.

That was that. It was over. I went back to work with just the daily dose of tamoxifen to remind me. I went back to running every day or two, to working out in the gym: there was nothing I had done before which I couldn't now do again. After a couple of months I stopped taking tamoxifen, because the side-effects were bothering me. I had had cancer. The support group continued for a further two years. Eventually we found that we had helped each other to tell our cancer stories to the end. It was time to end the group, too, though some of us have remained close friends ever since.

Suspicious developments

Well, it wasn't over, of course. In the summer of 1997 I went to one of our GPs with a small, hard lump on my upper back. He thought it was probably a boil and that I needed to wash more carefully. I was a bit indignant, but didn't question his diagnosis. However, a week later I found another lump, this time under my arm on the other side from where the cancer had been. I went back to the doctor and found myself fast-tracked back to the surgical outpatients. I had a needle aspiration again. The doctor missed the lump. I told him, politely, that I thought he had and he told me patiently that he hadn't. A week later, the day before we were to go on holiday, we returned for the results. He told us it was benign, but asked us to come back on our return from holiday four weeks later for a further check-up. We were jubilant! I hadn't realised how scared I had been. The idea that the cancer would come back was just not on my agenda. With hindsight, I wonder why we were not suspicious that he had given us another appointment so soon.

While we were on holiday I did something to my back. I thought it was because the bed was a bit hard or perhaps because I went for a run in soft sand, or piggy-backed one of our little nephews once too often. It was really painful. I slept fitfully, sitting up, with the help of painkillers, and with J. reading aloud to me until I managed to doze off. What I remember most is that as I lay propped on pillows, woozy with the drugs, she read randomly from old copies of women's magazines that were lying around, and I laughed so much it hurt.

On our return home, I went to the GP about my back. There was no obvious explanation and he furnished me with a prescription for anti-inflammatory medication and painkillers. However, at our health centre, patients are handed their medical records at reception. Waiting for my appointment I had time to browse. There was a letter from the surgeon I had seen just before going away. It said, 'The lump was small and I was unable to get a cell sample.' He had missed it, just as I had suspected!

Back to the hospital. I had three lumps on my back now, as well as the one under my arm. It was the solemn surgeon from before, this time. He had a group of students with him, so they all inspected and prodded. I asked them their names, which they seemed to find most disconcerting. The view expressed by the surgeon was that it was unlikely to be cancer. Subcutaneous lumps are not a usual form of recurrence. However, 'given my history' he would like to take out a couple to check.

I was given an appointment for outpatient day surgery three weeks later. By then I had seven lumps. I negotiated with the surgeon who did the business: I wanted him to take out the four largest (they were peanut-size). He thought two would be sufficient. We settled on three. Perverse though it may sound, I found the experience of being wide awake while he cut out the lumps really fascinating. I liked being involved, rather than being reduced to something inanimate. He showed the lumps to me. They were small and white, like gristle, with tassels of bloody fibre hanging from them. He popped them into little labelled jars.

Getting the results this time was grim. We were ushered into the consulting room and told to wait. I went to the toilet. While I was gone a nurse went into the room. She asked with obvious concern 'How has she been?' and J.

knew immediately that it was going to be bad news. When I came back we chatted in a desultory way. She kept to herself what was not her information to give me. The solemn surgeon gave it to me instead. Then the nurse came and enveloped me in a huge and unwelcome embrace and did not let go, and I had to reach behind her back to hold J.'s hand.

I wonder whether the nurse, or her colleagues, had had any training in breaking bad news, or in using non-verbal behaviour or communication skills! I think medical staff need more help in these areas. As for the patient: this was another point at which the offer of counselling would have been welcome and appropriate for J. and me.

Things swung immediately into an action phase. I started taking tamoxifen again. Taking it as a preventative measure had been an unconvincing proposition, but with palpable tumours to be dealt with, I was willing to give it another go. I had brain scans and bone scans and X-rays. I swallowed dye to show up the presence of anything that shouldn't be there. I was fed through a large polo mint. I was clamped into a helmet and shoved into a roaring tube. (They invited me to choose some music to accompany me on this particular journey, which involved keeping very still for half-an-hour, but actually the machine was so loud that I couldn't hear a thing.) From here on in, anything and everything which was remotely untoward in my body became a matter for investigation.

Now it emerged that I had 'activity consistent with the presence of disease' (don't you love that expression?) in my knee and lower leg, six vertebrae and a rib or two. Well, that explained the back problem: bone metastases.

Our relationship with our oncologist entered a busy phase. It wasn't easy: I think we displaced a good deal of our dismay onto her and for some time she couldn't do anything right. It is also true, though, that she continued to be defensive as we continued to ask questions and to quote from the research that we had access to. However, as we got to know each other better, she seemed to accept our approach more easily and to respond more readily.

I had radiotherapy on the bones. This stopped the back pain miraculously. Now I just had to keep taking the medicine and monitor the situation, to see what would happen over the next three months.

It was awesome. I grew new lumps at the rate of two or three a week. Our oncologist's verdict in December was typically circuitous: 'It's not that the tamoxifen isn't working. It's just that it isn't working as quickly as I would have liked it to.' Chemotherapy was scheduled to start in the New Year.

The poison: Chemotherapy once

The chemotherapy day unit was a light, bright, cheerful place. There were huge, squashy chairs with footrests. There was music. There were cups of tea and coffee and sweets to suck when you were having the particularly foul-tasting drugs (even though they entered the body intravenously, they permeated the taste buds). Best of all, though, the nurses were a stable, specialist team who seemed to enjoy their work. They didn't work shifts, so the same people were always around. There was time to be friendly, as they sat and coaxed large amounts of toxic fluid into the veins.

Some patients wore strange helmets which were taken out of a fridge, and replaced every half-hour or so. Eventually my curiosity overcame me. It turned out that these helmets were freezing cold, and were meant to stop the hair falling out. It was up to the oncologist as to whether or not one was allocated a helmet, as supplies were limited. Actually, I felt that losing my hair was a novelty which, on a time-limited basis, quite appealed to me, so I wasn't bothered about not having the freezer treatment.

It happened quickly but patchily. One memorable evening I appalled J. and friends who were visiting, by nonchalantly plucking out clumps of hair until the floor round my chair was adrift with it. I wasn't even really aware of what I was doing until I noticed their distress. I went and had my head shaved the next day.

The next three months were characterised by constipation and piles, mouth ulcers and fatigue, hats, scarves and a bright blue wig. I have photos of most of my friends and family in that wig. It was stunning!

IN ORDER NOT TO DRAW ATTENTION TO HERSELF, ROSIE PUT A LARGE PAPER BAG ON HER HEAD TO HIDE HER HAIR LOSS...

··· UNFORTUNATELY, THIS TECHNIQUE WAS NOT ALWAYS SUCCESSFUL

When I felt nauseous I just had to stop what I was doing and lie down. As I was so weary, this wasn't hard to do. But such exhaustion was hard for someone who usually has a lot of energy and likes to have a finger in every pie.

The novelty of the headgear wore off. It was hot. Because I got used to my bald pate, I would bare it when I was at home or amongst friends, and I became insensitive to how this was for other people. In retrospect I think I must have looked pretty grim: bald, yellow and drawn.

I finished the three-month course of chemo in May. The lumps had shrunk and no new ones were coming. I grew new hair: curly and with blonde streaks! I was back at work in June 1998. I even began to menstruate again, which I had been given to expect would not happen, as the treatment can bring on an early menopause.

I was now on medication which controlled the intermittent pains in my bones and was also meant to keep them from becoming crumbly, by preventing the calcium from draining out. This was not offered to us routinely, perhaps because it is expensive. But we had done our research and the oncologist prescribed it readily when we asked. I wonder whether people who do not know about bisphosphonates (the relevant drug group), and don't ask, don't get given it, or whether we just anticipated the doctor. I hope it is the latter! Anyway, I felt great.

By August I was growing new lumps again. Then I got a slight cough. It persisted and grew steadily worse. I was sucking cough sweets during sessions with my clients, and keeping a glass of water on hand. I couldn't lie down without coughing and had to sleep propped up. Soon coughing led to sudden vomiting: a reflex action as a nerve in the throat is triggered. I was still cycling to work, but having to stop and throw up when my laboured breathing stimulated this reflex.

We were seeing the oncologist on a monthly basis, and in November she listened to my chest and acknowledged that she thought there was 'something there'. I was sent for a chest X-ray. Getting the results this time was a complete shambles.

The waiting-room was crowded. We waited half an hour past our appointment time and were then ushered into a freezing cold room next to an extremely noisy building site. Another wait, and then a doctor we did not know, and who had not looked at my notes, came to see us. We had to explain that we had come for test results, and then he opened my file and told us that the cancer had spread through my mediastinum, just like that. This, we then learnt, is the soft tissue that envelops the lungs and other tubes and organs in the upper chest. He went off to see our oncologist and ask her what she thought we should do next. He returned with the recommendation that I start another course of chemotherapy forthwith. We scuttled off home, unable to think or respond in that environment, and to try once again to lend meaning to the concept of 'informed choice'.

We had to talk to our oncologist. Whatever emergency had led to her being unavailable, we felt abandoned and confused. If chemo had had such a short-lived effect before, what was the point of going through it all over again? Perhaps it was time to concede defeat and allow the disease to take its course. We wrote to her with our questions and concerns, and to her credit she phoned and talked to me one evening, when she had done a full day's work and was probably longing to get home. She recommended a stronger and longer course of treatment. She led me to understand that having been in remission for three months constituted 'successful' chemotherapy, and that, contrary to my view, the results of the last course were good. This was a sobering thought. The people close to me were careful not to put pressure on me to have more treatment, and I found it hard to know whether I was clutching at straws. But the oncologist thought it was worth another shot. I did too.

Chemotherapy twice: Keeping the best 'til last

Chemo was scheduled to start early in the New Year. We had a lovely week away in the country with friends. I coughed and threw up fairly often, but they tolerated this with humour and affection, and I was well able to enjoy my holiday. But I did think I was probably going to die.

During the next couple of months we went to meet various humanists who officiate at secular cremations, so that we could choose whom we felt most comfortable with. We also checked out a couple of funeral parlours, both run by women. One of these was a retired lesbian Jungian therapist. Perfect! I chose a cardboard coffin, and a bright pink flower design for decoration. I would be dressed in a long, bright pink African gown, which I love, for the occasion. I chose the music for the service and we looked at both the local crematoriums and picked one. Eventually J. had had enough of this, and I was satisfied with my preparations and felt able to let it go. All the relevant information was gathered and safely filed, with my will and other documents.

The nurses at the chemotherapy day unit welcomed us back with the appropriate degree of regret. The medicine was duly pumped in. I slipped back into my non-working routines: reading, painting, seeing people, resting a lot. I had the most wonderful gift from friends, family and colleagues: membership of a health club, so that I could swim and steam and bubble to my heart's content. The hair went again and this time I was ready for it!

Somewhere about halfway through this period, I fell into a hole. I experienced a feeling of depression such as I had not encountered before. It wasn't about death, or not directly so. It was a feeling of disillusion about myself. I seemed to lose the ability to imbue my life with meaning, or to recognise the world as meaningful. There was nothing I wanted to do with my acres of unstructured time. I had always thought I was an artichoke: that if layers and layers were peeled away, as they now were, I would uncover a shiny, vital kernel or core or heart. Instead I found I was an onion: that there were many layers, but that the layers were all. No layers, no onion, no self. This was painful and oddly humiliating, a hard lesson. Luckily, the despair didn't last. It evaporated as the end of treatment came into view.

After four doses of the new cocktail, my white blood cell count refused to climb to the required level for the fifth one and I had to have a reduced amount for the last two of the six. But slowly and surely, my chest cleared. I stopped throwing up. The lumps shrank and many disappeared completely. I was better! By June I had new hair, fair and curly with blonde streaks again, changing to very dark over the next three months: another first. I went back to work and to play.

The tyranny of alternative treatments

Having cancer is bad enough without being told that it is one's own fault. There is a theory in the psychobabble of New Age philosophy, that happy people don't get cancer; that it is the result of having a negative attitude, repressing emotions, harbouring grudges (LeShan 1989). There is the equally iniquitous view that one contracts cancer because one 'needs to learn something'. Then there are those sad souls who claim that getting cancer was the best thing that ever happened to them: who had, presumably, never loved their lives and had never before relished anything or revelled in anything until they got ill and realised they might lose it all. I find all this offensive and oppressive. I think that stress may well have a part to play in causing cancer, and probably most other illnesses. That is as far as I would go down that path. It is also well documented that dietary and environmental factors are relevant too.

The trouble was that everyone we knew, and people we didn't know too, had theories about what I should do or take, where I should go, whom I should see. None of my friends implied that I had brought it all on myself, and if anyone thought that, they kept it to themselves. But everyone knew someone who had had some treatment or some diet or some therapy or other, which it was essential I pursue immediately. I'm exaggerating, but it felt like that sometimes.

J. and I went to Bristol Cancer Help Centre for an expensive two days. Here we were 'marinated in love' (not really our style, although the staff really were very warm and welcoming). We ate delicious food and learnt how to alter our diet and exclude various things which are not good for us. We learnt about spiritual healing, visualisation and meditation. We did some art therapy. We talked to other people with cancer and to their partners and carers. We were introduced to a series of vital food supplements which it was recommended we take every day (at vast expense). It was a good two days, on balance. The approach was one of working to enhance one's health generally: of building up the immune system to give the body the best chance of managing the cancer. Enhancing one's mental health was seen as part of this too. But they never claimed to 'cure' cancer, and I appreciated the pragmatism which accompanied their 'marinade'.

On one occasion, we participated in a 'healing circle' with a rather charismatic spiritual healer, which was a positive, if bizarre, experience. We also went for a series of private healing sessions with a pleasant and ordinary woman. It made us both feel relaxed and helped J. with her insomnia. We had reflexology, which helped me with the awful constipation which resulted from the chemotherapy.

Many other options we rejected. I always felt slightly guilty that I was being ungrateful to the person who recommended whatever it was, and anxious in case this was the one thing that would have effected a cure. Sometimes we rejected things because they were only available somewhere abroad, or because they were too gruesome for words (or both). The norm, though, was that they were all extremely expensive. While I have some choice about spending money on treatment (and while I have had really generous gifts of treatments from friends), this is not possible for many people. What becomes of those on a low income, or who are living on benefits? Absolutely no hope of any of these options for them!

I settled for a selection of pills and potions. I am on three homeopathic remedies: one for the hot flushes and one for the joint pains I have had since the second course of chemo did indeed induce an early menopause. The third is meant to inhibit the growth of the cancer. I am lucky to be able to see a homeopath on the NHS. I also take the 'bone medicine' I talked about earlier (disodium clodrinate) every day. I take five varieties of vitamins and other supplements each day, with various others in the cupboard, which I use when I feel inspired.

I feel that we have been able to negotiate our way through many things which have been made known to us: some useful and some dubious. I am not knocking any of them particularly. What I get angry about is the implication, or worse, the insistence, that if only I embraced whatever treatment or elixir it is, or had the 'right attitude', I would be cured. This gets in the way of what I am most importantly doing, which is getting on with my life.

It's not over 'til the fat lady sings:
Living with advanced cancer

Well I can't go running any more, or use the gym, or stand on my head. The last of these is no loss, though the first two are. I can swim and cycle. I can't ride a horse, and when I go walking I can't jump down from the stile because my bones may not be able to take the jolt. I am not supposed to lift and carry, though I don't know how life would be possible if one was to take this literally. I was thrown out of a yoga class by the instructor. When I explained why I wasn't joining in with the shoulder stand, he couldn't get rid of me quickly enough. I thought I saw fear of litigation written all over his face. I forgot to mention my condition to a shiatsu masseur, who duly leaned into my back and caused me days of pain, which was not her fault at all.

We asked our oncologist for a prognosis at some point. She asked us why we wanted to know. It was as though I had to pass some sort of test before she would say anything. I convinced her that it would be useful to me because of my job. Then she said, 'If there are things you want to do in your life, do them sooner rather than later, and don't take on long-term work.' I suppose it was an unreasonable question, and she chose to be cautious in her response.

It was only after completing the second course of chemo that I read a book (Mayer 1998) which contained a series of first-hand accounts of women who had lived for 12 or 15 years with advanced breast cancer. Still more recently I read about a couple of people who have had it since the 1970s and are completely well. It would have been helpful if I had been told that this was a possibility, even if not a probability. The book changed my perspective, and instead of feeling that I was living on borrowed time I began to feel completely ordinary again. It is not about unrealistic optimism. It is not being 'in denial'. It is about reinvestment in life. Without even the possibility of some years' survival, I think I would have scaled down my plans and aspirations in terms of work, holidays, relationships: in all areas. I might have been in danger of not living fully. As it is, getting holiday insurance is a real problem, and going out of the UK costs as much in cover as the rest of the holiday expenses put together. Applying for another job is also pretty unrealistic, as no sensible employer wants a new member of staff who is, technically at least, terminally ill. This I can accept.

Information, support and counselling

What do a cancer patient and those in her circle need? Personally, I love talking to people with cancer. I want to hear their stories. I want to know how they found out, what they and the people in their lives think and feel, how they are approaching it. What treatment are they having? What is it like? What are the differences and similarities in our experiences? I want to talk about it all. I love reading first-hand accounts. I loved the support group that we were part of, and I am really grateful to have people in my life who are absolutely up for it, when I want to talk about cancer and dying and my funeral. This talking, laughing, crying has been for me a wonderfully containing and sustaining part of my continuing survival.

There is a lot of information about cancer: it is not, in my experience, given routinely. The predominant view seems to be that people will ask if they want to know. This is all very well, but it requires a certain amount of confidence and assertiveness to ask, to ask again, to query decisions made by doctors, to challenge their views. In Britain we revere the medical professionals to a degree which is unhelpful to them and to us.

However, J. and I have access to information which is available to us because of our class. We have medical friends and family. We are on the internet. When I think how hard it has been for us to make 'informed decisions' with all the resources that are at our disposal, I can imagine how impossible some people may find it. I visited a friend in hospital recently and was introduced to a woman who had had an operation. She didn't know what she had had removed or why. Although the various cancer organisations have really useful helplines, they cannot help with individual issues: they cannot offer enough.

Counselling is something different, and when I got the secondaries I was lucky enough to be able to go to The Harbour, a local organisation which offers free counselling to people affected by a life-threatening illness. I needed to talk to someone outside my family and friends, and outside the medical team. I was, on the one hand, being a complete Pollyanna about the whole thing, not being 'real' at all, and on the other hand I was furious when people took their cue from me and said things like 'Well, we are all dying, life is terminal', because then I felt that they were making light of my illness. I was impossible. I needed, and got, a very boundaried and solid relationship with a counsellor who seemed to be able to survive me, as I was surviving the cancer. J. was already seeing a therapist privately. Had she not been, she would have needed to find one at this point.

My first bid, then, is for staff with counselling skills to accompany cancer patients and their companions through the necessary processes at the points where information is given and considered and decisions made.

There is much I could say in support of the argument for counselling. Cancer affects many parts of my life, though it is no longer something I think about a lot. It comes into my awareness unexpectedly sometimes: I am conscious of it when I choose what to eat, or when I see how it has altered my body, or when I resist the temptation to run for a bus. It is always there when my love and I talk about the future. It is there when I plan next year's work schedule with my colleagues. It is there for a few moments when I take my medicine every day. It is there when I speak to friends who are worried if we haven't been in touch for a month or two. But before I went to counselling, it was there, in the forefront of my mind, for long stretches of time, and I needed help in managing that weight. I was really lucky to get it. I wouldn't have done so had I not lived in a city. Even then, not everyone feels able to approach an agency, supposing they know of its existence. For many people, counselling is only realistically available, legitimate and appropriate if it is offered within the framework, and with the sanction, of the medical setting.

Gravy

This has been the story of my cancer so far. I hope this chapter, 'my remission', is a long one. It's been a good one: it's all gravy now. When someone rings the doorbell I look out of the window to see whether they are wearing a long, hooded cloak and carrying a scythe. If they aren't, I let them in.

Note

Parts of this chapter are reprinted from an article in *Counselling 6*, 2, 138–140, 1995, with kind permission of the British Association for Counselling and Psychotherapy, the copyright-holder.

Useful organisations

Bristol Cancer Help Centre

Grove House, Cornwallis Road, Clifton, Bristol BS8 4PG. Office: 0117 980 9500

CancerBacup

3 Bath Place, Rivington Street, London EC2A 3JR. Office: 020 7613 2121 Freephone: 0808 800 1234

CancerLink

11–21 Northdown Street, London N1 9BN. Office: 020 7833 2818

The Harbour

30 Frogmore Street, Bristol BS1 5NA. Office: 0117 925 9348

Further reading

Batt, S. (1994) *Patient No More: The Politics of Breast Cancer*. London: Scarlet Press.

Butler, S. and Rosenblum, B. (1994) *Cancer in Two Voices*. London: Women's Press.

Diamond, J. (1998) *Because Cowards get Cancer Too*. London: Vermilion.

French, M. (1998) *A Season in Hell*. London: Virago.

LeShan, L. (1989) *Cancer as a Turning Point: A Handbook*. Bath: Gateway Books.

Lorde, A. (1985) *The Cancer Journals*. London: Sheba.

Mayer, M. (1998) *Advanced Breast Cancer: A Guide to Living with Metastatic Disease* (second edition). Sebastopol, USA: O'Reilly.

Picardie, R. (1998) *Before I Say Goodbye*. London: Penguin.

Wadler, J. (1994) *My Breast*. London: Women's Press.

Wilber, K. (1991) *Grace and Grit: Spirituality and Healing in the Life and Death of Treya Killam Wilber*. Dublin: Gill and Macmillan.

Wittman, J. (1993) *Breast Cancer Journal*. Golden, USA: Fulcrum.

Chapter 11

Challenges of counselling in psychiatric settings

Rachel Freeth

Introduction

It is unusual to be both a psychiatrist and a counsellor. Many of my psychiatric colleagues who pursue an interest in psychological therapies do so by specialising and training in psychotherapy during their psychiatric training. However, I undertook counselling training as a separate enterprise away from the National Health Service (NHS) setting in which I worked. Furthermore, the approach in which I trained was a humanistic one, person-centred, unlike the more popular theoretical orientations in the NHS such as psychodynamic, cognitive-behavioural or cognitive-analytic. These were both definite and deliberate choices.

The setting in which I work is part of the mental health service provided by an NHS Trust. It aims to respond to the general psychiatric and psychological needs of adults mostly under the age of 65 years, rather than specific problems that require a more specialised service such as a drugs and alcohol team or eating disorders service. The mental health team takes referrals from within a specified geographical area. My role involves seeing inpatients, outpatients and day patients. This also involves working closely with a community mental health team (CMHT). Although I am employed as a psychiatrist and not as a counsellor, I use some of my time to offer one or two counselling sessions a week.

I have chosen to focus on some of the main topics and issues – theoretical and practical – that pose a particular challenge in my work. This chapter is, therefore, divided into several sections that can be read either separately or as a whole. What I have written is very much a personal perspective, drawing upon my own experiences and impressions of working in psychiatric settings, and reflecting my particular theoretical and philosophical standpoint. I hope that it will be of interest to many mental health professionals, not just to counsellors, who perhaps struggle with challenges and tensions similar to those with which I struggle.

A challenge of identity

Belonging to two professions, each using different skills and method and with different training paths, is perhaps one of my greatest challenges. The question of how far integration is possible is a major focus for personal and professional reflection and supervision.

A general distinction between the roles of doctor and counsellor can be made as follows: a doctor is someone who diagnoses and treats 'patients' (or symptoms), often with medication, according to a largely biological (physical) model of disease. The counsellor focuses much more on psychological processes and the relationship with the patient (or 'client'), and usually places far more emphasis upon attentive listening as the channel through which healing takes place. The counsellor's stance is more often one of 'being with' the patient rather than 'doing to' the patient, although this is not to imply that a counsellor's role is more passive than that of a doctor. Another distinction is the assumption that medicine is more concerned with 'objective reality' rather than the 'subjective reality' of the patient. As well as having different goals and a different kind of expertise, doctors and counsellors will also use different professional codes of practice, and may have different ethical considerations and approaches to confidentiality, not to mention differing support and supervision needs.

It is not very easy to make generalisations about the way a psychiatrist works, even though all psychiatrists are trained first as doctors. Psychiatrists will vary markedly in their styles of communication, both with patients and colleagues, and with how they view and attend to the quality of the psychiatrist–patient relationship. However, what is true for most NHS psychiatrists, as well as other doctors, is the extent to which pressures on time can influence our manner and style of communication. Unlike counsellors, most psychiatrists do not have the time to spend fifty minutes or an hour with a particular patient on a regular basis, unless part of their job description allocates time for offering psychological therapy, which I take to include counselling. The exceptions are likely to be in the case of a psychiatrist who has specialised in psychotherapy or a trainee psychiatrist expected to acquire some experience of psychotherapy.

Whilst not advocating that all psychiatrists should be trained to practise counselling or psychotherapy, it has nevertheless been argued that 'no psychiatrist worth the name should lack psychotherapeutic skills and understanding' (Holmes 2000). In other words, it is surely a basic requirement that psychiatrists know how to listen effectively, both in theory and in practice. Lamentably, though, one of the most frequent complaints made by patients of psychiatrists (as well as other doctors) is that they aren't listened to, as reflected by such comments as 'more talk and less pills' (Seligman 1995). (This is leaving aside those instances where a patient's illness manifests in a way that prevents 'normal' psychological contact and the ability to hold a conversation.) It is my impression that many psychiatrists are not well trained in the art of listening, or in the use of counselling skills. Even less are counselling skills used as a therapeutic and healing tool that is valuable and important in its own right. Counselling skills have often been taught to doctors merely as a method or lever for gaining information from the patient.

It was being drawn to working therapeutically with people that led to my desire to undertake counselling training. The value of listening in depth, the power of empathy and nonjudgemental acceptance of persons was impressed upon me early in my medical training, through my listening to others, but more through my own experience of being listened to as a client in therapy. At various points in my life, both before and since qualifying as a doctor, receiving counselling or therapy has been a 'lifeline'. It has also enabled profound personal change and growth, as well as professional development. In training as a counsellor I was also consciously rejecting a full-time career path as a psychiatrist and the heavy demands and threats to one's personal life and mental health that such a path can impose. When I began full-time psychiatric training I was required to provide out of hours (on-call) cover that could mean working anything from 60–80 hours a week.

Critical as I am of the lack of counselling skills within psychiatric practice, I wish to acknowledge that psychiatrists are only able to listen to the patient as much as the 'system' (e.g. the NHS) enables or allows them to. The psychological and practical demands of the role are very heavy. The responsibilities are great and the volume of patients passing through the ward or outpatient clinic can be overwhelming. As a psychiatrist I am aware of these pressures, many of which are imposed by poorly funded services, and, therefore, insufficient resources and time to meet increasing demand. It can often be simply too emotionally demanding to attempt to listen in a way that the patient experiences as therapeutic.

Another factor limiting the listening aspects of a psychiatrist's role is a general lack of adequate and appropriate support and supervision. Any work of a listening nature, and which conceives the relationship itself as potentially therapeutic, does make particular emotional demands, and needs to be underpinned by supervision – supervision which, amongst other things, makes room for exploring one's emotional reactions to patients and to the role of listening. In terms of its understanding of, and emphasis on, supervision, the psychiatric profession lags a long way behind the counselling profession. My own experiences of being supervised as a psychiatrist, when supervision has occurred, have not focused on the therapeutic aspects of my work in a way that has encouraged reflective practice, or been supportive and encouraging of my style of working. I do not think that my experience is unusual.

The sad fact is, then, that even if psychiatrists do have good listening skills and are able to communicate empathy and understanding, the demanding working environment and conditions, as well as lack of appropriate supervision, so often prevents the creation of a therapeutic space for the patient. This does open up a big area of debate and controversy concerning the aims and nature of psychiatry. Many psychiatrists would argue that their primary role is as an objective, scientific observer, not as someone who necessarily works in a relational way, and leaves this to other mental health professionals. Furthermore, even if one does hold ideals about the merits of listening and investing in the therapeutic alliance, one also needs to consider what is and is not practicable, given the current working environment and conditions within NHS mental health services. Add to the equation the fact that patients are more empowered to express dissatisfaction in the current climate of increasing patient expectations and patient's rights, and it is no wonder that patients so often complain about their psychiatrist's inability to listen and give them time.

From what I have said so far it is probably becoming clear that there are many instances in my psychiatric practice where my training as a counsellor influences and informs my role as a psychiatrist, particularly in trying to pay attention to the relational aspects of my work. One of the dangers of which I need to be aware, however, is the potential for role confusion. A particular challenge of having two professional identities is being alert to the different, and sometimes contrasting, pulls on me. For example, working as a counsellor (as distinct from deploying counselling skills only), I may not want to initiate discussion about treatment and diagnosis, believing this in some situations to be counter-therapeutic. I may prefer to give the client freedom to use the counselling session in the way that they feel is most constructive to them, believing this to be empowering for the client. However, if at the same time I have overall medical responsibility for that client, then not to address issues of medication or other medical issues would be a neglect of my clinical responsibility. I therefore need to be aware of the particular working context and what is expected of me by my employer in terms of the responsibilities that I am required to exercise.

Although I cannot separate my professional identities totally, I have come to the conclusion that in order to work most effectively as a counsellor, it is necessary for me not to have, at the same time, a medical responsibility for the patient. I am aware that my agenda as a counsellor may at times confuse or conflict with my agenda as a psychiatrist. This is especially so in using the person-centred approach (PCA) as my counselling orientation. I will describe later how this approach in particular differs from the medical model. However, in practice the people I usually see for counselling are those I have first seen in my clinic as a psychiatrist. When offering counselling it is necessary therefore to explain carefully the difference between my ways of working as a psychiatrist and as a counsellor. In the latter capacity I still retain medical responsibility, but I would no longer see myself as primarily providing a psychiatric intervention, although the possibility of this occurring remains. I have attempted to illustrate this in a vignette in the section 'Who should receive counselling?'.

Perceptions of counselling

What is counselling? The fact that it seems necessary to ask this basic question is indicative of the confusion that exists in psychiatric settings as to what counselling might involve and aims to provide. A particular and common problem for counsellors is that the word 'counselling' is used to describe many different types of activity. Some examples include career counselling in schools, which implies and involves guidance; or debt counselling, which involves providing practical assistance and advice; and so it becomes impossible to formulate an overall definition, since the counselling that I am describing in this chapter generally aims to give neither guidance nor advice.

Understanding the activity of counselling is further blurred by those who confuse counselling and counselling skills, i.e. by those people (including psychiatrists and other mental health professionals) who apply the terms interchangeably. The word 'counselling' is often very loosely applied in psychiatric settings. Then the danger is that counselling ceases to be understood as a clearly defined and specific activity offered by someone who has undergone a counselling training course. It has been argued that 'doctors in hospitals are much more likely to be familiar with the practice of psychology, psychotherapy and psychiatry than with counselling as a discipline in its own right' (East 1995). While mental health services and other professionals within them are not always clear about what counselling is, and misapply the term, it will remain difficult for counsellors to establish a clearly identifiable and credible role within such services. Therefore, if counsellors believe their work is important and of value, it is necessary for them to take responsibility for informing and educating colleagues and potential clients. Unless we communicate what counselling is with greater clarity, it will continue to be open to misinterpretation and criticism, as so often occurs in the current climate.

Any discussion about what counselling is must also consider psychotherapy, and how the two are frequently regarded differently, particularly within mental health services. There are, however, powerful arguments refuting the claim that counselling and psychotherapy are different activities (Thorne 1992). I am much persuaded by these arguments.

Traditionally, counselling services and psychotherapy services within the NHS are separate entities. While many mental health trusts have a psychotherapy department, NHS counselling services are a rarity. One of the reasons for this is that psychotherapy as a professional activity and academic discipline is much older than the counselling profession.

It is also rare for mental health teams to employ counsellors as individual professionals working alongside other mental health professionals. This is in line with other secondary health care settings where counselling has been said to be 'probably the most patchy and varied of all provision in medical settings' (East 1995). While psychological therapies play a key role in mental health service provision, it is much more usual for these therapies to be provided by clinical psychologists, counselling psychologists or psychotherapists than by people specifically employed as counsellors.

Increasingly, however, many mental health professionals, particularly community psychiatric nurses (CPNs) and social workers, undertake counselling or psychotherapy training and seek to integrate counselling into their daily role. But this can often create a far from ideal situation, given the many implications of assuming a dual role. I have already mentioned the potential for role confusion, the challenge of working towards professional integration and the need for appropriate supervision to explore these tensions. The need to communicate with clients clear boundaries and agreements about time are other important and potentially tricky issues.

'Psychological therapy' is such a broad term that it could encompass any activity based on communication between professional and client (usually talking) and the building up of a respectful, trusting relationship. The ultimate aim is to help the client with their psychological difficulties. Storr (1990) has similarly described the activity of psychotherapy, understood in its broadest sense, as the activity of 'alleviating personal difficulties through the agency of words and a personal, professional relationship'. Another overall but more precise definition of psychotherapy describes it as 'a form of treatment based on the systematic use of a relationship between therapist and patient...to produce changes in cognition [thinking], feelings and behaviour' (Holmes 1991). How, then, is this different from counselling?

One of the definitions that best describes the way I work views counselling as:

> ...an activity freely entered into by the person seeking help, it offers the opportunity to identify things for the client themselves... It is clearly and explicitly contracted, and the boundaries of the relationship identified. The activity itself is designed to help self-exploration and understanding. The process should help to identify thoughts, emotions and behaviours that, once accessed, may offer the client a greater sense of personal resources and self-determined change. (Russell, Dexter and Bond 1992, in Sanders 1996, p.3)

To me this doesn't sound very different from definitions of psychotherapy. Nevertheless, there is a prevailing attitude and belief within psychiatry and mental health services that counselling is not the same as psychotherapy. Furthermore, counselling is, in my experience, frequently regarded as inferior to psychotherapy.

Like many organisations the NHS has a deeply ingrained and rigid hierarchical structure, and the medical profession exemplifies this. It is not surprising then that psychotherapy, which originated from the medical profession and which has grown out of the 'medical model', should be preoccupied with its status. This status is generally derived from a lengthier training which, at the same time, tends to be of a much more weighty academic nature than counselling training. Given the fact that psychotherapists working within psychiatric settings tend also to be psychiatrists who have specialised further, it is no wonder that psychotherapy is often considered to be a much more 'expert' activity than counselling.

In my opinion, if there are differences, they are mainly in the way that counselling and psychotherapy are perceived and referred to, and in the terminology traditionally used. For example, NHS psychotherapists tend to see 'patients', while counsellors see 'clients'. Psychotherapists use more the language of 'treatment' in which they are the experts applying a treatment approach to patients, who are also often more severely disturbed. Psychotherapy departments tend to receive patients referred with the aim of resolving more long-standing personal issues. In practice, therefore, psychotherapists see patients on a more long-term basis than counsellors. It is usually more common practice for counsellors to receive clients referred with the intention that they be helped to focus on, and deal with, current problems. I realise that I am generalising, but this doesn't diminish the fact that psychotherapists are often perceived, both within professional circles and by the public, as more powerful, and therefore more effective and important than counsellors.

Both psychotherapy and counselling aim to offer a relationship and form a therapeutic alliance that is experienced by the patient or client as constructive and healing. Whether the practitioner refers to him or herself as a psychotherapist or counsellor can only obscure the issue. However, this emotive debate will continue, with the potential to threaten the helping endeavour in which the losers are our patients and clients.

A clash of language, values and philosophy

Psychiatric settings are ones in which a person-centred counsellor, or any counsellor adopting a humanistic philosophy, can often feel isolated and misunderstood, given the predominance of other theoretical orientations. Psychodynamic and cognitive-behavioural schools of counselling and psychotherapy are particularly popular.

The concepts of humanistic psychology assert the uniqueness of human beings and their intrinsic, innate capacity to change and grow, given favourable conditions, which to me is like the body's astounding capacity to repair itself and grow. It is an optimistic view that has been described by the American Association for Humanistic Psychology (1965) as 'an ultimate concern with...the dignity and worth of man and an interest in the development of the potential inherent in every person'. It has also been described as that which emphasises the 'uniqueness of the individual, the quest for values and meaning, and the freedom inherent in self-direction and self-fulfilment' (Hjelle and Ziegler 1992).

My experience in psychiatric settings is that these concepts, particularly 'the quest for values and meaning', 'self-direction' and 'self-fulfilment', do not resonate very deeply. Or if they do resonate with mental health professionals, they aren't given much weight in clinical practice, given other concerns such as 'risk management assessments', medication, formulating 'care plans' and dealing with bureaucracy. One of the other main reasons is that mental health services generally use a different paradigm of understanding mental distress. Psychiatric settings use the concept of psychiatric (mental) 'illness', or 'psychopathology', and classify disorders according to 'operational diagnostic criteria'. In other words, types of psychological disturbance and distress are given labels such as 'psychosis', 'neurosis' and 'personality disorder', with further subdivisions within these three broad categories according to particular symptoms, observed behaviours and mental state.

The 'medical model', as mentioned previously, refers, strictly speaking, to the nature of the doctor–patient relationship. Within this relationship the greater power and control rests with the doctor. A diagnostic framework for individual disorders is used as a central and determining factor in the management and treatment of the disorder. Doctors and other mental health professionals are regarded as authority figures. It is this power and control that makes psychiatrists and other mental health service professionals so often feared and hated, particularly given instances when psychiatry has subjected patients to abuse and has been used as a powerful social control agent.

The PCA provides a sharp contrast to the medical model. It is an approach that places the authority in the experience and person of the client rather than in an outside expert. From his own painful experience as a patient, Rufus May, now a clinical psychologist, recently quoted in the *Guardian: Society* (2000), believes that 'It is not right to say "doctor knows best". Psychiatrists and other professionals do have an expertise. But treatment will fail if they do not engage with clients who have an expertise about their own life.' The PCA is of value here, since it strives to redress the power imbalance in the relationship between the professional and the client and to engage with the 'expert' in the client. Bozarth (1997) states that 'it is this paradigmatic difference which differentiates the person-centred approach from other approaches'.

The PCA also aims to create a nurturing and growth-promoting environment through certain attitudes and a non-authoritarian or non-expert way of being in the relationship, exemplified in the 'core conditions' of empathy, acceptance (or unconditional positive regard, as it is also known) and congruence. Karl Gregory (2001), in Chapter 12 of this book, 'Integrating counselling within the mental health services', describes further the basic tenets of the person-centred way of working, including the core conditions. He also demonstrates effectively the importance of the quality of the relationship and the crucial factor of trust between the professional and the client.

The PCA, I believe, has a lot to say to the psychiatric profession and mental health services generally. I do not advocate dispensing with the medical model, nor with notions of diagnosis and treatment – far from it. What I would like to witness is far more constructive dialogue between professional groups schooled in different therapeutic approaches. Psychiatric settings are ones in which different terminology, models and paradigms of understanding human experience and disturbance abound. There are many languages spoken, often with different meanings for the same term. Communication between professionals, therefore, can often be characterised by misunderstanding, as well as conflict and professional protectionism. What is needed is a much greater readiness to understand each other's language, values and philosophy. A more shared understanding would enable health professionals to work more effectively alongside each other with more respect for their individual roles, models and approaches to care. Counsellors, particularly those who do not use a medical model, need to be able to respond positively to these challenges when working in psychiatric settings.

Mental health policy and the current political climate

In July 2000 the government launched *The NHS Plan* (Department of Health 2000), the purpose and vision of which is 'to give the people of Britain a health service fit for the 21st century'. It is a comprehensive document that promises a great deal, such as the NHS shaping 'its services around the needs and preferences of individual patients, their families and their carers'. As part of a drive to a cycle of continuous quality improvement, 'Quality will not just be restricted to the clinical aspects of care, but include quality of life and the entire patient experience.' Amongst things such as investment in staff, there seems also to be a new focus on prevention: 'The NHS will focus efforts on preventing, as well as treating, ill-health.' Furthermore, mental health is one of the government's top priorities, along with cancer and heart disease. There would seem much at first glance to fill counsellors and many health professionals with a long awaited sense of optimism.

It is important, though, to look in more detail at the NHS Plan, particularly where it sets out its aims for modernising mental health services. When looking in addition at the National Service Framework for Mental Health launched in 1999 (Department of Health 1999), counsellors in mental health settings might well anticipate a difficult and increasingly challenging time ahead. The current political climate and mental health policy has many implications for counsellors in these settings. In what follows I discuss a few of these implications which, if I am honest, leave me feeling rather gloomy about future counselling provision within mental health services.

'Simple solutions for complex needs'

This catchy slogan aims to summarise the latest corporate plan of one mental health trust. If only there were simple solutions for complex needs! I sometimes wonder if there is a process of denial in operation amongst politicians, mental health policy-makers and managers when it comes to addressing mental health needs. It is the nature of mental health to be complex, particularly if the aim is to provide a service that is truly 'patient-centred', as NHS health policy promises to do. It therefore seems contradictory to talk about simple solutions, especially if one is to tailor services around individual needs, which must surely take into account the uniqueness of individuals and their circumstances.

Counselling is rarely simple, and even more rarely is it regarded as a 'solution' to various mental health problems. There is at the same time a powerful drive towards short-term working, not just in counselling but across a whole range of activities within psychiatric services. Increasingly the emphasis seems to be on providing a 'quick fix'. Many counsellors, and I include myself, are uncomfortable fitting in with the prevailing philosophy of 'short-termism', which in practice means offering counselling that is time-limited. A time-limited approach will usually need to be more structured, with less flexibility to work in a way that values the individuality of both the client and the counsellor. It is, then, not much of a step to offer counselling that is totally protocol-bound, and then, before one knows it, counselling becomes as prescriptive and regimented as drug therapy.

Of course, there are many approaches to counselling or therapy whose design is deliberately prescriptive and structured, e.g. 'problem-solving counselling', 'cognitive-behavioural therapy' or 'rational-emotive behavioural therapy'. Other approaches are deliberately brief, such as 'solution-focused brief therapy'. In these approaches there is usually a specific focus envisaged as a result of the client being able to articulate clearly the problem, as well as work towards a tangible goal. Given that these approaches do lend themselves to a time-limited structure, as well as the fact that outcomes can be defined and thus more clearly measured, it is not surprising that such approaches are immensely popular amongst managers and policy-makers.

While short-term, very focused work is appropriate for some people and for certain problems, unfortunately many people, particularly those who find it difficult to articulate their distress and whose distress cannot be 'medicalised' into a clinical syndrome, will be excluded. Furthermore, there are many people referred to psychiatric services, often via their general practitioner (GP), for whom it is clear that short-term, quick-fix therapeutic work will be wholly inadequate and may sometimes be harmful. This is especially the case for people who come into contact with services carrying a deep sense of mistrust or fear of services and mental health professionals.

Clinical governance

'Revolutionary changes have occurred in NHS culture, such as clinical governance and use of performance indicators...' (Leung 2000). These terms and the activities they describe are becoming commonplace in the NHS and they also have direct implications for counsellors and counselling practice. At the very least, counsellors need to be familiar with these terms.

Clinical governance is part of the efficiency agenda of the NHS. It is a term used to 'capture the range of activities required to improve the quality of health services' (Rosen 2000). Such activities include the development of processes for continuously monitoring and improving the quality of health care and developing systems of accountability. Evidence-based practice, audit, risk management and mechanisms to monitor the outcomes of care are all part of this. The National Service Framework for Mental Health sets out standards in specific areas, implementation strategies, as well as mechanisms that aim to ensure progress.

The rhetoric used in mental health policy documents sounds at a superficial level rather utopian. Unfortunately, the reality is that the NHS and mental health services have finite resources, and this will continue to be the case despite the large financial investment promised by the prime minister in March 2000. Mental health need (however one defines need), as well as patient and public expectation, will always outweigh service provision.

Standards are an important aspect of care but in my opinion they soon become a dirty word when applied in the form of regularly subjecting employees to surveillance, regulation and evaluation of performance. The motivation to reduce costs is also clear to see. In spite of the promise of delivering a 'patient-centred' service, the reality is that services are currently 'cost-driven' rather than 'needs-driven'.

Who should receive counselling?

This question has become a routine and difficult one. Given that the NHS is a publicly funded institution, it has become necessary to decide, somehow, to whom the limited resource of counselling should be offered. Making these decisions is not just about considering which sort of patients or clients might benefit according to evidence-based research, which is currently limited. It is not easy to adopt clearly defined categories of suitability for counselling because such clarity does not always exist. Nor is it often the case of being presented with concrete problems to which 'simple solutions' can be applied, as mentioned previously.

Psychiatric services are increasingly geared towards people who can be understood by using a diagnostic framework, i.e. who are regarded as having a clearly diagnosed mental illness. Furthermore, psychiatric services are focusing on, and putting more resources into, determining 'service models' to meet the needs of the seriously mentally ill, particularly those in the community. In reality, though, mental health professionals, and GPs even more, see many people to whom a diagnosis cannot easily be applied, but whose levels of distress are nevertheless high. Should psychiatric services be resourced to respond to people with generalised distress, as well as those who are known to have a mental illness? Counselling is usually considered more appropriate for the former rather than the latter. This is another thorny issue with a long history. Suffice it to say that as long as the priorities of psychiatric services are to respond to the needs of people with serious mental illness (which largely excludes those with personality disorders), counselling will remain a neglected and under-resourced activity. Furthermore, many people will continue to be directed to the private sector for counselling, which will exclude those without the necessary financial means.

Deciding who should receive counselling means deciding who is likely to benefit most from what is on offer. In other words, it is about setting priorities. Rationing might be a less nice way of putting it. It is also still to a large extent a lottery as to who receives counselling, whether according to post code or according to policy and resource decisions made by individual mental health teams, which vary nationally and locally.

Certain factors can be taken into account when assessing whether someone might benefit from counselling. Motivation of the client is important, as well as realistic expectations on the part of the client, according to the particular counselling orientation used. It is also important that the client is able to enter into some form of contractual arrangement with the counsellor, although the parameters of that arrangement might vary over time or from client to client.

As mentioned previously, my counselling clients are usually people whom I have first seen in my outpatient clinic. A typical scenario might be:

> Steven is in his thirties. He is single and works full-time. For about a year his GP has been treating him for depression and anxiety with antidepressants, with partial success. His symptoms of anxiety have lessened, enabling him to concentrate better on his job, and he has more energy. However, he still regularly experiences bouts of despair, during which he feels suicidal. He doesn't think he would end his life, believing it would 'crush' his parents, but he cannot see the point in living and he experiences a sense of meaninglessness in which he feels both himself and his life to have no value. He also describes himself as a lonely and misunderstood person.
>
> Over the course of a couple of visits to my clinic, Steven acknowledges that medication has helped him but he feels he needs something more. He believes he needs to be able to talk through with someone his thoughts and feelings. He has found talking to me helpful but both of us acknowledge that our 15- or 30-minute appointments every 2–3 months (depending on my clinic load) wouldn't be sufficient. I therefore mention the possibility of my offering some counselling sessions that could take place weekly. He seems keen on this idea.
>
> Steven seems motivated and he also feels ready and able to explore further at some depth some of his thoughts and feelings, even though this might be painful for him to do. Motivation and a certain 'psychological readiness' are key indicators for my offering counselling. What is also important has been his willingness to trust me, and I have been impressed by his openness and honesty during our two meetings. I feel warm towards him and I sense that there is a good rapport between us. He has also understood that as a counsellor I am likely to be a lot less directive, and that my style of working with him will be different. I am not concerned that he will be unable to utilise the therapeutic space provided in counselling.

This fictional vignette describes the 'ideal' potential client, regarding whom sex, age, marital status, employment and diagnosis are factors that are not necessarily significant in deciding whether to offer counselling. I am aware, however, that in describing what is ideal there may be many 'less ideal' potential clients for whom counselling could provide an equally favourable outcome. These might be people who perhaps find it difficult to trust me initially, or who may be scared at the prospect of further exploring their thoughts and feelings on a more regular basis, or who might initially have been hoping for some clear answers or solutions to their problems from me.

Supervision and support needs

It is interesting to observe that of all the issues I have chosen to address in this chapter, I have left the issue of supervision and support to the last. It seems to me that this is probably a good reflection of how psychiatric settings regard the supervision and support needs of mental health professionals. It is also a reflection of how considering one's own needs as a carer can often be neglected or become a low priority.

As a doctor and psychiatrist I am used to dealing with the frustration of working in an environment that is not particularly alert to the supervisory and support needs of staff. This is true of the medical profession and of NHS culture in general. Supervision of junior hospital doctors, for example, has tended to be provided by the consultant on whom one relies for a reference. This 'line-management' supervision has severe limitations, yet it is not an unusual model within mental health services. Consideration of training and supervision needs often comes a poor second to meeting service requirements. This is despite the National Service Framework for Mental Health promising to provide more 'care for carers' (Department of Health 1999). However, the irony has been noted that 'while acknowledging the burden on family and informal carers there is no mention of the burdens facing professional carers' (Deahl, Douglas and Turner 2000). The ultimate irony is that the mental health needs of professionals working in increasingly stressful environments are often ignored. If the mental health needs of professionals are neglected, then the whole caring endeavour is threatened and we become unable to tend others' needs effectively.

Any method of working therapeutically that involves a heavy use of one's self requires a great deal of space for personal reflection, as well as a safe place in which to offload. I have become increasingly aware as I have been writing this of the many aspects of my work for which I need 'pit-head time':

> The British miners in the 1920s fought for what was termed 'pit-head time' – the right to wash off the grime of the work in the boss's time, rather than take it home with them. Supervision is the equivalent for those that work at the coalface of personal distress, disease and fragmentation. (Hawkins and Shohet 2000, p.51)

My impression of mental health services (including the medical profession) is that the need for pit-head time is grossly under-recognised, at least by managers and policy-makers. The counselling profession, however, is much more alert to the supervisory needs of counsellors, which it views as a fundamental, ethical component of good practice. This is just one of the areas in which counsellors can make a valuable, educative contribution to psychiatric settings.

For my own supervisory and support needs I use a mixture of group supervision, peer supervision and individual supervision which I finance myself, and which takes place outside normal working hours. Sometimes it is easy to resent this, but without these supports I am sure I would be jeopardising the level of care I provide, as well as my own health needs. It has also been important to build up good working relationships with colleagues, and I am grateful for the informal support that these relationships provide. Part of my supervision involves looking at how my personal life impacts upon my work, as well as how my various roles impact upon my personal life. I continually need to examine and reflect upon my priorities in attempting to achieve a healthy balance between my personal and professional life. Receiving my own counselling, too, can be of great importance here.

Conclusion

I do find myself very engaged in the work I do – intellectually, emotionally and spiritually. It is immensely challenging to explore the border areas between psychiatry, counselling and the person-centred approach. It is also at times very uncomfortable. The emotional demands are high and sometimes exhaustion, frustration and despair set in. However, these are outweighed by the rewards of meeting people (patients and clients) often at a profound level of human relating, and the privilege of being entrusted with their feelings and thoughts.

I am aware, though, that in struggling with some of the many challenges that I have highlighted, and which are relevant to my own work, it is all too easy for the client or patient to somehow get 'lost'. There is a danger that the therapeutic relationship becomes 'muddied' by my own frustrations and struggles, particularly within the working environment of the NHS and current mental health policy. This is one of the greatest pitfalls that the pressures and tensions of working in psychiatric settings produce. Therefore, as a reminder to myself of what I believe is important concerning most of the work I do, I will end with the following quotation about a psychiatric hospital called Mount Misery from a novel of that name by Samuel Shem (1999): 'The delivery of psychiatric care is to know as little as possible and to understand as much as possible about living through sorrow with others.' This, for me, says something about simply caring, and in a way that transcends technical skill and academic knowledge. Caring can be the greatest challenge of all, when, in a society that seems so troubled, it would often be so much easier not to.

Acknowledgements

My thanks to Jane Brown, Karen Clements, Sandra Cooper and Mary Taylor for their helpful comments during the writing of this chapter.

References

American Association for Humanistic Psychology. *Brochure for 1965–66.*

Bozarth, J. (1997) 'The person-centred approach.' In C. Feltham (ed) *Which Psychotherapy?* London: Sage.

Deahl, M.P., Douglas, B.C. and Turner, T.T. (2000) 'Full metal jacket or the emperor's new clothes? The National Service Framework for Mental Health.' *Psychiatric Bulletin 24*, 207–210.

Department of Health (1999) *A National Service Framework for Mental Health. Modern Standards and Service Models.* London: DoH

Department of Health (2000) *The NHS Plan. A Plan for Investment. A Plan for Reform.* London: DoH

East, P. (1995) *Counselling in Medical Settings.* Buckingham: Open University Press.

Gregory, K. (2001) 'Integrating counselling within the mental health services.' In K. Etherington (ed) *Counsellors in Health Settings.* London: Jessica Kingsley Publishers.

Hawkins, P. and Shohet, R. (2000) *Supervision in the Helping Professions* (second edition). Buckingham: Open University Press.

Hjelle, L. and Ziegler, D. (1992) *Personality Theories: Basic Assumptions, Research and Applications* (third edition). New York: McGraw-Hill.

Holmes, J. (1991) 'Introduction: analytic psychotherapy.' In J. Holmes (ed) *Textbook of Psychotherapy in Psychiatric Practice.* Edinburgh: Churchill Livingstone.

Holmes, J. (2000) 'Fitting the biopsychosocial jigsaw together.' *British Journal of Psychiatry 177,* 93–94.

Leung, W. (2000) 'Career focus. Managers and professionals: competing ideologies.' *British Medical Journal* classified ads, 14 October.

May, R. (2000) 'Spying on the psychiatrists. Profile: Insider who has challenged the treatment of mental illness.' *Guardian Society,* Wednesday 20 September.

Rosen, R. (2000) 'Improving quality in the changing world of primary care.' *British Medical Journal 321,* 551–554.

Russell, J., Dexter, G. and Bond, T. (1992) 'Differentiation between advice, guidance, befriending, counselling skills and counselling.' *Advice, Guidance and Counselling Lead Body.*

Seligman, M. (1995) 'The effectiveness of psychotherapy: the Consumer Reports Study'. *American Psychologist 50,* 965–974.

Shem, S. (1997) *Mount Misery.* London: Black Swan.

Storr, A. (1990) *The Art of Psychotherapy* (second edition). London: Heinemann Medical Books.

Thorne, B. (1992) 'Psychotherapy and counselling: the quest for differences.' *Counselling 3,* 4, 242–248.

Further reading

Davies, B., Gask, L. and Usherwood, T. (1997) *Medical and Psychiatric Issues for Counsellors.* London: Sage.

East, P. (1995) *Counselling in Medical Settings.* Buckingham: Open University Press.

Hammersley, D. (1995) *Counselling People on Prescribed Drugs.* London: Sage.

Hawkins, P. and Shohet, R. (2000) *Supervision in the Helping Professions* (second edition). Buckingham: Open University Press.

Tyrer, P. and Steinberg, D. (1993) *Models for Mental Disorder: Conceptual Models in Psychiatry* (second edition). Chichester: John Wiley and Sons.

Chapter 12

Integrating counselling within the mental health services

Karl Gregory

The less I control others, the more they become themselves. (*Anon*)

Introduction

Counselling was just beginning to influence the British psychiatric system when I started psychiatric nursing in the early 1980s. In this chapter I shall chart my journey through the system, from psychiatric nurse to counsellor, integrating counselling with medical, social and other psychological models. The history of the system is important, so I will briefly describe how I have experienced it and what the literature has to offer. The subject title to this chapter is vast, so I have concentrated on the core aspects of counselling. There is not the space to detail other approaches that are integrated. References used will provide further detailed information.

The main focus of this chapter is about the therapeutic relationship. I have used a client case study to demonstrate how I integrate counselling within psychiatry. The reason for using this heuristic style is that in counselling, the therapeutic relationship is subjective. My relationship with the psychiatric system is subjective, so this account too is openly subjective.

A brief historical perspective

People experiencing disturbing thoughts or perceptual difficulties, or exhibiting behaviour not acceptable to their society, have been rounded up and removed from society since the 1600s, in one way or another (Porter 1987). It was not until the 1800s that attitudes began to change. Charitable institutions (born out of religious and moral considerations) began providing more humane asylums. Then, with the rapid advance of science, it was perceived that science would eventually provide a 'cure' for what was beginning to be seen as an 'illness'. After World War II another development emerged in the shape of a social theory of 'illness'. Two army psychiatrists, Tom Main and Maxwell Jones, along with others, began achieving results by working with traumatised servicemen in therapeutic groups. Some commentators see this as the beginning of community-based mental health care (Coppock and Hopton 2000). Between 1952 and 1959 came the discovery of major tranquillisers, now renamed neuroleptics. After the establishment of the National Health Service in 1948 psychiatry began to follow two paths: a social model of care in the community and the development of new treatments in hospitals (Nolan 1993).

Training as a psychiatric nurse in the early 1980s meant learning a confusing yet exciting array of concepts, from diagnostic medical approaches to psychoanalytic theories. The medical model predominated and was presented as fact; counselling skills were taught alongside models, theories and techniques. As we developed as student nurses, these approaches were applied in the world of wards and community, individuals and groups; psychiatric hospitals were old and away from the community; 'community care' was developing (beginning in the 1950s and still continuing today!). Counselling was the 'in' word, often seen as a shift of focus that could rebalance some of the criticisms levelled at the patriarchal, authoritarian approach of the medical model.

Carl Rogers began developing his client-centred work in the USA from 1930 to the early 1940s (Kirschenbaum and Henderson 1990) and published his definitive work on client-centred therapy in 1951 (Rogers 1951). Yet it was not until the late 1970s and early 1980s that the mental health services in Britain began to see its impact. Coppock and Hopton (2000) offer some interesting reasons why this may have been so, but in truth there are no clear reasons. A common observation within the psychiatric services is that any new way of working takes years to be assimilated into the services (Georgiades and Phillimore 1975).

The counselling approach was person-centred, and emphasised self-development of the nurse. As a nurse I found it difficult to pursue counselling on a ward with any seriousness. My role was mainly that of a caring custodian, administering the medication, observing effects and side-effects as the psychiatrist requested. The core textbook of the time, discussing counselling, reads: '...neither should the nurse undermine the doctor/

patient relationship by offering advice or suggestions which are contrary to those given by the doctor' (Darcy 1984).

The nurse was expected to 'control' the behaviour of the patient while working on the ward. I remember my first introduction to these wards as a student nurse armed with theories, diagnosis and expectations, and feeling totally incompetent because I could not tell the difference between someone who was psychotic and someone who was depressed. They all appeared to be people in varying degrees of distress.

The teaching at that time was that if a patient heard voices, the nurse must not engage the person in conversation about these for fear of colluding. Yet how did I know what the patient was struggling with unless I could enter into some in-depth conversation? I could not communicate with the patient very easily using the terminology or attitudes of the medical model; this had the effect of creating a distance between the patient and me. I will explain this by describing the medical model.

The medical model

The term 'medical model' is often used to describe the approach used within the psychiatric services. Psychiatry is the study and treatment of mental disorders, and a psychiatrist is a medically qualified physician specialising in mental illness. In the nineteenth century the experience of mental distress began to be defined in terms of a somatic model, giving birth to the idea of mental *illness*. Following the work of Kraepelin and Bleuler in the late nineteenth century, mental illness was classified into two groups – psychosis and neurosis. Generally speaking, psychoses are mental disorders said to involve a lack of contact with 'reality' (experiencing hallucinations and delusions), while neuroses are disorders in which there is too much contact with 'reality' (creating anxiety or depression) (Hayes 1994).

Professionals working in psychiatry came into mainstream medicine with the creation of the National Health Service. Bringing with them social, psychological and medical theories, psychiatric professionals entered the world of scientific medicine. The medical model in psychiatry has never been purely about medicine but has incorporated, evolved through and embraced different models. This has been offered as a reason why psychiatry strengthened its professional position (Fennell 1996).

The word 'scientific' is important to understand. The science of the day (which still is the main influence in psychiatry) assumed a positivist perspective, in which only that which can be scientifically verified or is capable of mathematical or logical proof is 'true'. This involves the condition of objectivity, e.g. setting up studies in which the subject is observed within an environment of controlled variables. The observer (or researcher) attempts to be 'rigorously objective'; therefore they separate and distance themselves from the observed. To professionals within the medical model, this objectivity is important.

Although psychiatry could not claim to be exclusively a natural science, the profession was assimilated into mainstream medicine and the concept of mental illness was established (Coppock and Hopton 2000). In general, a psychiatrist works from the belief that mental illness is a physical condition caused by metabolic, genetic or biochemical abnormalities and treatable by physical methods.

However, it is not only psychiatrists who influence the psychiatric system. Although the psychiatrist is, by law, clinically responsible for the care of the patient, he or she is one of a team of professionals – clinical psychologists, nurses, social workers and occupational therapists. In fact, in today's system referrals are usually made to a mental health team. Some commentators argue that these team members have benefited from being under the umbrella of the medical model in such a way as to gain their own power and voice within the psychiatric system (Ingleby 1983).

Problems with integrating counselling skills in psychiatry

In following this concept of the medical model, I was in conflict with one of the major principles of counselling, 'congruence'. I could not be myself with the patient. I was able to appreciate that diagnostic criteria were a way of articulating experiences in terms that mental health professionals could understand and then possibly treat, but these classifications did not translate well enough to explain the experience. The relationship between the person and myself became more important.

After initial training, it is up to the nurse to continue his or her own development. Many of the nurses who were developing a counselling approach gravitated towards community care and became community or day hospital nurses. Working in the community in the 1980s as a community psychiatric nurse (CPN), I was largely left to my own devices. Basic criteria had to be fulfilled, like accepting *all* referrals, assessing for mental illness, monitoring patients who had been discharged from hospital, administering medication as prescribed and generally keeping the communication flowing between hospital, GP and the patient.

General distresses with life events were becoming increasingly medicalised; the classifications of mental illness under the medical model were ever increasing (Rose 1986). Because emotional and social difficulties were being interpreted in medical terms, an expectation arose that the psychiatric services should provide professional support. As patients with long-term mental health problems (generally diagnosed with a psychosis) were gradually transferred back into the community, the numbers of CPNs increased. As the nurses developed their practice in the community they came more into contact with GPs who valued counselling skills and could see an opening to refer patients with distressing life difficulties. The patients being discharged from the long-stay wards in hospitals generally had their own support via a rehabilitation team or continuing care nurses. Those who did not, often through lack of motivation, remained silent, and either on their own or with families or other carers taking the burden of care. There was also a myth that one could not use counselling with patients diagnosed with psychosis.

A myth explored

In the 1990s there was a dramatic change when a combination of political, economic, social and clinical developments coincided. Although caring for patients with severe mental distress in the community began in the 1950s, it was not until 1990 that the government began to legislate for this with the National Health Service and Community Care Act. There were more opportunities for community nursing with patients with continuing care needs. Having decided to work in this area I was willing to develop new skills and I was surprised at the positive response I gained with this group of people when using counselling skills. I discovered that counselling skills were absolutely necessary to begin to work with the issues ahead of us. Carl Rogers also observed this:

> Neurotic clients appear to perceive the understanding and genuineness of the therapist and thus it is natural that their central focus appears to be on self-exploration. Our schizophrenic patients on the other hand perceived primarily the levels of warm acceptance (positive regard) and genuineness. Their focus appeared to be on relationship-formation. (Rogers 1967, cited in Binder 1998, p.217)

Moving further into this work, I gained a position within a rehabilitation team for people with severe and enduring mental illness. I worked with a consultant psychiatrist who valued counselling and the skills used to work alongside people with a diagnosis of psychosis. I gained funding to study on a diploma in counselling (integrative counselling) course and obtained supervision. I began to understand why using counselling with people diagnosed with a psychosis is useful.

Principles of counselling

At this stage it is important to discuss what I mean by counselling. What defines the counsellor is the set of values and philosophical underpinning of the approach. Counselling comes from humanist beliefs about human beings, essentially stating that we all have the potential to be psychologically healthy. It is based on the 'actualizing tendency present in every living organism – the tendency to grow, to develop, to realize its full potential' (Rogers 1986, cited in Kirschenbaum and Henderson 1990).

The importance of self-regard born out of self-perception is crucial to developing and maintaining a state of psychological well-being. A person has an incredible amount of inner resources and everything that is necessary within them to reach their potential. Counselling is based on the belief that these resources exist in the person. The role of the therapist is to convey trust in the person's own innate ability and promote an environment in which they can realise their potential. To do this there are basic 'core' conditions that are necessary for a growth-promoting climate.

> The first element is genuineness, realness, or congruence... The second attitude of importance in creating a climate for change is acceptance, or caring, or prizing... The third facilitative aspect of the relationship is empathetic understanding. (Rogers 1986, cited in Kirschenbaum and Henderson 1990, pp.135–6)

I will discuss these core conditions in more detail later. Within all of this is the implicit message of the person's worth and respecting for the person's right to exist. This I feel is so relevant with today's attitude towards people who have a medical diagnosis of psychosis. Besides developing skills and understanding theory, a counsellor's training involves working on one's own self-awareness, so as to be able to offer the core conditions to the best of one's ability.

Counselling is not a technique to be applied to the patient but a basic, living philosophy of a way of being with the person. In my experience there is a tendency within the NHS to teach basic counselling skills as a technique; that is, treatment is seen as something done *to* the patient rather than *with* the person. Carl Rogers said that 'as the therapist lives these conditions in the relationship, he or she becomes a companion to the client in this journey toward the core of self' (Rogers 1986, cited in Kirschenbaum and Henderson 1990). The work in the sessions is to bring the 'will' of the core self into consciousness (Assagioli 1974). In my view the 'real therapy' is testing this out in life itself and then bringing it back to reflect on during the session.

It is important to acknowledge at this point that humanist values are not the sole domain of counsellors. As Coppock and Hopton (2000) reason, critics of the medical and behavioural models forget that 'throughout the history of British medical psychiatry it is possible to identify important humanitarian advances at both the structural and ideological levels' (Coppock and Hopton 2000). Behavioural therapists are motivated by humanitarian considerations (Skinner 1973) but counselling is more about how these principles are 'lived' within the relationship (Corey 1996). In counselling the most important tool is the therapeutic use of the self – the core self (Clarkson 1995; Wosket 1999). I believe that it is possible to integrate other medical, social and behavioural models with these principles. I shall now proceed to demonstrate this.

Pre-therapy

The following is an example from a patient case study, of how I have used counselling with a person medically diagnosed with a psychosis.

When I met John (I am not using his real name, so as to preserve his anonymity) he was very suspicious of me. I later asked him: 'John, how do you remember the first meeting we had?' And this is what he said:

I did not trust you,
I thought you were going to trick me
Into taking more medication.
Nursing staff in hospital –
Visiting nurses –
Extensions of authority.
Not my nurses.

I was sectioned,
Forced to take medication.
It was poison
No one listened to me.

I was possessed
Small parts of me separating
I had to gain control.

Good and evil manifesting
Itself in me
Evil, a counterattack
To the good that I was.

Voices winding me up
Making me shout
I was sectioned.

When I first started working with John he would not talk to me about any of this. John was diagnosed as having a psychosis, specifically classified as paranoid schizophrenia with persecutory religious delusions. His condition was perceived as resistant to medication, meaning that neuroleptic medication appeared not to be effective in treating his symptoms. He was described as having no insight into his condition, meaning that he did not accept or acknowledge that he was 'ill', and he was poor at engaging with the services. These factors had led to him being referred to the rehabilitation team.

John had isolated himself in a dingy basement flat. Socially withdrawn, he spent most of his time battling with malevolent voices. At times these would come out of his mouth with force in the shape of animal noises or violent swearwords. He did not own these actions and felt distressed and frightened at their manifestation.

When in hospital he had a particularly severe side-effect from the medication (postural hypotension) and in his words 'collapsed'. He did not trust the medication or have any experience of safety in talking about his experiences. Our first meetings were consequently hit-and-miss affairs. Sometimes John would let me into his flat; often he would refuse his medication, at other times accepting it with an attitude of resignation. I continued to offer contact, whatever his response to me. What I was offering was a 'pre-therapy' relationship (Prouty 1994).

Dion Van Werde (1998) terms this the 'contact facilitator' role. As Van Werde explains, the basic principle is that all people possess a healthy core self which can be accessed and strengthened, however small it may appear. As seen in the above conversation, John had some awareness of this himself: 'Evil, a counterattack to the good that I was.' My role was to offer a relationship in which to make contact with the healthy part of John. I used to hear professionals within the psychiatric service argue that counselling was not effective as a therapy with people diagnosed with a psychosis because this core self was fragmented and therefore not accessible. I have not found this. I believe the core self is buried under a fragmentation of self-concepts that conflict with the core self. Again, John highlights this: '…small parts of me separating, *I* had to gain control.'

To explain the contact facilitator concept further, Van Werde uses the image of a tree in which the branches, leaves, etc., are seen as everything 'up in the air' (dreams, hallucinations, daydreams, and so on), while the roots represent everything grounded with the elements needed to nourish the tree – constructive social contacts, a place in society, physical health, and so on. He argues that 'if you have a large top to carry, you also need a vast bed of roots' (Van Werde 1998). Roots, in this concept, are perceived in terms of 'anchorage'. The task in the pre-therapy relationship is to make contact with the core self of the person, then facilitate the nourishment of the roots so as to provide a stable base from which to explore the 'psychotic' experiences later.

Whenever I met with John in the early stages, I rarely discussed his problems with his hallucinations, or his belief system around them. The task in this pre-therapy relationship was to make contact with John's core self; I needed to facilitate the nurturing aspects of our relationship to provide a stable base from which later to explore psychotic experiences. So we talked of his interests: music, poetry and his scholastic knowledge of the Bible (without entering into antagonistic debate). After a while John agreed to meet me at a local café. As John explains:

> We used to go down the café
> You didn't try to talk about
> Hospitals,
> Illness
> Medication.
>
> We played badminton
> You didn't make it a
> Routine job
> You took interest in *me*
>
> We had a few things in common
> We talked about
> Music
> Poetry
> Christianity.

Then later:

> I can sense when someone is just being polite
> Not really wanting to know
> Except to write down schizophrenia
>
> The saying 'sticks and stones' is rubbish
> I know words can have a detrimental effect
> And hurt me
>
> You did not criticise me
> You were not a threat
> I had to weigh up the cost
> Of speaking my mind
>
> I thought I've got someone
> Who is here to listen
> Doesn't use authority
> To increase the medication.

This was part of building the core pre-therapy relationship. Every human being has the right to exist, the right to contact with the world around them, places, people, and so on (Van Werde 1998). Prouty (1994) describes the building of the core pre-therapy relationship as the 'pre-experiencing activity'. This has the effect of strengthening the anchorage and self-identity in a concrete here and now.

During this time John began to discuss some of his basic needs. He was not claiming the full benefits he was entitled to, so survived on very little money. He did not like or feel safe in his flat, and his relationship with his family had deteriorated. Gradually these issues needed to be addressed. Within the team we claimed for his benefits, worked with social services and secured more appropriate accommodation, and as I got to know John he agreed to begin including his family in support from the services – family work (see Barrowclough and Tarrier 1992).

John highlights the importance of the relationship. He can sense when people are only interested in finding out the symptoms, and not so genuinely interested in him as a person. To be able to trust me, John needed to feel safe in my company; for this I needed to feel rooted in myself, and sincere enough to communicate that to John in our conversations – in counselling terms, congruent. I needed to be open and willing to engage in sharing some of my own experiences – in counselling terms, appropriate self-disclosure –

and endeavour to understand the world as John construed it to be. This is 'empathetic understanding'.

Empathy is not a technique to employ every now and then; in itself it is not a technique at all. Binder (1998) suggests that empathy serves as 'an affective–motivational frame of reference'. Empathy is a 'lived' process in which one person is genuinely connecting with another through their core selves, thus being able to get a sense of what the other is experiencing; the person has a feeling of 'being seen' through this empathic listening. Empathy belongs within the 'context of a frame of reference which is structured according to the dimensions closeness–distance, known–unknown, friend–foe, clarity–confusion' (Binder 1998). John had a sense that I really wanted to know him and we both felt safe enough to choose to be in relationship with each other.

Integrating other approaches

As John engaged further into our relationship he began discussing his experiences with the voices that he heard and the beliefs he had about them. He did not perceive this as an illness, but certainly did feel that the voices were causing him problems. I understand this as insight. We were at a point in our relationship where John began to include me in the exploration of the problem. The process that is understood in the concept of anchorage is that as the roots are strengthened the person becomes strong enough to let the therapist become involved in working towards integrating the struggles and frightening experiences (Van Werde 1998). Thus the patient no longer 'is' the problem, but the problem is distanced enough for both patient and counsellor to explore collaboratively. The task of the therapist in exploring the problem is to keep the core relationship in sight. As John and I began to explore the problems, I began searching literature to discover if there was anything useful in other people's experience.

At this time, with some colleagues, I set up a group, Practical Approaches to Working with Schizophrenia (PAWS), in which a number of professionals from all aspects of the service showed interest. There was an increase in research on the social and psychological experiences of patients and their families, out of which developed what are now known as psychosocial interventions. Educational courses began to proliferate, and we developed the PAWS interest group into a diploma course for professionals in the training of psychosocial methods.

Stress vulnerability models (Nuechterlein and Dawson 1984; Zubin and Spring 1977) emphasise several factors that interact, e.g. inherited and environmental. The relationship between stress and vulnerability underpins psychosocial interventions (Clements and Turpin 1992). Using these models, psychosocial interventions integrate medical, social and psychological approaches; cognitive behavioural therapy (CBT) is the main psychological input. (Literature in this area in now massively increasing, so it will not be possible in the confines of this chapter to present an in-depth discussion of this.) Cognitive behavioural approaches provide researched, specific assessments and techniques for working with people with mental disorders, using a phenomenological approach. Cognitive approaches pay attention to the patient's experience and bring the importance of the experience into prominent view within psychiatry, as did Laing (1959, 1982) and Rogers (1967).

The cognitive behavioural view is that the patient–therapist relationship, although important, is not sufficient for behavioural change to occur. The problem with this view is that it often leads to an assumption that the therapeutic relationship exists between the patient and therapist: as Corey argues some therapists are 'so anxious to work towards resolving problems that they are not fully present with their client', consequently 'focusing on the presenting issues instead of listening to the client's deeper messages' (Corey 1996). (In today's 'blame culture' within the NHS, often emphasised by the media, it is understandable why some clinicians are driven by anxiety to resolve problems.)

However, also on the theme of empathy in a therapeutic relationship, Binder (1998) argues that empathy alone may be inadequate. If empathy were the only behaviour available to protect ourselves, we would be overwhelmed emotionally and socially, no longer being able to regulate our own basic needs. (People with psychosis often experience this.) Binder suggests that a cognitive/social perspective is also necessary. However, a cognitive/social perspective, being rationally focused, 'can produce, on the one hand, flexible and quick decisions and evaluations, which are based on life experiences, and on the other hand rigid, narrow-minded patterns of expectation and judgement which block access to genuine experiencing' (Binder 1998). In reality both empathic and cognitive/social perspectives need to be intergrated.

Within the psychosocial model the importance of the therapeutic relationship is addressed by focusing on counselling skills in terms of engagement (Gamble 2000). Gamble reports the views of users of psychiatric services when she asked them to brainstorm what qualities they thought practitioners required. Nearly all the qualities named matched the principles of counselling!

As the relationship between John and me developed, we began exploring elements of the voices he was hearing and his beliefs about them. I integrated some appropriate CBT assessments and techniques, which John found useful to explore. (There is now a whole range of assessment tools within the CBT approach (Gamble and Brennan 2000).) To work with these within our relationship, John and I had to reinterpret some of them in language that was acceptable to John. In research terms this would render them invalid, but in practical terms their validity was in the usefulness of the assessments for *both* John and me. Cognitively we explored the number of voices, frequency, duration, location and content (Chadwick and Birchwood 1996; Romme 1998). We discussed what John believed about the voices, and he constantly checked with me how I valued him for having these beliefs. I would own and offer my own belief system without forcing it onto John, thus always keeping the relationship between us central.

Miller (2000) explores the work done by Monty Roberts (1997) in humane aspects of horse training, in which Roberts uses a method called 'join up'. Miller and Rollnich (1991) combine humanistic, client-centred approaches with cognitive behavioural therapy, calling this motivational interviewing. In his paper, Miller (2000) argues that the relationship must always be kept within view of the therapist and the patient: 'An important common point here is that it is the *relationship* that provides the atmosphere within which rapid change is possible' (Miller 2000).

As John explained:

> The way we discussed my life
> Demanded me to be honest
> For you to accept me
> As I am
>
> You weren't just a professional
> With techniques
> Like a child
> Playing with a tank
>
> You kept your private life
> But
> You didn't shut the door
> On

Letting me know
What
You were like
You still said how you felt.

In this exploration we were both in a state of wonder, both equally able to examine John's experiences. I would offer different perspectives as hypotheses; I did not know how they would work for John, but he would discuss them within his own belief system and test them out. He developed different strategies, which he consolidated after further discussion. John's evaluation of them focused not so much on the techniques but, again, more on the therapeutic relationship:

You let me open up about the voices
The manifestation was out
In the open

The shock was out
You didn't react
Negatively

You didn't get me back into hospital
You were listening and understanding
Not talking me out of it
Not telling me to be responsible
Or get in control

We talked of spiritual things
You didn't make me feel an idiot
For believing
What I believe

Other people just think I'm strange
There is purpose to our conversation
If you're not on the same wavelength
It must sound strange

Medication

John and I examined the effect of his medication (Brennan *et al.* 2000; Day *et al.* 1995; Healy 1997). As previously mentioned, John had no trust in what the doctors were prescribing. In his experience, medication did not have any beneficial effect on the voices, in fact he discovered that it blocked the 'will' of his core self to respond. This frightened him further, to the point that he believed he was being poisoned. He stated that he would take medication to keep the 'authorities' off his back. This put our relationship under a certain amount of strain whenever the subject arose.

> I don't think the medication
> Has done anything
> To help my problems
>
> You would talk about it
> As if the medication
> Was helping me
>
> Which is what the doctors did
> This wasn't from
> My point of view.

Recently researchers and clinicians have been using the Health Belief Model (Becker and Maiman 1975) in exploring levels of compliance in taking medication (Kemp, Hayward and David 1997). What has been discovered is that 'perceived benefits' and 'perceived severity' are the two most important issues for people diagnosed with a psychosis, when considering medication (Adams and Scott 2000). John felt the medication had no perceivable positive effect on his experience; it made him feel worse, so he was not willing to take it. Ironically, the 'perceived severity' for him was that when he did not take the medication and then expressed the severity of his experience with voices, he would be admitted to hospital.

When working with issues of compliance, clinicians now see the necessity of developing a collaborative relationship in which the patient is able to act on informed choice rather than coercion (Faulkner 1999). Again, the therapeutic relationship is central to the issue.

As John began to explore any benefits from taking medication, he discovered that if he took at night the doses prescribed throughout the day, then the side-effects of sedation actually helped him sleep better. In collaboration with the consultant psychiatrist John adjusted the dose and found some benefit from taking medication.

So, by integrating medical, social and psychological models (the psychosocial model) within the counselling relationship, John began benefiting from engaging with the psychiatric system and, as he comments:

Some things
> I began to see
> I could
> Work out
> For myself

Conclusion

For three years I managed a rehabilitation team for patients experiencing severe and enduring mental illnesses, and I observed that we were at our most effective when approaches were integrated within an atmosphere of respect.

Every relationship, every need expressed, every counselling process, every 'psychotic' experience, *every person* is unique. In this chapter I have attempted to demonstrate that uniqueness, and at the same time to show how, by using the principles underpinning counselling, we may be invited to 'join in' with a person's experience of 'psychosis'.

It seems probable that an individual's experience of psychosis 'represents a complex interaction between genetically transmitted capacities and environmental influences' (Birchwood, Hallett and Preston 1989). Consequently our approaches need to reflect this. Within the psychosocial model different approaches are being integrated, with increasing awareness that the quality of the therapeutic relationship is central to communication with people experiencing psychosis.

An integrated model maintains that psychiatry is not an exact science and that the causes of psychosis are multi-factorial. The approach used in psychiatry needs to be geared to the needs of the individual person in the context of the society in which she or he lives. The appropriate models need to be integrated to help the person achieve their maximum potential with the minimum disruption to their biological, psychological and social systems.

Postscript

On a final note, the communication between John and me has not been one-sided, with me showing him 'the way'. We have come a long way on the journey, and at times I have found his beliefs profound as I explore my own position in life. The other day, when we were discussing the contents of this chapter, he asked:

You know all this
Empathy
Stuff

Isn't it
Another word
For
Love?

References

Adams, J. and Scott, J. (2000) 'Predicting medication adherence in severe mental disorders.' *Acta Psychiatrica Scandinavica 101*, 119–124.

Assagioli, R. (1974) *The Act of Will: A Guide to Self-Actualisation and Self-Realisation.* Woking: Platts.

Barrowclough, C. and Tarrier, N. (1992) *Families of Schizophrenic Patients: Cognitive Behavioural Intervention.* London: Chapman and Hall.

Becker, M. H. and Maiman, L. A. (1975) 'Sociobehavioural determinants of compliance with health and medical care recommendations.' *Medical Care 13*, 10–24.

Binder, U. (1998) 'Empathy and empathy development with psychotic clients.' In B. Thorne and E. Lambers (eds) *Person-Centred Therapy: A European Perspective.* London: Sage.

Birchwood, M. J., Hallett, S. E. and Preston, M. C. (1989) *Schizophrenia: An Integrated Approach to Research and Treatment.* New York: New York University Press.

Brennan, G., Roberts, C., Gamble, C. and Chan, T. F. (2000) 'Chemical management of psychotic problems.' In C. Gamble and G. Brennan (eds) *Working with Serious Mental Illness: A Manual for Clinical Practice.* London: Baillière Tindall and Royal College of Nursing.

Chadwick, P. and Birchwood, M. (1996) 'Cognitive therapy for voices.' In G. Haddock and P. Slade (eds) *Cognitive-Behavioural Interventions with Psychotic Disorders.* London: Routledge.

Clarkson, P. (1995) *The Therapeutic Relationship.* London: Whurr.

Clements, K. and Turpin, G. (1992) 'Vulnerability models and schizophrenia: the assessment and prediction of relapse.' In M. Birchwood and N. Tarrier *Innovations in the Psychological Management of Schizophrenia: Assessment, Treatment and Services.* Chichester: Wiley.

Coppock, V. and Hopton, J. (2000) *Critical Perspectives on Mental Health.* London: Routledge.

Corey, G. (1996) *Theory and Practice of Counselling and Psychotherapy.* London: Brooks and Cole.

Darcy, P. T. (1984) *The Theory and Practice of Psychiatric Care.* London: Hodder and Stoughton.

Day, J. C., Wood, G., Dewey, M. and Bentall, R. P. (1995) 'Self-rating scale for measuring neuroleptic side effects validated in a group of schizophrenic patients.' *British Journal of Psychiatry 160*, 650–653.

Faulkner, A. (1999) 'Weighing the evidence.' *Mental Health Nursing 19*, 3, 3.

Fennell, P. (1996) *Treatment without Consent.* London: Routledge.

Gamble, C. (2000) 'Using a low expressed emotion approach to develop positive therapeutic alliances.' In C. Gamble and G. Brennan (eds) *Working with Serious Mental Illness: A Manual for Clinical Practice.* London: Baillière Tindall and Royal College of Nursing.

Gamble, C. and Brennan, G. (2000) 'Assessments: A rationale and glossary of tools.' In C. Gamble and G. Brennan (eds) *Working with Serious Mental Illness: A Manual for Clinical Practice.* London; Baillère Tindall and Royal College of Nursing.

Georgiades, N. J. and Phillimore, L. (1975) 'The myth of the hero-innovator and alternative strategies for organisational change.' In C. C. Kierman and F. P. Woodford (eds) *Behaviour Modification with the Severely Retarded.* London: Associated Scientific Press.

Hayes, N. (1994) *Foundations of Psychology: An Introductory Text.* Surrey: Nelson.

Healy, D. (1997) *Psychiatric Drugs Explained.* London: Mosby.

Ingleby, D. (1983) 'Mental health and social disorder.' In S. Cohen and S. Scull (eds) *Social Control and the State.* Oxford: Blackwell.

Kemp, R., Hayward, P. and David, A. (1997) *Compliance Therapy Manual.* London: Institute of Psychiatry.

Kirschenbaum, H. and Henderson, V. L. (eds) (1990) *The Carl Rogers Reader.* London: Constable.

Laing, R. D. (1959) *The Divided Self.* London: Tavistock.

Laing, R. D. (1982) *The Voice of Experience.* Harmondsworth: Penguin.

Miller, W. R. (2000) 'Motivational interviewing: some parallels with horse whispering.' *Behavioural and Cognitive Psychotherapy 28*, 285–292.

Miller, W. R. and Rollnich, S. (1991) *Motivational Interviewing: Preparing People to Change Addictive Behaviour.* London: Guilford Press.

Nolan, P. (1993) *A History of Mental Health Nursing.* London: Chapman and Hall.

Nuechterlein, K. H. and Dawson, M. E. (1984) 'A heuristic vulnerability–stress model of schizophrenic episodes.' *Schizophrenia Bulletin 10*, 300–312.

Porter, R. (1987) *A Social History of Madness: Stories of the Insane.* London: Weidenfeld and Nicolson.

Prouty, G. (1994) *Theoretical Evolutions in Person-Centered/Experiential Therapy.* New York: Praeger.

Roberts, M. (1997) *The Man who Listens to Horses: The Story of a Real-Life Horse Whisperer.* New York: Random House.

Rogers, C. R. (1951) *Client-Centred Therapy.* London: Constable.

Rogers, C. R. (ed) (1967) *The Therapeutic Relationship and its Impact: A Study of Psychotherapy with Schizophrenics.* Madison: University of Wisconsin Press.

Rogers, C. R. (1986) 'A client-centred/person-centred approach to therapy.' In I. Kutash and A. Wolf (eds) *Psychotherapist's Casebook.* San Francisco: Jossey-Bass

Romme, M. A. J. (1998) *Understanding Voices: Coping with Auditory Hallucinations and Confusing Realities.* Cheshire: Handsell.

Rose, N. (1986) 'Law, rights and psychiatry.' In P. Miller and N. Rose (eds) *The Power of Psychiatry.* Cambridge: Cambridge University Press.

Skinner, B. F. (1973) *Beyond Freedom and Dignity.* Harmondsworth: Pelican.

Van Werde, D. (1998) '"Anchorage" as a core concept in working with psychotic people.' In B. Thorne and E. Lambers (eds) *Person-Centred Therapy: A European Perspective.* London: Sage.

Wosket, V. (1999) *The Therapeutic Use of the Self: Counselling Practice, Research and Supervision.* London: Routledge.

Zubin, J. and Spring, B. (1977) 'Vulnerability: a new view of schizophrenia.' *Journal of Abnormal Psychology 86,* 260–266.

Chapter 13

Training and supervision issues for counsellors working in health settings

Kim Etherington

Introduction

During the planning phase for this book I placed an advertisement in *Counselling*, the journal of the British Association for Counselling and Psychotherapy (BACP), asking if there were people working in health settings who would be interested in writing a chapter. I had already chosen most of the contributors and just needed a couple more, so I was a bit overwhelmed by the number of responses I received from all sorts of interesting people: counsellors working in occupational health, a doctor/counsellor who offered counselling to junior doctors, someone who combined being a homeopath with being a counsellor, an accident and emergency nurse who also offered counselling, a counsellor working with people with ME, and others whose contributions were eventually included in this book. There were so many I wanted to include that I rethought my original idea and decided to create two books instead of one! (Even this did not allow me the space to use all of the contributions that were offered.) *Counsellors in Health Settings* is the first book; the second, *Rehabilitation Counselling in Mental and Physical Health*, which will be published later in 2001, aims to provide insight into how counselling is integrated into the field of rehabilitation. Rehabilitation counselling is a vast subject and deserves a separate book.

As I read the chapters that became this book and thought about what counsellors were explicitly or implicitly identifying as concerns, I began to recognise that two clear categories were emerging: training and supervision.

So in this chapter I will focus mainly on training and add some thoughts about supervision.

Training

As you may have noticed, many of the chapters of this book are written by counsellors who have previously trained in other helping roles. In general, it is not unusual for counselling trainees to hold previous qualifications and have a wide range of life experiences. Sometimes people retrain as counsellors because their working lives are no longer satisfying, or because some life crisis has awakened their interest in counselling through their own experience of being counselled. Sometimes the job they initially trained for has changed beyond recognition and moved them into areas in which they have no interest. Social workers, teachers, nurses, for instance, finding themselves buried in paperwork, can feel that they have lost the contact with people that previously made their work so satisfying.

Others, mostly women, might never have had a prior training but may have extensive life experience, having reached a stage in their lives when they have time for their own development, perhaps after their children have flown the nest. Emmy van Durzen (1998) says of this group: 'I now know that there is one group of people better qualified than others, not through professional knowledge, but through biology, to claim an intimate knowledge of the transitions of life and death.' However, motherhood and fatherhood are not the only life experiences that qualify people to become counsellors – rather, that people are open to whatever those experiences have brought.

Traditional training

Generally, counselling training focuses on providing trainees with skills, theories and personal development that will equip them to engage with individuals or couples in a boundaried relationship over time. When I say 'boundaried' I mean that this relationship is usually one-to-one, or maybe one-to-two; it also means 'separate' in that there is no other relationship with the client(s), and that the 'edges' of the relationship are clearly defined and held in terms of regularity, time and place.

Although training often includes a 'people-in systems' approach (Egan and Cowan 1979) to help counsellors understand how family, social and cultural systems impact on lives, it is not directed to helping counsellors who will end up working in systems where they are members of a team. Counselling training does not usually cover in any depth organisational issues and dynamics; team working; awareness of the differences between working with a medical model and a biopsychosocial model; the possible impact of medication on counselling; an understanding of a variety of models of health and illness; time-limited approaches – all of which are important for counsellors working in health settings. Susan McDaniel, an American professor of psychiatry writing in the foreword of Bor *et al.* (1998), says: 'Health care has its own culture, its own rituals, its own practices, that require counsellors to adapt the style and even the substance of their treatment to be effective.'

Contextualised training

In response to the increasing number of GPs who employ counsellors in their surgeries, a few courses have been designed to provide specific training. The Counselling in Primary Care Trust (CPCT) commissioned research to discover what was offered by training organisations to ensure that counsellors who wanted to work in primary care were adequately informed (Einzig, Curtis-Jenkins and Basharan 1992). This research revealed that little attention had been paid to training for this context, the belief being that generic training was adequate in any context. Following on from this, twenty five counsellors, who were already experienced in primary care, were asked what counsellors should be taught to prepare them well for the context (Einzig, Curtis-Jenkins and Basharan 1995). The message was clear: there were several areas of need that were highlighted, namely: team membership and collaboration; models of health and illness; time-limited approaches; and personal and professional development.

In response to this information the CPCT commissioned Penny Henderson to design a one-year course that would attract qualified counsellors who wanted additional, contextualised training to support them in primary care. Back in 1995 I was employed by the University of Bristol to set-up and run one of these courses. Four other centres also attempted to establish the course, and for several years course leaders met to develop their ideas with the support of the CPCT, who also gave generous start-up bursaries to students applying for the first three courses. Since then the Bristol course (one of the few to survive) has developed into a two-year professional counselling qualification which has now received BACPP accredited status. At that time the course also broadened its aims to include education for counsellors who were working, or wanting to work, in health settings other than GP surgeries, such as hospitals, hospices, rehabilitation centres and voluntary, charitable or private organisations concerned with matters of health and illness. It was hoped that this would encourage a wider range of people than those simply wishing to work in primary care, including perhaps health professionals involved in rehabilitation, such as occupational therapists, psychologists, physiotherapists, speech therapists, nurses and perhaps doctors, to gain a counselling qualification. It was also our intention to raise awareness of counselling as a resource for everybody during a period of illness, loss or major transition, and to interest people in the idea that the psychological and emotional needs of patients are equal in importance to their medical needs, not just in primary care but in other health settings too.

However, currently there are very few courses that provide training for counsellors who work in both primary and secondary care, notably the Diploma/MSc in Counselling in Primary Care/Health Settings (Bristol University) mentioned above, and MSc in Rehabilitation Counselling (Brunel University). New courses are becoming established for primary care counsellors. Other courses have focused on the needs of counsellors in other organisational settings, commerce and industry, e.g. Diploma/MSc in Counselling at Work, run by Bristol University.

From modernist to postmodernist perspectives

Counselling training that has traditionally taught students to work within tight boundaries is based on the belief that a client needs a safe place in which to find the 'true' self. This belief arises from the teaching of the earliest psychoanalysts, who described the core of the person as dangerous, violent and sexual (McLeod 1997), and is based on a pathological view of a person as needing to gain insight which may be provided by the 'expert' analyst. This is built upon the assumption of progress: that the person will be better in the future because we have expert help at hand. This modernist view reflects the essentially positivist philosophy that grew up during the first half of the twentieth century and has underpinned Western European therapeutic approaches – unchallenged until very recently.

Behaviourism and cognitive behaviourism are approaches that also developed within the positivist culture of experimentation, science and modernism. Within these models people are encouraged to develop techniques and strategies to deal with the constraints of external forces that have influenced their behaviour in certain situations. Behaviourists consider a well-adjusted person to be someone who can take control of these external forces, and make choices and appropriate decisions for dealing with them.

Lenny (1993) suggests that when a person becomes ill or disabled their problems are caused not only by their inability to make choices or appropriate decisions, but 'because every aspect of the world in which they live denies them any form of control over their lives'. Illness and disability, in these terms, is not so much a problem of the individual but of the society in which we live.

Later Carl Rogers challenged both the psychoanalytical and behaviourist views, seeing instead the core of the person as full of positive potential. He was much more concerned with helping people explore their personal situations and the meanings these had for them. He proposed that, given the right conditions, the 'core' of the person could emerge; he saw the main vehicle for change as a therapeutic relationship that would provide the safety in which the 'real' self could actualise. This approach still implies that individuals are responsible for their difficulties and require professional expert skills to put them right.

For people who are already struggling to overcome the effects of illness or impairment, any or all of these beliefs, if offered as 'facts' or 'truths', may serve to compound their problems. Postmodernism is a term that usually implies an abandonment of such certainty and 'truth' (Speedy 2001), challenging the idea that there is a reality that can be proven with the idea that 'reality' and knowledge are socially constructed (Gergen 1994). We are also challenged to search for moral frameworks that are expanded by global thinking now made accessible through the use of technology (Frank 1995).

We need to remember that psychological theories have evolved within the context of knowledge available at the time and that these 'stories' may not necessarily fit with a person's experience of their current lives. Postmodern thinking encourages us to view the person within the context of the stories available to them through family, culture, religion and organisation. When we explore with them how their beliefs, constructs, language, assumptions and myths may influence and limit their ways of viewing their identity and their problems, this can assist the development of new perspectives on their ability to cope (Gergen 1992, 1994). Counselling can then be regarded as a social rather than a purely psychological process (McLeod 1999).

Viewing the problem from a different position can free clients from identifying *themselves* as the problem, thus allowing them to gain some leverage, power and agency. People can sometimes describe themselves as 'a cancer victim' or 'a depressive' rather than a person who has cancer or depression. Through questioning and deconstructing this limiting identification people can create alternative, perhaps richer, stories that might allow them to become more aware of their strengths and resources as well as their difficulties. Narrative therapists describe this process as 'thickening' a previously 'thin' story (Freedman and Combs 1996; Monk *et al.* 1997; Speedy 2001; White and Epston 1991).

The context

In the preceding chapters authors have described how it is rarely possible in health settings to create the conditions normally required for the practice of traditional therapy, both in terms of working over a long period of time and/or of having the private space that seems to be required. Intensive care units are full of noise, bright lights, crying children, bustling activity, and the client may be seen only once or intermittently, alone or with other members of the family or friends. Clients who are seriously ill or disabled may need to be seen in their own homes or on the hospital ward – requiring flexibility from the counsellor, who may need to deal with interruptions over which they have no control, but which may mirror the reality of the client's daily life. Counsellors working in general practice might see clients in a different doctor's room every week; several members of the same family might be referred to them concurrently; they might have to deal with questions from receptionists or cleaners who see their neighbours heading off towards the counselling room.

Counsellors who have been trained to believe that useful work can only be done if clients can commit to regular, weekly fifty-minute or one-hour slots over a period of months, or maybe years, might feel undermined by this approach, fearing that others will not value their work as 'proper counselling'. In the context of health settings, however, clients may disappear for weeks on end back into the care of surgeons or other health professionals, or they might be discharged from hospital between one session and the next without any consultation with the counsellor. Young people attending a sexual health clinic sometimes have a lifestyle that makes a regular or long-term commitment impossible or unnecessary.

Another major factor for people working in health settings is that the counselling relationship is often not 'boundaried' in the sense that it is exclusive or separate. Counsellors frequently have dual roles within the same organisation, e.g. a nurse working in an accident and emergency department who offers a separate counselling service to clients whose friends or relatives may have died following an emergency admission; a patient advocate who offers herself in a separate counselling role to those who have brought a complaint about the service that they or their relatives have experienced during a stay in hospital. Working across dual roles entails extra skills and awareness that can be developed by relevant training.

Gillian Grant (2000), who has a background in nursing and is now trained as a counsellor, has set up an inpatient counselling service in a hospital in Northern Ireland. She wonders if perhaps 'those providing forms of counselling within hospital settings are feeling confused as to what it is they are doing'. Penny Cook, herself having been a nurse, states in her chapter that good attention should be paid to the difference between being a nurse who uses counselling skills to enhance her communication without taking on the role of counsellor, and someone who has a clear contract with a client who perceives her in the role of counsellor.

Team membership

It is important for counsellors to have an understanding of the unconscious dynamics that may be called into play in organisational settings and sufficient self-awareness to recognise when these dynamics threaten their relationships with other team members or clients. Counsellors in health settings who are aware of their internalised boundaries might more quickly recognise their part in situations where blurred boundaries might endanger the work.

Wiener and Sher (1998) suggest that counsellors generally work in a closed system and that many have an antipathy towards institutions and organisations. If this is the case then it is likely that they will not seek to explore ways to take full advantage of the setting, with its possibility of collaboration with other professionals and clients who are rarely seen in other settings.

Collaboration challenges the modernist assumption that therapeutic success depends upon a boundaried relationship, by recognising that 'one person's contribution may complement and strengthen the contributions of others' (Seaburn *et al.* 1996). The identity of the other contributors depends upon who, within the particular context, shares a commitment to clients' goals, whether they are other professionals, family or friends. Seaburn *et al.* suggest that even people with different backgrounds and experiences can work collaboratively if they are able to make good relationships with one another. This is particularly pertinent when those trained in the medical model work collaboratively with counsellors who are more at home with the biopsychosocial model. Generally counsellors are at an advantage when forming relationships because of their training and skills in building relationships.

I believe that a training that invites counsellors to explore the values that they might have in common with other professionals, and how they might work together, will develop their interest and confidence in their ability to make a fuller contribution in health settings. This is a view shared by others (Bor *et al.* 1998; Curtis-Jenkins *et al.* 1997; Einzig *et al.* 1995).

Confidentiality

The boundaries of confidentiality are complex for counsellors working in health settings. The British Association for Counselling and Psychotherapy has recently amended its codes of practice in response to the difficulties created by an earlier document for counsellors in health settings. In general, traditional health care providers understand 'confidentiality' to mean that information about patients can be shared with one another.

Julia Segal describes this in her chapter as 'unit confidentiality', which she sees as different from 'counsellor confidentiality'. Unit confidentiality is information that is shared by other workers in the unit, while counselling session notes are kept separately. Even though a considerable amount of thought has gone into this matter it is clear from Segal's writing that it is an issue with which she continues to struggle and debate. The newly proposed amendments to the BACP code of ethics base decisions about confidentiality upon ethical principles that each counsellor must work through with her colleagues and her clients (BACP Draft 2001). All counselling clients have a right to confidentiality and there can be serious legal ramifications if personal material is disclosed without the patient's consent.

Gillian Grant (2000) describes how she overcame a hurdle about contracting with patients about confidentiality when setting up a hospital counselling service. She had to try to convince ten consultants that what she proposed 'would not only be beneficial but would not be harmful to the patients in their care'. The consultants were anxious that they would be excluded from having information about their patients which, if known, might alter the care and treatment they provided. After careful consideration of the implications for her clients and her own integrity, and discussion with each consultant, Grant resolved the issue by including in the counselling contract a clause which stated: 'If information discussed during counselling might change the course of treatment then, after discussion with the client, this would be brought to the attention of their consultant.'

In health settings clients are frequently surprised by the notion that information will *not* automatically be shared with other team members, as this is the 'norm' within the medical culture. However, the most important factor is that the counsellor should clarify, at the stage of contracting with the client, any limitations on confidentiality. It is the counsellor's responsibility to ensure that clients fully understand and agree to the contract. Agreement should be reached about what information can be shared, and with whom; it is particularly important for counsellors working in a hospital or hospices to consider this in terms of information that might be sought by concerned family members. Counsellors need to seek permission to speak to family or friends, in the same way as they need to seek permission to speak with other professionals. With this clarity the client can then make a choice about whether or not they wish to enter into a counselling relationship. In health settings it is particularly important to make clear the difference between 'using counselling skills' and 'counselling'.

Time-limited counselling

It has been recognised that there are cultural, professional, training and economic forces that influence our attitudes and readiness to engage with the practices of time-limited counselling (Elton-Wilson 1996; Feltham 1997; Hudson-Allez 1997; Thorne 1999). Brian Thorne asks if by offering short-term therapy we are colluding with the frantic busy-ness of people's lives: 'Could it be...that short-term therapy is the inevitable dysfunctional response to a sick society and that it seems to work for that very reason?' Yet he also recognises that when he offered three-session therapy it seemed to work well when clients were able to focus on a specific issue, prepare for the first session in advance and remain single-minded.

Others have looked for ways of maintaining their fundamental person-centred beliefs, which on the face of it seem to militate against the incorporation of solution-focused, time-limited approaches, by exploring the similarities and differences between the models and arriving at a way of valuing both (Hales 1999). However, de Shazer, a co-founder of solution-focused therapy, states that it is not possible to integrate solution-focused therapy into other models, as the focus on problems rather than solutions changes the ethos of what we are doing (O'Connell and de Shazer 2000).

Time-limited counselling can encompass a variety of meanings; there are those who have described a single-session model (Talmon 1990) and those who normally offer multiples of from four to sixteen sessions (Ryle 1990).

Many employee assistance services, GP surgeries and student counselling services offer between six and eight sessions as a way of meeting the demands on their services. However, the term 'time-limited' usually implies an attitude rather than a prescription of a required number of sessions.

Attitudinally, planned time-limited counselling requires that the counsellor and the client agree to accept a set of values as to what therapy can and cannot do. These values almost always develop and gain credibility because of system demands for low-cost care and a large population of treatment users. Because of the pressures on all mental health professionals at this time, we may have to think increasingly 'brief', realistically and efficiently. Patients in health settings are used to time-limited interventions and are often surprised to be offered a whole hour or fifty minutes of a counsellor's time, being more used to seven to ten minutes of attention from their doctors. It may be beyond their expectations to be offered even more hours. Clients' ability to value time-limited work is likely to be influenced by the manner in which the contract is made. A counsellor who apologetically offers 'only six sessions' will impart a message of deprivation rather than plenty. However, this will depend upon whether the counsellor herself is able to value time-limited approaches.

Budman and Gurman (1988) suggest that counsellors seem most ready to value time-limited counselling when they can think systemically, believing that by effecting change in one area, people can make changes in other areas of their lives through the 'ripple effects'. They also suggest that the most successful time-limited counsellors believe that:

- people are always changing and developing – rather than believing that there is a hardened character structure that has usually been laid down by the age of 6: the time-limited counsellor maintains an adult developmental perspective assuming a degree of continuing change throughout a person's life, and sees the counsellor's role as helping the client negotiate some of those tasks

- 'least is best': the less time people spend in therapy the more time they will spend living their lives

- the concept of 'cure' is inconceivable: the human condition is such that anxieties, doubts, losses, changes and conflicts are pervasive

- health rather than an illness is a preferred orientation, while maintaining appreciation of the role of diagnosis and appropriate medical intervention

- the client's presenting problem should be taken seriously and hopes affirmed of helping them make changes in some of the areas specified: the problem should be collaboratively and consensually defined and a planned approach agreed

- changes occur after therapy has ended, and the counsellor will not necessarily observe them

- therapy may be 'for better or for worse', and not everybody who requests therapy needs or can benefit from it

- being in the world is more important than being in therapy. Most brief therapists are interested in emphasising current relationships, present-centred problems and ongoing life situations.

Working in this way requires the maintenance of a clear and specific focus and realistic goals. The attitude of 'not having to do it all now' allows the counsellor to centralise a particular problem without becoming bogged down in the task of total personality reconstruction. Believing that the person is not the problem, but that the problem is the problem, means that we dispense with notions of 'damaged personality'.

Feltham (1997) suggests that there are certain people, rather than certain problems, who may not benefit from time-limited counselling. He includes in this list:

- people who are not willing to take responsibility for their own lives

- people for whom brief work might become a collusion with what he called 'hurry sickness' or who have difficulty in allowing themselves to contact their dependency needs

- people he believes to be psychologically damaged, who are without support or resources

- people who have an agenda of 'personal growth'.

Although I can understand the reasoning for such exclusions, I would not like to dismiss any client as potentially unable to make use of time-limited work. There are indeed those who seem to require long-term therapy, but I also recognise that short, focused intervention can have an important part to play in the overall therapeutic process, including a process of working towards further referral.

Steve de Shazer, who co-founded solution-focused brief therapy with his partner, Insoo Kim Berg, says that clients who are attracted by the description 'brief therapy' will benefit from brief therapy (O'Connell and de Shazer 2000). I would agree with that, provided that the counsellor also values brief therapy. If client and counsellor have shared attitudes and expectation of the work, this will surely increase the potential for success.

Assessment

It is clear from the above that assessment is an important skill for time-limited counsellors in health settings, but it is also important to bear in mind that assessment can involve other people who have insight and information that can be helpful – members of the team, particularly the person who referred the client for counselling; and the client (Cummings 1998).

The client needs to be centrally involved in the assessment process. We need to find out if the client is self-referred, and if not, why he thinks he has been referred. His answer will inform the assessment. From which position does the client view the problem? Does she see the problem as being located within herself, in others, or the situation in which she finds herself? Is he currently receiving help from any other source? If so, how does he think counselling might be different?

The referrer is also involved in assessment. It is important to find out what their expectations are; their reasons for referring, and whether these reasons say more about the referrer than the referred. If it is an 'urgent' referral, what is the meaning of the urgency?

A counsellor involved in assessment within health settings also needs to assess herself; her level of competence to deal with the issues involved; her confidence in using, and her commitment, to brief work; her commitment to partnership and collaboration; and her access to suitable supervision. Counsellors need to be able to refer on clients they do not feel competent to work with, and to recognise the limitations of their training and ability and their own mental health and personal resources at any given time.

In order to make referrals, counsellors should provide themselves with knowledge of resources within the team and the system, which may be the psychiatric or psychology services, including psychotherapy, the community mental health team, or private practitioners, and voluntary agencies when patients have been discharged. Counsellors also need to inform themselves about recognised referral procedures. In the meantime counsellors will need to contain clients until appropriate referral sources can be accessed.

Solution-focused approaches

Solution-focused brief therapy has had a major impact on the therapeutic community in the UK over the last ten years (Saunders 1995, 1996, 1998). It is an approach that deals with solutions rather than problems, emphasises the person's strengths, abilities and resources and attempts to explore the whole person within the context of their lives, including their achievements and successes. For these reasons it is clearly an approach that is eminently useful for people who are ill or disabled.

Solution-focused brief therapy lays a great emphasis on clients making decisions and setting agendas, on future directions and goals, on creative visualisations of possibilities that may lead to positive outcomes. The 'miracle question' asks clients to think about how they would be different if a miracle occurred, unknown to them, during their sleep and their problem was solved – how would they know that such a miracle had occurred, and how would others know? This invites clients to examine in detail how their attitudes might affect their behaviour and helps them link inner and outer experience through visualisations.

The approach has been criticised during the early days for avoiding the painful feelings attached to people's stories, and this is a view I held myself after a training session with de Shazer. However, it seems that although less time is spent empathising with a person's problems, they are certainly acknowledged: practitioners would spend as much time empathising with these feelings as seemed useful to the client. Jane Lethem (1994) says 'acknowledgement is the hidden ingredient of therapy' and in her moving and powerful book on working with the grief of women and children she demonstrates her ability to acknowledge feelings, empathise and move on to find ways to leave the pain behind. Traditional therapy often encourages people to go back over painful experiences; in solution-focused therapy clients are asked if they would choose to move on or look back.

Finally: About training

The traditional culture of counselling may have impacted negatively on some people's sense of identity as 'counsellor' by offering a limited view of the role. Colin Feltham argues that training should include an opportunity for students to think deeply and challenge the dominant cultural forces imposed by theories of psychology and therapeutic models. He suggests: (1) a general change of attitude, allowing for the legitimacy of serious questioning of fundamental counselling ideology; (2) the injection into training of a specific critical component; (3) the recognition within counselling institutes and authorities of their own fictitious, philosophical oppressions and other 'shadows' (Feltham 1996).

John McLeod reminds us that counselling training is 'grounded in multi-culturalism; it is only from a comparative perspective that the cultural construction of one's own identity can become apparent. It is necessary for counsellors to locate their approach within its social and historical context' (McLeod 1999).

Some of the joy of being a trainer comes from seeing students leave our courses with a greater sense of who they are and what they are offering, what they can ask for in terms of pay and conditions, and a clearer sense of their rights and responsibilities as members of a team. They learn, through their essays and presentations, to articulate what they do and why. With a clearer grasp of their role they gain self-respect. Students are taught how to audit and evaluate their service. In the process of doing this they gain a clear view of how much they mean to clients and fellow professionals. All this increases their self-confidence, which in turn increases others' confidence in them. But perhaps the most enduring need is for counsellors to examine themselves – their personal relationship with power and authority; to be open to challenge and criticism, and so earn the right to challenge and criticise anything that is unhelpful to their practice.

Supervision

All of the contributors to this book who are writing from the counsellor's perspective have drawn attention to the importance of supervision in helping them maintain their clarity and psychological health. Rachel Freeth comments on the fact that supervision is one of the major differences between the expectations of her roles as counsellor and psychiatrist: 'As a doctor and psychiatrist I am used to dealing with the frustration of working in an environment that is not particularly alert to the supervisory and support needs of staff. This is true of the medical profession and of NHS culture in general.' I believe this reflects one of the fundamental differences between the medical model and the psychosocial model and the movement away from the modernist view of health and illness. Where supervision does occur in the medical world it is more often concerned with 'case management' than with reflexive practice, therapeutic aspects of the work or the worker's emotional responses to patients – although there are now a few exceptions.

Some of the supervision issues that have been raised in this book are concerned with:

- boundaries and role conflict
- potential for 'splitting' between team members
- confusions about responsibilities/loyalties
- strength of feelings in the face of trauma
- the danger of burnout
- the balance between personal and professional life
- transference and counter-transference
- time-limited working and the sometimes 'bitty' nature of the work
- the importance of choosing a supervisor and type of supervision.

Boundaries and role conflict

Counsellors in health settings who have been taught by their training that boundaries of time, place, confidentiality, role and relationship are sacrosanct will inevitably struggle when faced with the reality of the context in which they find themselves. However, these ideals need not be sacrificed altogether to the nature of this work; rather they will be challenged, questioned and re-negotiated – as they should be in all counselling arenas. Jonathon Smith suggests that what is needed is 'flexibility, a degree of elasticity with regard to the boundaries whilst at the same time having a sound and firm structure' (Smith 1999).

It is certainly important that clients should feel safe enough to explore what troubles them, and I believe we can ascertain *with* them what they require to achieve that level of security, rather than make assumptions or impose taken-for-granted ideas about what those requirements should be. Dealing with the uncertainty of ill-health will inevitably cause counsellors to question issues related to boundaries: how do we end counselling when a person is dying? What does it mean to a patient who has lost control over his life that he cannot choose when and where his counselling takes place and how many sessions he can have? What is it like for a client to know that the counsellor, in her role as nurse, was present at the death of a loved one when he was not there himself?

As I have shown earlier, many counsellors in heath settings have other roles within the same setting. Supervision can provide a space in which counsellors can reflect on the impact on the client, themselves and the counselling process of belonging to two professions, sometimes with different skills and training pathways, and underpinned by different philosophies.

Back in 1992 when I was training as a supervisor I found myself questioning the teaching on boundaries. I was at that time receiving supervision from my therapist – something that I was almost afraid to admit to, although in knowing me so well, with all my potential blind spots and transference issues, my therapist made an excellent supervisor and our relationship worked well. We talked about this issue and frequently checked out how this overlap might be affecting our relationship, my own therapy and my work with clients. I knew that others in my training group would challenge me with ideas that I was 'avoiding an ending', that I was acting out 'a problem holding boundaries' in this relationship, etc. I decided to write an essay about it – as a way of admitting it, at least to my tutors and peer assessors who would read it. It would also give me a chance to reflect, and focus some of my thinking. It was in preparing for this essay that I came across *No Boundary: Eastern and Western Approaches to Personal Growth* by Ken Wilber (1979). This book stimulated me to question even further the usefulness of rigid boundaries.

Wilber suggested that boundaries were a useful way of describing, naming, defining differences, but went on to say, 'when you establish a boundary so as to gain control over something, at the same time you separate and alienate yourself from that which you attempt to control'. A boundary line both separates and unites, but it is often at the edges, where overlap occurs, that the most useful and interesting things happen. Wilber describes a boundary as a potential battle line, an area of conflict. If we treat boundaries as real we may imagine that the opposites created by the boundaries are irreconcilable, separate, and forever set apart. Counsellors working in health settings may find supervision a useful place to 'patrol' the boundaries and explore the tensions inherent in membership of a multidisciplinary team. Counsellors can become confused about accountability and responsibilities and may be pushed and pulled emotionally in many directions when faced with the conflicting agendas of patients, their family, and/or other professionals. In supervision counsellors can be reminded that the patient's needs are paramount, whilst balancing accountability to the organisation and clarifying responsibilities.

Transference and counter-transference

Ill people often regress, especially when removed from their familiar surroundings. The power of the patient–healer relationship might arouse feelings that they felt towards their care-givers during childhood. Counsellors might find themselves being used as a repository for the negative and/or positive feelings patients have towards other team members as representations of parental figures. Patients may take their negative or positive feelings about the counsellor to other team members, who may not have the same level of understanding of the need to contain the potential split between 'good parent' and 'bad parent'. Team members may have their loyalties shaken in the face of powerful unconscious dynamics, and it may be only the counsellor who has an opportunity to untangle these responses in supervision. Splitting may best be avoided or dealt with by the counsellor sharing her knowledge about these dynamics with other members of the team. Supervision can ensure that counter-transference does not further complicate matters, and can become the container for opposing forces.

Counter-transference responses can create problems between fellow workers and the counsellor as some of the above dynamics are acted out unwittingly. Counsellors may see themselves as the 'champion' of the client's cause, they may want to protect clients from being misunderstood, blamed or referred on to others who they do not think are able to give the client what they believe they need. They may become caught up in conflicts, particularly when clients/patients have been referred to specialist services in an attempt to treat the symptoms without treating the underlying issues. Judith Herman notes the potential for further harm to patients:

> In institutional settings the problem of staff splitting or intense conflict over the treatment of difficult patients frequently arises. Almost always the subject of the dispute turns out to have a history of trauma. The quarrel among colleagues reflects the unwitting re-enactment of the dialectic of trauma. (Herman 1992, p.152)

Danger of burnout

Counsellors working in health settings will usually have to deal with powerful emotions, trauma, and a rapid turnover of clients, frequent endings, loss and the pressures of the organisation. The danger for people working in this situation is that they may become overwhelmed or suffer 'burnout'. Supervision can provide a haven of safety in what may seem like an unsafe world. A supervisor may notice that the client seems to have intruded into the counsellor's life; or that the counsellor sounds disconnected from her clients. Counsellors who are survivors of trauma may have increased capacity for empathic resonance with clients and become a source of hope and validation; but they may also be more at risk of vicarious traumatisation (Follette, Polusny and Milbeck 1994; McCann and Pearlman 1990).

Vicarious traumatisation can cause disruptions in the counsellor's sense of security, self-esteem and identity. Her faith in humanity may be challenged and her sense of personal vulnerability heightened. She may become more fearful and mistrustful of people in general – especially in close relationships. She might become cynical about the motives of others and pessimistic about the future of the human condition. Counsellors need a safe place where thoughts and feelings can be named, even those that may be counter to the caring culture with which they identify. Their identity as a caring human being may be shaken – they may question themselves at the deepest spiritual core. In supervision these feelings can be explored in terms of the 'counter-transference–vicarious traumatisation' cycle (Pearlman and Saakvitne 1995).

Sometimes counsellors experience uncanny, grotesque, bizarre imagery, dreams or fantasies while working with severely traumatised people. They may experience various forms of dissociation while listening to the client, including numbing, perceptual disturbances, depersonalisation and derealisation. The counsellor may feel in a state of constant suspense – having a sense of dread, or fear of the future – much as people describe as a consequence of post-traumatic stress disorder, and is in line with the criteria outlined in the American Psychiatric Association's Diagnostic and Statistical Manual of Mental Disorders (1994). With this in mind, supervisors might notice patterns that occur in the material that supervisees present; it may be that particular images recur in supervision, with the counsellor frequently bringing cases that have some underlying shared theme. The supervisor can invite supervisees to explore the reasons why those particular images/cases are troubling, and raise the possibility of unconscious material that may be being triggered from the counsellor's life (Etherington 2000a).

Strength of feelings in face of trauma

When counsellors become deeply immersed in counter-transference they may experience powerful negative feelings that are difficult to acknowledge – either to themselves or to their supervisor. The supervisor may sense the counsellor's withdrawal and may begin to feel intrusive as she seeks to connect with her.

Negative feelings that are not addressed in supervision may accumulate over time and counsellors may become tired, stressed and less able to be with the client in helpful ways. They may also become less able to care for themselves and therefore expose themselves to the danger of burnout. Being overwhelmed with negative or distressing feeling may be felt as shameful for counsellors who pride themselves in being resilient. In denying these feelings counsellors might lose the opportunity to process them and therefore lessen their availability to themselves and their clients. For example, the supervisor might notice counsellors speak of horrific events in their client's lives with no expression of feeling – having defended themselves against their own negative feelings they might be less able to resonate empathically with those of their client. In this state the counsellor may lose sight of the client's strengths and resources and assume the role of rescuer – doing more and more for the client, thus implying that the client cannot act for himself. The more the counsellor accepts this role, the more she may be in danger of disempowering the client. This may lead to the counsellor feeling grandiose and omnipotent – thinking she is the only one who can help this client because she alone understands (Herman 1992). Delicate issues like this can be raised within a supportive and restorative supervisory relationship, enabling counsellors to recognise issues for further in-depth exploration in personal counselling (Inskipp and Proctor 1995).

Supervision on time-limited work

Counsellors who offer time-limited work can be affected by what one counsellor referred to as the 'bitty' nature of the work, as well as the fact that some very deep issues are being worked with. Sometimes time-limited therapy can also mean 'holding' a client over a long period, although being in counselling contact only intermittently or briefly. In health settings clients can return for counselling at different stages of their lives, perhaps in response to new treatment, deterioration in their medical condition or other changes in their lives. Cummings and Sayana (1995) provide an excellent example of how a client and his family can use a psychotherapy service in this way.

Single- or six-session models mean that counsellors face a very high turnover of clients, with numerous beginnings and endings. In these situations counsellors need to be capable of creating a working alliance very quickly; they will need to be skilled at making immediate connections, getting to the heart of the matter quickly and choosing, in the light of a speedy assessment, the interventions that are most likely to meet the client's needs (Henderson 1999). It may be that in between supervision sessions counsellors will have begun and ended with several clients who have not been attending long enough to be taken to supervision. Caroline Stedman refers to this in Chapter 6 on her work with young people in a Brook advisory clinic. She recognises that discussion in supervision about a client who has been and gone can help her deal with the next time she comes across a client with similar issues.

Choosing a supervisor

Francesca Inskipp draws attention to the fact that prior to 1988 supervision was provided by counsellors who had enough experience to oversee the work of other counsellors: 'They usually took on their new role by modelling that which they received, and often [supervised] using counselling values and assumptions' (Inskipp 1996). She goes on to say that nowadays, since the proliferation of supervision training courses, it is increasingly recognised that supervision has become a discipline in its own right.

However, there are still many people offering supervision who trained as counsellors within the traditional models of psychodynamic, cognitive-behavioural or humanistic counselling and may not have challenged their attitudes by further training in time-limited approaches, or indeed by training as a supervisor on a recognised course. It is becoming clearer that supervision needs to take context into account (Carroll and Holloway 1999), much as I have suggested that counselling needs to take context into account.

From what has gone before in this chapter it will be understood that supervisors who do not share counsellors' understanding and the values that inform their work in health settings will probably be unable to provide a 'safe haven' for their supervisees. Penny Henderson says:

> Supervisors who can support brief and continuing but intermittent work as a treatment of choice for some patients will be able to help their supervisees to work in a focused way. Supervisors who do not accept these limits cannot support the counsellors to wrestle positively with the implications of them. (Henderson 1999, pp.85–6)

To this I would add that a supervisor who has an understanding of organisations (particularly the NHS) and their impact on counsellors and their work, knowledge of models of health and illness, skill in focusing and assessment, and the ability to work well with differences, will be best able to support the work of supervisees in health settings.

In a study of the experiences of primary care counsellors in supervision it was noted that 62 per cent of supervisors were not themselves counsellors. Eighty-seven per cent of the counsellors chose their supervisors (Burton, Henderson and Curtis-Jenkins 1998), and 89 per cent reported a good match between their theoretical approach and that of their supervisors, although it was acknowledged that differences did sometimes cause problems for supervisees. Counsellors in health settings are also likely to have a line manager, especially when working within the NHS. Because of lack of understanding of the different purposes of counselling supervision and line management, it is important for supervisors and supervisees to clarify contracts carefully with the organisation. Confusion can arise when counsellors also have another role within the health setting, for which line management or consultancy may be a more appropriate option. Clarity can be gained by good supervision training that takes organisational issues into account (Inskipp 1996).

As well as choosing an appropriate supervisor, counsellors may need to consider the type of supervision forum that will best suit their needs. Individual, peer and group supervision can provide a range of opportunities for support, challenge and sharing information. Peer and/or group supervision, especially within an organisational context in which counsellors may feel 'alien', can help create networks of like-minded people who have similar philosophies and training pathways. This can enable a counsellor to feel less isolated and empathically understood.

Conclusion

I have written above about the views on the nature of 'self', the nature of 'problems' and how to deal with them, which inform different psychological, social and philosophical theories. I have questioned the thinking that underpins the belief that people can only be helped psychologically and emotionally within a long-term, private, therapeutic relationship. It has taken me a long time to come to this point and even now, as I write, I remember how important it was for me to have a long-term therapeutic relationship of this kind. However, I also remember several important occasions when I was helped by single meetings with a hospital chaplain, a nun, a teacher, etc. My first experience of counselling extended over a few months – perhaps ten sessions; my second was five sessions; my third about six sessions. My last counsellor was someone I worked with for three years. I then worked with a body therapist for a further year-and-a-half. All of these interventions were different and useful and met my needs at the time. In between I worked on myself in training groups, through writing, feedback from supportive colleagues, leisure pursuits and personal relationships. My needs changed as I continued to reconstruct my identity.

During my own counselling I know I needed to feel safe, respected and understood and that I wanted my personal feelings, thoughts and unfolding understanding of myself to be honoured as confidential. However, I also remember that I struggled against the sense that I needed the help of an 'expert'. Although all of my counsellors helped me to feel empowered, to have a sense of my untapped potential and understand that choices were available to me that I had not recognised, I still felt troubled by the thought that at my 'core' there was a 'self' that was damaged by my earlier life experiences.

Although I find it difficult to break away entirely from the idea of a 'core' or 'essential' self, I know that I have always felt that I am many selves and that these selves have changed, developed and grown over time and in varying contexts. As I write this today (and I may have changed my thinking by the time you read this) I believe that I have within me a 'spirit' that makes me uniquely who I am, and that that spirit is a constant in my life, and beyond damage or repair. It is the part of me that will survive beyond my bodily existence, perhaps within the memory of others or through my writing or in other ways that I have not yet understood. I also believe that I am many selves that are constantly reconstructing and evolving over my lifetime; there are selves I do not yet know – my elderly self, my great-grandmother self, perhaps my widowed self.

I have also realised that my occupational therapist (OT) self has many parts that I can reclaim and that I have learned to value anew. I now believe that when I gave up my work as an OT I was reacting against the constraints of the context within which I was working. Being a community OT within the system of a local authority social services department did not allow me to live out the part of me that valued people's life stories as a way of assisting them to take agency in their lives and find solutions to their problems. Even though I recognised that their stories were as important as providing aids and adaptations to overcome practical difficulties in their daily lives, without permission from those in authority I could not work as I wanted to.

However, by rejecting my OT role and becoming a counsellor who was trained to accept the concept of the 'autonomous bounded self', I gave up some of the flexibility of that role, in which I had visited clients in their homes, in hospital, in nursing homes, met with some people only once and with others over a period of years, etc. I did not fully value then that OT training was the first holistic training to begin to challenge the values of the medical model even whilst working alongside others who espoused it, understanding people in terms of body, mind and spirit, and recognising how disabling environments condemn people to limited lives. Neither did I truly value the opportunity the OT role had given me to gain a wide variety of experience over the years, working in a child guidance clinic; a psychiatric day hospital; a charity that provided residential care for people with autism; an NHS general hospital; and as a teacher in a college of occupational therapy. In producing this book I have reconnected with that part of myself and have a sense that I have almost come full circle. I have reclaimed those values and seen how they can also enhance my role as a counsellor, supervisor, trainer and researcher – and I am grateful.

References

American Psychiatric Association (1994) *Diagnostic and Statistical Manual of Mental Disorders* (fourth edition) (DSM-1V). Washington DC: APA.

Bor, R., Miller, R., Latz, M. and Salt, H. (1998) *Counselling in Health Care Settings.* London: Cassell.

British Association for Counselling and Psychotherapy (2001) Draft: 'Statement of fundamental ethics for counselling and psychotherapy.' Rugby: BACP.

Budman, S. and Gurman, A. (1988) *Theory and Practice of Brief Therapy.* New York: Guildford Press.

Burton, M., Henderson, P. and Curtis-Jenkins, G. (1998) 'Primary care counsellors' experiences of supervision.' *Counselling 9*, 2, 122–130. London: Counselling in Primary Care Trust.

Cade, B. and O'Hanlon, W. H. (1993) *A Brief Guide to Brief Therapy.* London: W. W. Norton and Co Ltd.

Carroll, M. and Holloway, E. (eds) (1999) *Counselling Supervision in Context.* London: Sage.

Cummings, N. and Sayana, M. (1995) *Focused Psychotherapy: A Casebook of Brief, Intermittent Psychotherapy throughout the Life Cycle.* New York: Bruner Mazel.

Cummings, P. (1998) 'What do service providers want?' Paper delivered to Counselling in Primary Care Trust Conference, April, at Royal Society of Medicine, London.

Curtis-Jenkins, G., Burton, M., Henderson, P., Foster, J. and Inskipp, F. (1997) 'Supplement no. 3 on supervision of counsellors in primary care.' Staines, UK: Counselling in Primary Care Trust.

Egan, G. and Cowan, M. (1979) *People in Systems: A Model for the Development in the Human-Service Professions and Education.* Pacific Grove, CA: Brooks/Cole.

Einzig, H., Curtis-Jenkins, G. and Basharan, H. (1992) 'The training needs of counsellors in primary medical care: the role of the training organisations.' *CMS News 33*, 9–13.

Einzig, H., Curtis-Jenkins, G. and Basharan, H. (1995) 'The training needs of counsellors in primary medical care.' *Journal of Mental Health 4*, 205–209.

Elton-Wilson, J. (1996) *Time-Conscious Psychological Therapy*. London: Routledge.

Etherington, K. (2000a) 'Supervising counsellors who work with survivors of childhood sexual abuse.' *Counselling Psychology Quarterly 13*, 4, 377–389.

Etherington, K. (2000b) *Narrative Approaches to Working with Adult Male Survivors of Child Sexual Abuse: The Clients', the Counsellor's and the Researcher's Story*. London: Jessica Kingsley Publishers.

Feltham, C. (1996) 'Beyond denial, myth and superstition.' In R. Bayne, I. Horton and J. Bimrose (eds) *New Directions in Counselling*. London: Routledge.

Feltham, C. (1997) *Time-Limited Counselling*. London: Sage.

Follette, V. M., Polusny, M. M. and Milbeck, K. (1994) 'Mental health and law enforcement professionals: Trauma history, psychological symptoms, and impact of providing services to child sexual abuse survivors.' *Professional Psychology: Research and Practice 25*, 3, 275–282.

Frank, A. (1995) *The Wounded Storyteller*. London: University of Chicago Press.

Freedman, J. and Combs, G. (1996) *Narrative Therapy: The Social Construction of Preferred Realities*. New York: Norton.

Gergen, K. (1992) 'The post-modern adventure.' *Family Therapy Networker 52*, 56–58.

Gergen, K. (1994) *Toward Transformation in Social Knowledge* (second edition). London: Sage.

Grant, G. (2000) 'Counselling in a hospital setting.' *Journal of Faculty of Health and Counselling Practice,* Spring, 11–13. Rugby: BACP.

Hales, J. (1999) 'Person-centred counselling and solution-focused therapy.' *Counselling 10*, 3, 233–236.

Henderson, P. (1999) 'Supervision in medical settings.' In M. Carroll and E. Holloway (eds) *Counselling Supervision in Context*. London: Sage.

Herman, J. (1992) *Trauma and Recovery*. New York: Basic Books.

Hudson-Allez, G. (1997) *Time-Limited Therapy in General Practice*. London: Sage.

Inskipp, F. (1996) 'New directions in supervision.' In R. Bayne, I. Horton and J. Bimrose (eds) *New Directions in Counselling*. London: Routledge.

Inskipp, F. and Proctor, B. (1995) *The Art, Craft and Tasks of Supervision. Part 2. Becoming a Supervisor*. Twickenham: Cascade.

Lenny, J. (1993) 'Do disabled people need counselling?' In J. Swain, V. Finkelstein, S. French and M. Oliver (eds) *Disabling Barriers – Enabling Environments*. London: Open University Press and Sage.

Lethem, J. (1994) *Moved to Tears, Moved to Action: Solution-Focused Brief Therapy with Women and Children*. London: BT Press.

McCann, I. L. and Pearlman, L. A. (1990) 'Vicarious traumatisation: A contextual model for understanding the effects of trauma on helpers.' *Journal of Traumatic Stress 3*, 1, 131–149.

McLeod, J. (1997) *Narrative and Psychotherapy*. London: Sage.

McLeod, J. (1999) 'Counselling as a social process.' *Counselling 10*, 3, 217–222.

Monk, G., Winslade, J., Crocket, K. and Epston, D. (eds) (1997) *Narrative Therapy in Practice: The Archaeology of Hope.* San Francisco: Jossey-Bass.

O'Connell, B. and de Shazer, S. (2000) 'Solution-focused brief therapy.' *Counselling 11*, 6, 343–344.

Pearlman, L. A. and Saakvitne, K. W. (1995) *Trauma and the Therapist: Countertransference and Vicarious Traumatisation in Psychotherapy with Incest Survivors.* London: W. W. Norton and Co.

Ryle, A. (1990) *Cognitive Analytical Therapy: Active Participation in Change.* Chichester: Wiley.

Saunders, C. (1995) 'Berg, de Shazer and friends; an American training experience.' *Counselling 6*, 2, May.

Saunders, C. (1996) 'Solution-focused therapy in practice: a personal experience.' *Counselling 7*, 4, November.

Saunders, C. (1998) 'Solution-focused therapy: what works?' *Counselling 9*, 1, February.

Seaburn, D. B., Lorenz, A. D., Gunn, W. B. and Mauksch, L. B. (1996) *Models of Collaboration – A Guide for Mental Heath Professionals Working with Health Care Practitioners.* New York: Basic Books.

Smith, J. (1999) 'Holding the dance: a flexible approach to boundaries in general practice.' In J. Lees (ed) *Clinical Counselling in Primary Care.* London: Routledge.

Speedy, J. (2001) 'The storied helper: an introduction to narrative ideas and practices in counselling and psychotherapy.' *European Journal of Counselling, Psychotherapy and Health 3*, 3.

Talmon, M. (1990) *Single Session Therapy.* San Francisco: Jossey-Bass.

Thorne, B. (1999) 'The move towards brief therapy: its dangers and its challenges.' *Counselling 10*, 1, February, 7–11.

van Durzen, E. (1998) *Paradox and Passion in Psychotherapy.* Chichester, UK: Wiley and Sons.

White, M. and Epston, D. (1991) *Narrative Means to a Therapeutic End.* New York: Norton.

Wiener, J. and Sher, M. (1998) *Counselling and Psychotherapy in Primary Health Care: A Psychodynamic Approach.* London and Basingstoke: Macmillan.

Wilber, K. (1979) *No Boundary: Eastern and Western Approaches to Personal Growth.* London: Shambala.

Contributors

Helen and George Boxer (pseudonyms) were in their mid-30s when they realised they might need fertility treatment. They had been together six years before starting treatment in 1995 and both had successful careers. They are now the proud parents of two little girls, and Helen balances motherhood with running her own career. Helen and George live in the West Country.

Pete Connor (BA Dip Couns MSc) is a BACP accredited counsellor and BACP recognised supervisor. He has worked in the HIV field for almost 15 years and is currently employed as coordinator for Terrence Higgins Trust West. He also teaches part-time on the Diploma in Counselling at the University of Bristol and is an individual and group supervisor, mainly working with counsellors in the voluntary sector. Pete has particular interests in bereavement and grief counselling and research, lesbian and gay issues within counselling, and power and oppression within counselling and supervision relationships.

Penny Cook is a paediatric nurse with intensive care experience, UKRC (United Kingdom Register of Counsellors) Occupational Registered Counsellor, and counselling supervisor. For over ten years she has been the Family Liaison Sister, working with the families of sick and critically ill children, at Addenbrooke's Hospital, Cambridge. She has written her own book *Supporting Sick Children and their Families* (Baillière Tindall, London, 1999) and contributed to other books and publications.

Kim Etherington is a BACP accredited counsellor and supervisor in private practice. She is a lecturer at the University of Bristol with a special interest in teaching research. Having started out in the early 60s as an occupational therapist, Kim worked in NHS general and psychiatric hospitals and in charitable organisations, including a child guidance clinic and a community for autistic people, and in the 80s as a community OT for social services. She then trained as a counsellor at the University of Bristol. Her previous books *Adult Male Survivors of Childhood Sexual Abuse* (1995) and *Narrative Approaches to Working with Adult Male Survivors of Child Sexual Abuse* (2000) follow from the research she undertook for her PhD. She has three adult sons, three daughters-in-law and three grandsons, and has been married for nearly 40 years.

Rachel Freeth (BM DCP Dip Couns) works part-time as a staff grade psychiatrist for an NHS Trust. She has a longstanding interest in the psychological therapies. However, rather than pursuing psychotherapy training within the NHS as a psychiatric speciality, she gained a diploma in counselling at the University of East Anglia. Since then she has spent some time working voluntarily as a counsellor within an NHS counselling service. Now she offers some counselling sessions within her post as a psychiatrist, where she incorporates and integrates, where possible, person-centred values and concerns into the NHS psychiatric setting. Rachel is a registered associate of BACP, the British Association for the Person-Centred Approach (BAPCA), and the Bridge Pastoral Foundation. The latter promotes education and training in pastoral care and counselling, and with the Foundation Rachel is developing a Pastoral Team for her local churches. For recreation she enjoys singing with a chamber choir and travelling to countries of a non-western culture.

Heather Goodare worked as an academic editor before her diagnosis of breast cancer in 1986. On her recovery she trained as a counsellor, working with her local cancer support group, Crawley Cancer Contact. She is a UKRC (United Kingdom Register of Counsellors) Occupational Registered Counsellor, and for four years edited the newsletter of the National Association of Cancer Counsellors. She is also active in national consumer movements, has served on the editorial board of the *British Medical Journal* as a consumer representative, and has contributed to the Cochrane Collaboration and Consumers in NHS Research. She chairs Breast UK (Breast-cancer Research Ethics and Advocacy Strategy).

Karl Gregory (RGN RMN Dip Couns MSc) divides his time between private counselling work, lecturing and tutoring on the diploma in counselling course at the University of Bristol, working part-time in NHS settings, and teaching on the Thorn Initiative Psychosocial Interventions programme. He also takes part in a training programme for personnel in the RAF and Army through the University of Bristol. Karl has 18 years' experience as a psychiatric nurse in acute and rehabilitation psychiatry. He has worked in both hospital and community settings and was a manager of a rehabilitation team for three years. As a member of the Community Psychiatric Nurse Association he has co-run workshops at their annual conferences on issues of psychosocial interventions.

Rosie Jeffries was born in 1955. She works as a student counsellor at the University of the West of England. She lives in Bristol with her life partner, J. She is a feminist. She enjoys her work and loves holidays, singing, reading, swimming, painting, walking and her wonderful network of friends and family.

Kate Kirk has worked for Salford Palliative Care Counselling Service for four years. Her interests in holistic medicine, psychoneuroimmunology and psychodrama influence the way she works with clients. Her PhD research was into the worker's experience of working with clients who have been sexually abused. She would like to continue her post-doctoral studies by focusing on workers in hospice, oncology and palliative care settings.

Maria Lever originally set up the Salford Palliative Care Counselling Service six years ago. She recently completed her MSc study into nurses' professional development in palliative care. Her interests are professional development, ethical dilemmas and the efficacy of counselling in palliative care. She is currently involved in a qualitative research study exploring the needs of bereaved people locally.

Sue Santi Ireson (BEd Dip Couns) is a BACP accredited counsellor. Sue manages a counselling service in a GP practice and is also involved with GP and psychiatric registrar training. She has a private practice in which she offers counselling, supervision and training to individuals and organisations. She was until recently chair of the Personal, Relationship and Family Division of the British Association for Counselling and Psychotherapy.

Julia Segal (MA) trained originally with Relate and is a BACP accredited counsellor who works within the North West London Hospitals NHS Trust counselling people with multiple sclerosis and members of their families. She also works privately training professionals who work with people who have various disabilities. She is particularly interested in using the insights of Melanie Klein and her colleagues to increase understanding in relationships, particularly those involving mental or physical disabilities. She has written extensively on counselling people with disabilities (including *Helping Children with Ill or Disabled Parents*, Jessica Kingsley Publishers, London, 1992) and on the work of Melanie Klein.

Caroline Stedman (BA CQSW MA Dip Couns) was a social worker for many years before becoming ill with ME in 1990. Retraining as a counsellor formed part of her recovery and she discovered the career she should have had all along. Although passionate about counselling adolescents, she has also worked in the field of HIV/Aids and in smoking cessation with adults.

Gill Woodbridge has been a counsellor for twenty years, working in private practice and NHS settings. Her particular interest lies in relationship and women's health issues, and she has experience of working with women with unplanned pregnancy, gynaecological problems, divorce and conciliation as well as infertility. Her dissertation for an MSc in counselling at Bristol University focused on the emotional responses of men whose partners were infertile as a result of premature menopause. She was recently a member of the executive committee of the British Infertility Counselling Association and she is a member of BACP.

Subject Index

Author index